A Value-Driven European Future

P.I.E. Peter Lang

Bruxelles • Bern • Berlin • Frankfurt am Main • New York • Oxford • Wien

Léonce BEKEMANS (ed.)

A Value-Driven European Future

Series "Europe of Cultures"
n° 5

Università degli Studi di Padova | Interdepartmental Centre on Human Rights and the Rights of Peoples

Jean Monnet European Centre of Excellence
"Intercultural Dialogue, Human Rights & Multi-level Governance"

This project has been funded with support from the European Commission. This publication reflects the views only of the author, and the Commission cannot be held responsible for any use which may be made of the information contained therein.

Lifelong Learning

Cover picture : "Finding the pathway", 2012, © Daniele Canedo.

Éditions scientifiques internationales
Brussels, 2012
1 avenue Maurice, B-1050 Brussels, Belgique
www.peterlang.com ; info@peterlang.com

ISSN 2031-3519
ISBN 978-90-5201-890-4

D/2012/5678/88

Printed in Germany

Library of Congress Cataloging-in-Publication Data

A value-driven European future / Léonce Bekemans (ed.).
p. cm. — (Cultures of Europe ; no. 5) Includes bibliographical references and index. ISBN 978-90-5201-890-4
1. European Union. 2. Social values—European Union countries.
I. Bekemans, Léonce, editor of compilation. II. Bunjes, Ulrich. Future perspective on intercultural and interreligious dialogue.
JN30.V355 2012 341.242'2—dc23 2012033340

CIP also available from the British Library, UK.

Bibliographic information published by "Die Deutsche Nationalbibliothek"
"Die Deutsche Nationalbibliothek" lists this publication in the "Deutsche National-bibliografie"; detailed bibliographic data is available on the Internet at <http://dnb.d-nb.de>.

Editorial Note

I would like to express my sincere gratitude to the Jean Monnet Programme of the European Commission. It has allowed for an ongoing support to teaching and research activities on the cultural and value dimensions of Europe's future from a multi-, inter- and transdisciplinary perspective. The Interdepartmental Centre on Human Rights and the Rights of People of the University of Padua, in particular Prof. Antonio Papisca and Prof. Marco Mascia, provide a permanent stimulating content and context setting for a human rights, value-based European future. Last but not least, I wish to thank the students who have followed my courses throughout the years – not only at the University of Padua, but at various European universities. They were a continuous source of motivation and feedback. The continuous exchange and interaction in teaching, meetings and conferences throughout Europe, bridging concepts with differentiated realities and transmitting commitment and ideas for Europe's future within a globalising context, has resulted in a fruitful process of lifelong mutual learning. It gave ample satisfaction and content strength for practising change and building responsible citizenship in a value-driven and thrust-worthy path towards Europe's future destiny.

I would also like to thank the various collaborators of the Interdepartmental Centre for their continuous support and assistance. A particular word of gratitude to Claudia Pividori, a PhD student and research assistant, who once more assisted with caring dedication in the finalisation of the various versions of these contributions, through to the formatted result. A last word of thanks goes to the International Publishing House P.I.E. Peter Lang, for producing the final outcome as part of its "Europe of Cultures" series.

Léonce Bekemans

Jean Monnet Chair "Globalisation, Intercultural Dialogue and Inclusiveness in the EU," Academic co-ordinator of the Jean Monnet Centre of Excellence "Intercultural Dialogue, Human Rights and Multi-level Governance," University of Padua

"The European Union is based on a large set of values, with roots in antiquity and in Christianity, which over 2.000 years evolved into what we recognize today as the foundations of modern democracy, the rule of law, and civil society. This set of values has its own clear moral foundation and its obvious metaphysical roots, regardless of whether modern man admits it or not. Thus it cannot be said that the European Union lacks its own spirit, from which all the concrete principles on which it is founded, grow. It appears, though, that this spirit is rather difficult to see. It seems too hidden behind the mountains of systemic, technical, administrative, economic, monetary and other measures that contain it.[....] That is why it seems to me that perhaps the most important task facing the European Union today is coming up with a new and genuinely clear reflection on what might be called European identity, a new and genuinely clear articulation of European responsibility, an intensified interest in the very meaning of European integration in all its wider implications for the contemporary world, and the recreation of its ethos or, if you like, its charisma."

"I would welcome it, for instance, if the European Union were to establish a charter of its own that would clearly define the ideas on which it is founded, its meaning and the values it intends to embody. If the citizens of Europe understand that this is not just an anonymous bureaucratic monster that wants to limit or even deny their autonomy, but simply a new type of human community that actually broadens their freedom significantly, then the European Union need not fear for its future..."

Extract from the speech "About European Identity" made by Václav Havel, the President of the Czech Republic to the European Parliament in Strasbourg on March 8th, 1994.

Table of Contents

Preface

José Maria GIL-ROBLES

Former President of the European Parliament, President of the European University Council for the Jean Monnet Programme, Jean Monnet Chair and Chairman Jean Monnet Centre of Excellence, Complutense University of Madrid

The book I am introducing represents a step further in the long and successful fight of the Jean Monnet Centre of Excellence of the University of Padua, for a European Union rooted in solid values, i.e. the values that the French Revolution established forever: liberty, equality and fraternity (now named usually "solidarity").

One might query the successful part of this fight – how can we speak of success, when Europeans only care or seem to care about their welfare (or unwelfare) state, trade, and finance? It is only economic values that seem to be at the forefront of European discussion. This is absolutely right. It is the landscape if we remain only at the surface of the very profound process of transformation occurring in our societies. That is the landscape if we only observe the media noise and nothing more.

However, the essence of the EU must be searched for more deeply. The EU is a device that, by means of creating economic links and common interests between peoples, drives them to remain at peace with one another, to work for a common prosperity and try to put into practice, in their daily lives, the ideals of freedom, equality and solidarity. Their achievement represents a big challenge. Responses are not found in a simple and easy way. They are not even institutionally established, but need to be explored, identified and tested every day. This trial and error system needs to be guided with a compass: human rights.

The Jean Monnet Centre of Excellence of the University of Padua has excelled in reminding us, year after year, of the need for using that compass. This book is the fruit of applied reflections and contributions presented at the international Workshop: "*Cultural and Value Roots for Intercultural Dialogue in a European Context.*" organised on 25-26

October 2011, in the framework of the activities of the Jean Monnet Centre "Intercultural Dialogue, Human Rights and Multi-level Governance." Intercultural dialogue is a privileged tool for establishing peaceful links between persons and between peoples, provided it is based on solid value roots.

The European Union is a ship that was launched only half built. It has to be completed in an ongoing way but, at the same time, has to be manned carefully for it to survive in rough seas. This book represents a formidable appeal for us to always keep to the compass of our human rights values, even in the more frightening waves of today's world.

General Introduction

Léonce BEKEMANS

I. Premises

The current European reality is confronted with the preoccupation and the responsibility to maintain its socio-economic model of integration and diversity, but also to meet these challenges within a world of drastic changes, a world in a complex crisis of governability at various levels. In other words, Europe presents itself to the world with a wealth of cultural, social, linguistic and territorial diversities but also with an urgent need for concerted action, for social and economic cohesion to deal with the gravity of the crisis.

Europe is currently at a turning point in its history. Challenges will only be overcome with a new common purpose and responsibility, defined by the needs of the current age. The EU is more than a common market, and of course we need increased economic governance and the treaty on the European budget pact (the fiscal compact) might be an important tool in building a stability and growth agenda based on the Europe 2020 strategy. But it is in the first place a community of destiny and a Union of values embodied in a commitment to human rights, peace, freedom and (internal and external) solidarity. These values have universal significance. If Europe wants to become a Community and Meeting Place of Multiple Identities, it will need a morally acceptable political structure and policies that strengthen its sense of common purpose and democratic citizenship.

We all have multiple identities, which include local, regional and national elements. There is no doubt that these primary forms of identity will remain the key reference points for citizens. But these elements have to go hand in hand with an emerging "European" identity, based on a shared understanding of EU history, the practical benefits deriving from EU citizenship, and a common vision of Europe's future and place in the world. It is only by clearly spelling out the EU's common agenda and purpose in the 21st century, that citizens will develop a stronger sense of ownership of the European project.

In this perspective, the EU governance model – "governing in partnership" – can be perceived as an example of effective regionalism:

a common public space with pooled sovereignty and the capacity to define common interests, strong institutions and the primacy of the rule of law. Therefore, delivering "good governance" is by far the EU's most powerful means of ensuring continuous commitment and the engagement of its citizens. The EU endeavours to deliver on these principles through a system of "multi-level governance," where competences are shared between various levels of authority. Therefore the paradigm of multi-level and multi-actor democratic governance should be further developed according to the principle of territorial and functional subsidiarity and be firmly anchored in the International Law of Human Rights. In the coming years, the EU will need to pursue an ambitious agenda to deal with the current challenges of favouring a culture of good human-centric governance.

Think long-term but act with determination now – this message must shape European leadership in this current age of insecurity. It presents a political opportunity to offer new ways of establishing European multi-level governance, accepting a sustainable statehood, built with interconnecting levels of authority. Regional and local contexts and actors become more and more crucial instruments for an active conviviality between citizens and institutions. In other words, good European governance means the recognition that globalisation, the emergence of a multi-polar world and the management of complex interdependencies, are shaping factors of Europe's future, but it also means a continuation/strengthening of the process of European integration whilst respecting diversities and preserving identities. This form of governance recognises diversity as a value worth preserving and solidarity as a value to be defended within the European and global context.

Managing diversity is done through intercultural dialogue and mutual learning. In an era of interdependencies, it touches many aspects of and problems in our societies. It presents one of the major challenges in the development of a new, plural and democratic citizenship.[1] But dialogue here is meant only in the sense that the sharing of values are translated into a "doing together" – into inclusive policies at international, European, national, regional and local levels, stimulated by democratic citizenship building. The European Citizens' Initiative is a good step forward.

---

[1] I refer to the European interuniversity research project "The role of intercultural dialogue for the development a new (plural, democratic) citizenship," a major contribution to the European Year for Intercultural Dialogue 2008. The result of the research work was Bekemans, L. *et al* (eds.), *Intercultural Dialogue and Citizenship. Translating Values into Actions. A Common Project for Europeans and their Partners*, Venice, Marsilio, 2007.

II. Setting

This publication is carried out in the framework of the Jean Monnet Centre of Excellence "Intercultural Dialogue, Human Rights and Multi-level Governance" of the University of Padua, located at its Interdepartmental Centre on Human Rights and the Rights of Peoples. The Centre was launched in September 2000; it was reaffirmed in the summer of 2009 when the University was one of the few institutions to have the title and funding re-awarded and has now finalised a 3 year cycle. Its purpose has been to strengthen and consolidate the European and international profile of the existing curriculum of teaching and research activities in the broad area of intercultural dialogue, human rights and multi-level governance. This is done from an interdisciplinary and policy-oriented perspective within and beyond the University, in co-operation and networking with the civil society, the regional authorities and other Jean Monnet Centres and Chairs.

The Jean Monnet Centre greatly benefits from the activities and international networking of the Jean Monnet Chair *ad honorem* held by Prof. Antonio Papisca, the Jean Monnet Chair on "European Union Political System," held by Prof. Marco Mascia, the Jean Monnet Chair on "Globalisation and Inclusiveness in the European Union," held by Prof. Léonce Bekemans and the Jean Monnet Module on "Sport and Human Rights in European Union Law," held by Prof. Jacopo Tognon. It can also rely on a small but committed, pluridisciplinary staff, able to relate and respond to its multidisciplinary and multidimensional programme.

The activities and events cover teaching modules (Territorial Dialogue, Intercultural Dialogue, Immigration and Trafficking, City Diplomacy and Sports), public lectures by international experts on policy-related topics and an action-oriented research programme focussed on the interconnecting fields of intercultural dialogue, human rights and multi-level governance.[2] It operates in a pro-active synergy within and outside the university and possesses a wide-ranging expertise in international relations, human rights, political sciences, intercultural dialogue and interdisciplinary studies.

III. Structure

The book presents a structured and interdisciplinary in-depth analysis of culturally oriented and value-driven applied reflections on Europe's future. It collects a number of contributions of which many

2 Bekemans, L. (ed.), *Intercultural Dialogue and Multi-level Governance in Europe. A Human Rights Based Approach*, Brussels, P.I.E. Peter Lang, 2012.

were originally presented at the international Workshop "*Cultural and Value Roots for Intercultural Dialogue in a European context*" organised on 25-26 October 2011 in Padua. The various authors present valuable, wide-ranging and diversified contributions to the debate on the future of Europe, analysing and assessing aspects and dimensions of a European Union rooted in solid values. They provide applied as well as critical reflections, some with a sectoral or geographical scope, on the complexities of transforming realities, oriented towards a common destiny of sustainable and cohesive societies in a globalised world, i.e. the building of a European future.

The book is structured along three parts. The first part provides a conceptual framework for understanding and contextualising intercultural and interreligious dialogue, with a focus on an in-depth institutional and international law approach. The second part consists of contributions concerning the value-driven foundations of Europe, ranging from historical, value and human rights perspectives. The last part proposes applied reflections on the (future) perspectives of a value-oriented Europe in the world. It introduces various understandings of a value-driven European future, including policy analysis, a social market economy, a common goods and education perspective, as well as sectoral and geographical approaches.

The book offers a general applied reading to policy-oriented academics, international relations and human rights scholars, regional, national and European institutions, as well as to the interested reader committed to the European project. Its interdisciplinary and interconnecting approach addresses crucial issues and challenges to a value-based European future. Through its diversity of contributions, from scientific and critical reflections to policy papers and case studies, the message of the book clearly refers to the fundamental importance of a human-centric development, being the cross-cutting and cross-border compass for the Europe of the future.

Part I

Conceptual Framework

A Conceptual Context: Introduction

Léonce BEKEMANS

Part I on the "*Conceptual Framework*" presents two complementary views and analyses of the contextual understanding of intercultural and interreligious dialogue, both of which are equally important for a value rooted European future.

Ulrich Bunjes, the current Head of the Youth Department at the Council of Europe, presents an institutional and policy-oriented view of the "*Future Perspective on Intercultural and Interreligious Dialogue.*" His starting point is the role of the Council of Europe in the reflection and policy-making on intercultural dialogue. Its strong involvement is perceived as part of a deep security concern to build deeper and more sustainable relations between individuals, cultures and religions. In the first section, the value basis and policy areas of the "White Paper on Intercultural Dialogue," are set out. Next, reference is made to the Report "Living together – Combining diversity and freedom in 21st-century Europe," written by an independent group of eminent persons. In the third section, the author focuses on the religious dimension of intercultural dialogue, in particular the protection of human rights, and the care and protection of cultural heritages. In the final part, the role of academia is seen as important for building up intercultural competencies, not only among the elites, but with a wide reach.

Antonio Papisca, Jean Monnet Chair *ad honorem* and UNESCO Chair "Human Rights, Democracy and Peace" at the University of Padua, focuses on the legal aspects of intercultural and interreligious dialogue in his paper "*International Law of Human Rights for Fostering Religious Freedom and Intercultural Dialogue.*" The author starts from the ontological argument of the wholeness and integrity of the human being – human dignity as the supreme value – implying the principle of the interdependence and indivisibility of human rights. He argues that current developments and events present a historic opportunity to better understand the strength of universal ethics – at the core of which are religious values – and to use them to develop social cohesion, inclusion and peace. He refers to the "supra-constitutional" relevance of international human rights law. The international normative reality recognises that rights of a religious nature belong to the essential core of human rights, and that religious values are an integral part of a just and peaceful "glocal" order. However, he clearly states that the exercising of specific rights to religious freedom must be compatible with the general principles of the universal code of human rights. The author further argues that the effects of religious inspiration on the development of intercultural dialogue may well be of fundamental importance, especially as regards processes of inclusion and the acceptance of the new concept of plural citizenship within an intercultural and inclusive European space. The final part of the paper illustrates some of the implications of this emerging concept at the local level. In the model for a sustainable city, intercultural dialogue is needed to reach an agreement on a shared code of rules and to therefore build an inclusive city. An identikit of the intercultural city is presented, being an inclusive city and laboratory for the development of plural citizenship. As a consequence, Papisca pleas for a redefinition of the concept and status of citizenship, taking into consideration the respect of multiple identities and the acquisition of a transcending civic identity. Moreover, the intercultural city also implies a redefinition of the category of territoriality, which can allow forms of cross-border territorial co-operation. Finally, the intercultural city is said to be a city committed to educating its citizens in human rights, dialogue, solidarity, beauty, artistic creativity, respect for nature and the environment and therefore a laboratory for a new "Humanism," opens to transcendence and positive secularity.

Future Perspective on Intercultural and Interreligious Dialogue: an Institutional and Policy-oriented View

Ulrich BUNJES

Head of the Youth Department, Member of the Office of the Co-ordinator for the Intercultural Dialogue, Directorate of Democratic Citizenship and Participation, Council of Europe

In recent years, the Council of Europe has been strongly involved in the reflection on intercultural dialogue, and has encouraged policy-making in the spirit of intercultural dialogue all over the continent and beyond. In fact, it was the Council of Europe that first introduced the term "intercultural dialogue" in an international legal text. In 1995, the member states of the Council of Europe adopted the "Framework Convention for the Protection of National Minorities," which instructs the ratifying state to:

> encourage a spirit of tolerance and intercultural dialogue and take effective measures to promote mutual respect and understanding and co-operation among all persons living on their territory, irrespective of those persons' ethnic, cultural, linguistic or religious identity, in particular in the fields of education, culture and the media.[1]

It is useful to mention at the very beginning of this paper, that, for reasons of day-to-day politics, intercultural dialogue is almost exclusively linked to questions of migration and globalisation. In reality however, the term has a much wider relevance, because cultural diversity as we experience it today has a deep historical context.

Looking back at its historical heritage, Europe's only way forward is to learn to understand each other. Drawing the right conclusions from the past is to build democratic societies, where everyone has a fair chance to participate in the life of the community and where everyone enjoys all the rights that belong to every human being. The final aim is the building of a Europe that protects the commonly shared values of the

---

[1] Article 6.

European civilisation, namely human rights, democracy and the rule of law.

This constant effort to protect our fundamental values is nothing less than an essential part of security policy. The Secretary General of the Council of Europe calls this "deep security" – "something that comes in addition to the traditional security arrangements, a deeper level of security that we build among individuals." Deep security is about building deeper and more sustainable relations between individuals, cultures and religions.

I. The White Paper on Intercultural Dialogue 2008

A central aspect of the policy of "deep security" is intercultural dialogue. Three years ago, the Council of Europe launched a significant "*White Paper on Intercultural Dialogue*," called "*Living Together as Equals in Dignity*."[2] This policy initiative was unique at the global level, at least in the form of a wide and intensive consultation of all stakeholders. Its purpose was to frame a platform for collective action and to formulate the principles on which all can agree. It also drew ample inspiration from a long series of practical projects and programmes, developed in the past by the Council of Europe in the field of human rights, democratic institution-building, education, youth, social cohesion, cultural policy, etc. Some twenty international conventions and protocols developed by the Council of Europe have had repercussions on intercultural dialogue. Over the last two to three decades alone, the Committee of Ministers has formulated more than 80 recommendations to member states that are relevant to intercultural dialogue.

In the "history" of intercultural dialogue, the Third Summit of Heads of State and Government in 2005, was, in many ways, a turning point. That same year, the decision was made to bring all these experiences into focus and to develop a "*White Paper on Intercultural Dialogue*." The drafting of the White Paper was preceded by a wide-scale consultation of all major stakeholders within and outside the Council of Europe, in written form and through consultation events. This process was strongly encouraged by the substantial and positive response from public authorities at all levels – civil society including many minority organisations, religious communities, journalists and media organisations and social partners.

It is important to highlight some of the basic thoughts that inspire the White Paper, in particular the value basis of intercultural dialogue. The White Paper underscores the need to reconcile respect for different

---

2 Available on www.coe.int/dialogue.

identities with the need to strengthen social cohesion. This can only be achieved if the policy is based on universal human rights and fundamental freedoms. They are the common denominator for holding together our societies. They inspire our political institutions. They are the precondition for social trust. They are what one could call the "*ius humanitatis*" – to use a term used by Professor Papisca – the rights-based bond that unites us in all our diversity.

The White Paper also supports the notion that intercultural dialogue happens – and must be promoted – at all levels: at the local level, in the national context, between European societies, and between Europe and other world regions. Furthermore, promoting intercultural dialogue is a transversal policy and a common responsibility that needs to be shared by all: public authorities at all levels but also civil society and other non-state actors, including religious communities, private enterprise, the media and – above all – individual citizens.

The White Paper sets out what is needed to promote intercultural dialogue in five broad policy areas:

– Firstly, democratic governance of cultural diversity. We need to build a political culture of diversity that recognises the rights of minorities and migrants; and to promote policies aimed at the equal enjoyment of rights by all.

– Secondly, intercultural dialogue is dependent on a strong and widespread sense of democratic citizenship and on participation for all.

– Thirdly, intercultural competence. This has strong implications particularly for all parts of the education sector and for formal, non-formal and informal education alike.

– Fourthly, efforts must be made to create more – and more accessible – spaces for intercultural dialogue, be it physical or virtual spaces like in the media or the arts. Kindergartens, schools and universities are obviously of prime importance in this context.

– Finally, the principles of intercultural dialogue must also inspire international relations, including, for instance, the contributions that educational and other authorities, the media or civil society, can make in this context.

The White Paper argues that social justice and the equal enjoyment of rights are essential prerequisites for a successful democratic management of diversity. The White Paper invites everyone to engage in intercultural dialogue and shows how this can be realised. The following examples demonstrate that today, more precise knowledge is available for what needs to be done, and what can be done, in terms of policies, institutional arrangements and general sensitivity, to promote intercultural dialogue at local level.

The network of "Intercultural Cities," co-ordinated by the Council of Europe and a joint initiative with the European Union, provides us with numerous examples of best practice in all areas. The "Intercultural Cities" project has created a network of cities, which manage cultural diversity in an active and exemplary way. In its new phase, started in 2011, the programme supports a group of new cities joining the network, and the national networks that have been created in several member states. It also focuses on clearly demonstrating the benefits of the intercultural approach for urban cohesion and development.

In 2009-2010 the Council of Europe conducted a campaign with media professionals and trainers, called "Speak Out Against Discrimination." Large parts of the media industry are responsive to issues of cultural diversity, and many professionals are sensitive to their specific roles and responsibilities. Together with journalism training institutes, curricular material was developed. However, additional steps are required to make the media industry as diverse as the societies around them.

Today we are also much better equipped to adapt the educational systems to the requirements of multicultural societies. To quote the White Paper: "The competences necessary for intercultural dialogue are not automatically acquired: they need to be learned, practised and maintained throughout life." The Council of Europe has, for instance, developed modules for the training of teachers, covering democratic citizenship, human rights, mutual understanding in diversity, "multi-perspectivity" in history teaching, media literacy, prevention of crimes against humanity and prevention of discrimination and violence.

Better knowledge is also available on how to address the specific challenges of cultural diversity in non-formal education, particularly in youth work. The annual "Youth Peace Camps," which bring together young people from both sides of regional conflicts, have demonstrated how the peaceful future of Europe can be prepared by working intensely with enthusiastic, committed young people. A new youth project entitled "Human rights defenders online" will be starting very soon. Youth activists will be trained to combat the rampant hate speech against minorities that we find on the Internet today. Its objective is to combat this phenomenon not through repression, but through counter-arguments, through irony and through the example of good practice.

One of the current concerns for the Council of Europe's member states is the issue of intolerance against Muslims. Following an initiative from the OSCE, several international organisations – among them the Council of Europe and UNESCO – recently launched a project to develop "Guidelines for Educators on Combating Intolerance and Discrimination against Muslims through Education."

And yet, these projects have a limited impact. They are slow to trickle down to the grassroots, even if the "European Year of Intercultural Dialogue" – proclaimed by the European Union in 2008 – did help to popularise these ideas and approaches. In Europe today many feel threatened by the multitude of social, political, cultural and religious forces around them. Many develop mistrust and fear. There are many worrying signs, such as the political campaigns and political decisions to reduce individual and collective freedoms, arising from a fear of cultural diversity. Some political forces are exploiting existing anxieties for their political ends.

For some years already we have witnessed the emergence of a new cultural nationalism in many European countries, emphasising through public policies the "national cultural canon." These tendencies could turn out to be extremely counter-productive. They could threaten the progress made in recent decades. As the Secretary General of the Council of Europe said recently, "We are witnessing a process that weakens the culture of togetherness that we helped build after the war. A cold wind is blowing over Europe." In short, these developments have to be taken seriously. We would fail miserably if we allowed xenophobia, exclusion, discrimination and segregation to get the upper hand.

II. The Group of Eminent Persons 2011

In the summer of 2010, the Council of Europe asked an independent "Group of Eminent Persons," headed by the former German Foreign Minister, Mr Joschka Fischer, to prepare a report on the challenges arising from the resurgence of intolerance and discrimination in Europe. The report, published in May 2011 under the title "Living together – Combining diversity and freedom in 21st-century Europe," assesses the seriousness of the risks, identifies their sources and makes a series of proposals for "living together" in open societies.[3]

The conclusion of the report is very clear on two points: our societies are very diverse; and we are not very successful in managing that diversity. The report contains very specific recommendations on how to do better and on how to transform diversity from a potential threat to a real benefit for our societies. Europe must fully embrace diversity if it wants to remain a region of peace and prosperity. This can only work if we acknowledge what unites us as citizens of free democracies: that we are equal before the law, that we respect human rights, and that we share certain rights and obligations within our societies.

---

3 Available on www.coe.int.

The report identifies a number of risks: rising intolerance; rising support for xenophobic and populist parties; discrimination; the presence of a population virtually without rights – Roma and irregular migrants among them; the emergence of parallel societies; Islamic extremism; the loss of democratic freedoms based on the questionable assumption that security and civil liberties are somehow at odds with each other (here the report formulates that "the imposition of excessive controls [of migration flows] do indeed represent a serious risk to the health and strength of our European democracies")[4]; and possible contradictions (or a "trade-off") between religious freedom and freedom of expression. The report also looks at how the various stakeholders – such as education, mass media, social partners, civil society, the religious communities, towns and cities, national governments and international institutions – can and should react.

Currently, member states are in the process of evaluating the report. Obviously, 47 different states with 47 governments of widely different political "colours" can be expected to arrive at widely different conclusions, when it comes to sensitive issues such as those connected to cultural diversity. However, there is a strong conviction that the common values, embodied in and protected by the European Convention on Human Rights, will prevail and offer a common basis for action.

One example of the current debate illustrates the issues at stake. In early 2011, in his address to the "Munich Security Conference," UK Prime Minister David Cameron spoke about the roots of terrorism. One of the underlying reasons, he said, is that "under the doctrine of state multiculturalism, we have encouraged different cultures to live separate lives, apart from each other and apart from the mainstream. We have failed to provide a vision of society to which they feel they want to belong."[5]

Mr Cameron is not alone in this forceful criticism. In many parts of Europe, politicians express their misgivings about the slow, or failing, integration of migrants and other minorities. Terrorism may be the most terrifying aspect, but ghettoisation, educational failure, unemployment, discrimination, marginalisation and mutual stereotyping are widespread symptoms of the same problem.

This being said, it is important to distinguish, as Mr Cameron rightly did in his Munich speech, between two notions: the "multiculturality" of our societies – an indisputable fact throughout Europe – and the policy approach we call "multiculturalism." The Council of Europe makes this

4 GEP Report, p. 24 (printed version).

5 http://www.number10.gov.uk/news/pms-speech-at-munich-security-conference/.

distinction very clear in the White Paper on Intercultural Dialogue. It clearly states that "multiculturalism" is an outdated and insufficient concept, based on a schematic opposition of majority and minority, which endorses separation – instead of dialogue, interaction and shared values. Instead, arguments are made in favour of "interculturalism" and an "interculturalist" conception of politics, based on the equal dignity of everyone, on the universal values of human rights, democracy and the rule of law. I find it very interesting that Pope Benedict XVI (before becoming Pope) used the same term – "interculturalist approach" – in a 2005 text.[6]

III. The Religious Dimension of Intercultural Dialogue

Religion has always played a role in the policy of the Council of Europe and other intergovernmental organisations. Over many years, the Council of Europe has dealt with religion specifically under two aspects: the protection of human rights, and the care and protection of cultural heritage.

A. The Protection of Human Rights

Article 9 of the European Convention for the Protection of Human Rights and Fundamental Freedoms, consists of two sentences. They read as follows:

> 1. Everyone has the right to freedom of thought, conscience and religion; this right includes freedom to change his religion or belief and freedom, either alone or in community with others and in public or private, to manifest his religion or belief, in worship, teaching, practice and observance.
>
> 2. Freedom to manifest one's religion or beliefs shall be subject only to such limitations as are prescribed by law and are necessary in a democratic society in the interests of public safety, for the protection of public order, health or morals, or for the protection of the rights and freedoms of others.

The European Court of Human Rights has developed case-law in over 900 judgements and decisions.

The human right of religious freedom has led to the principle of non-discrimination on religious grounds, which can be found in many other conventions, e.g. in the conventions on cyber criminality, nationality, adoption rights, mutual recognition of educational diplomas, legal status of migrant workers, data security, the fight against terrorism, and in the European Social Charter.

---

6 Habermas, H. and Ratzinger, J., *Dialektik der Säkularisierung. Über Vernunft und Religion*, Freiburg [Germany], Herder, 2005.

B. Protection of the Cultural Heritage

The second aspect, being the treatment of religion as part of the European cultural heritage, is much less developed and lesser known. Examples are the appreciation of the Jewish cultural heritage by the Parliamentary Assembly in 1987; the colloquium of the Secretary General on the contribution of the Islamic culture to the culture of Europe; and a number of intergovernmental programs in the context of the Cultural Convention mentioned before.

The protection of religious freedom and the acknowledgment of religions' contribution to the European cultural heritage, are important, but they refer perhaps only to a small segment of the religious reality of Europe. Moreover, the Council of Europe has denied dialogue with religious communities for a long time. This may be interpreted as an expression of "abstentionist laïcité," as it has been called – a strict neutrality of the state, marked by an element of suspicion and by non-dialogue.[7] Charging political conflicts with religious meaning in the early 1990s, and the strong emergence of Islamist tendencies in some parts of Western Europe, probably did not help – rather, this produced the opposite result. Religion was kept at bay, outside the political discourse. As a case in point, the "Declaration on Cultural Diversity," adopted in December 2000 by the Committee of Ministers of the Council of Europe, neither includes the word "religion" nor the term "religious communities."

Only recently has the Council of Europe begun to deal with religion and religious communities in a political way. The 3rd Council of Europe Summit, Warsaw, 2005, expressed itself more comprehensively than ever before on the role of religions. The Summit used, for the first time, the formulation of "Europe's cultural, religious and human inheritance," and committed itself to the promotion of "political, intercultural and interreligious dialogue," in order to make cultural diversity a source of mutual enrichment. The Final Declaration says that:

> We shall systematically encourage intercultural and inter-faith dialogue, based on universal human rights, as a means of promoting awareness, understanding, reconciliation and tolerance, as well as preventing conflicts and ensuring integration and the cohesion of society.

From the text of the third summit in Warsaw, three conclusions can be drawn. Firstly, the Council of Europe is ready to go beyond its past approach, particularly in connection with the dialogue between cultures,

[7] E.g. Willaime, J.-P., "Teaching Religious Issues in French Public Schools," in R. Jackson *et al.* (eds.), *Religion and Education in Europe: Developments, Contexts and Debates*, Münster [Germany], Waxmann, 2007.

and to accept religion as a component of culture. Secondly, the value basis of the Council of Europe, i.e. human rights, integration, and cohesion – applies also to the dialogue between religions and cultures. And thirdly, the Committee of Ministers (like the Parliamentary Assembly before it) expresses itself for the first time on a question that on the surface concerns only the religious communities themselves: interreligious dialogue.

Implementing this in practice is not easy. Professor Gil-Robles Gil Delgado, the first Commissioner of Human Rights of the Council of Europe, did groundbreaking work in this area. He began in 2000 a series of annual discussions with representatives of the three largest religious communities traditionally present in Europe. The topics focussed on the basic values of Europe: What and how can religious communities contribute to peace and reconciliation in Europe? How can the mutual understanding between cultures be promoted? How is the relationship between religion and state to be organised?

The Parliamentary Assembly has increased its efforts, in recent years, to promote dialogue with representatives of religious communities. The Committee of Ministers of the Council of Europe has opened the way for an open and regular exchange of views with religious communities, beginning in 2008 with the first "Exchange" on the religious dimension of intercultural dialogue. This now takes place every year, looking at various aspects such as the role of the media and education.

In short, the significance and the role of religious communities are recognised more strongly than was usual in past decades. We are convinced that the aims of the Council of Europe can be achieved only together with the religious communities, not against or without them. This can only work if the religious communities are ready to engage in dialogue.

IV. The Role of Academia

An institutional and policy-oriented view on the future perspective on intercultural and interreligious dialogue also relates to the role of universities and the academic community. In a conference of the newly established "International Institute for the Alliance of Civilizations" of the United Nations University in Barcelona[8] the Co-ordinator for Intercultural Dialogue of the Council of Europe, Ms Battaini-Dragoni, said:

> We know some things about culture, education and youth, but we need to know much more. We need to share this knowledge with more people. And

---

8 http://unu.edu/institutes-and-programmes/institutes/unu-iiaoc.

knowledge is only one dimension – we also need to build up intercultural competencies, not only among the elites, but as widely as possible.

Higher education has an obvious and important role to play. Learning and teaching intercultural competences are part of the "core business" of higher education. Beyond the competences that higher education will give learners in their specific field of study, higher education must give all graduates a set of generic competences if they are to meet today's academic, political, cultural and economic requirements. These competences include analytical ability, communication skills and the ability to make decisions despite only having incomplete information. Higher education should provide its graduates with competence in one or more foreign languages – an important point not only because it makes communication easier, but also because learning a foreign language means understanding and accepting that the same concept can be expressed in different ways.

In a recent project, the Council of Europe explored the role of higher education in promoting intercultural dialogue on campus, as well as in broader society. This has led to several publications in our "Higher Education" series. One of these was issued jointly with the International Association of Universities and draws on contributions from all parts of the world.[9]

Universities are important in increasing our understanding and knowledge of less widely spoken languages and of the cultures they carry, of the history and of societies that are less well known to us, and of how majorities and minorities relate to each other. Are there situations that tend to accentuate tensions between majorities and minorities? How can such tendencies be defused?

Higher education also has a role in deepening and expanding the understanding of history, of our "own" history, which – as most if not all – academic disciplines will tell us, is never entirely our history alone; but also how other cultures and societies have evolved through history.

What we need to be reminded of is that we need competences not only to get a job, but also for our other roles as citizens and human beings. I cannot resist the temptation to refer to the Council of Europe's important work on defining public responsibility for higher education and research. This led to another political recommendation from our

---

9 Cf. Bergan, S. and Damian, R. (eds.), *Higher Education for Modern Societies: Competences and Values,* Council of Europe higher education series, no. 15, 2010. Bergan, S. and van't Land, H. (eds.), *Speaking Across Borders: the Role of Higher Education in Furthering Intercultural Dialogue*, Council of Europe higher education series, no. 16, 2010. Bergan, S., *Not by Bread Alone*, Council of Europe higher education series, no. 17, 2011.

Committee of Ministers, which spelled out the main purposes of higher education. Preparing for a sustainable place in the economy is one of those purposes – but it is only one among several others. Higher education also needs to prepare students for life as active citizens in democratic societies; for personal development; and for the development and maintenance of a broad and advanced base of accessible knowledge.

In view of these essential functions for society, it would be unthinkable that higher education and research is not fully engaged in the promotion of cultural diversity and the teaching and learning of intercultural skills. We need to know about other cultures but we also need to understand them and we need to be able to act on this knowledge and understanding – to be able and willing to conduct intercultural dialogue. This, not only as an academic exercise, but also in our daily activities. This is where the academic community of the University of Padua, in particular the activities of its Jean Monnet Centre of Excellence, have an important role to play.

International Law of Human Rights for Fostering Religious Freedom and Intercultural Dialogue

Antonio PAPISCA

Professor Emeritus, University of Padua, UNESCO Chair "Human Rights, Democracy and Peace," Jean Monnet Chair ad honorem

I. Human Dignity, the Universal of All Universals

The horizon of human rights promotion and protection is increasingly – and visibly – a global one. The more this is emphasised by interdependence, and the more it becomes globalised, the more human rights are invoked everywhere. Anywhere life and freedom are threatened, regardless of the country or cultural and political context, we hear the cry for "Human Rights." Those who suffer under dictatorships and poverty demand respect for their human dignity: this is what makes International human rights law an effective law and in no way a lesser law than judgments passed by the courts. It is the conscience of all members of the human family, and especially the weakest and most vulnerable, which becomes the World Supreme Court.

Human dignity is the supreme value – the universal of all universals. The Universal Declaration of Human Rights – as Amartya Sen has argued – proclaims that recognition of human dignity is a meta-juridical assumption, in the sense that the inherent rights of the human person are "the parents of law, not the son of law." This is not, however, an abstract concept, since it concretely postulates the incarnation of human rights in each individual human being, made of body and soul, of spirit and matter, of intelligence, conscience and will. And from this ontological argument of the wholeness and integrity of the human being descends the principle of the interdependence of all human rights: civil, political, economic, social and cultural.

The history of human improvement of societies and institutions is founded on universal values. In recent decades, this dynamic has gathered speed thanks to three factors: the interdependence-globalisation of the planet, the development of a new International Law, rooted in the first part of the United Nations Charter; and the Universal Declaration of Human Rights, the transnational actions of a vast number of civil society organisations and movements founded on the principle of solidarity. In 1989 the Berlin Wall collapsed, putting an end to the diarchal regime of world governance. No political scientist had ever even dared to forecast this event: only a world war – they all used to say – could ever overcome the division into an Eastern and a Western Bloc. And, since that war would have been thermo-nuclear, it would never happen. Therefore, preserving the *status quo* was the name of the game.

The sacrifice of Jan Palach, a 19-year-old student, on January 16th 1969, did not prevent the brutal repression of the Prague Spring; equally, the Budapest uprising in 1956 did not prevail over the Soviet tanks. Yet, the values of freedom and justice continued to blossom through the commitment of the so-called dissidents, Charter 77 and Solidarity.

On 4 January 2011 Mohamed Bouazizi, aged 26 – a graduate who was also an exploited street vendor – set himself on fire in Tunisia. The whole country followed, going up in flames, until a few days later the dictator Ben Ali was overthrown.

The revolutionary movements that started in Egypt and Tunisia – and are now spreading to other Near Eastern countries – are founded on the axiological triad "human rights, rule of law, democracy." The young leaders of these movements never tire of stating that what is happening is revolution, not merely rebellion. More precisely: "*la révolution de la dignité humaine, des droits humains, de l'état de droit et de la démocratie*."

We must not miss this historic opportunity. The events on the southern shore of the Mediterranean must be interpreted through a lens of the "sign of the times," as an opportunity to better understand the immanent strength of universal ethics – at the core of which are religious values – and to use them to develop social cohesion, inclusion and peace, in accordance with article 28 of the Universal Declaration: "Everyone is entitled to a social and international order in which the rights and freedoms set forth in this Declaration can be fully realised."

II. The "Supra-constitutional" Relevance of Article 18 of the Universal Declaration of Human Rights

International human rights law, which is rooted in the United Nations Charter, in the Universal Declaration of human rights and in the two International Covenants of 1966 – respectively on civil and political rights, and in social, economic and cultural rights – specifically confronts the question of religious freedom. An expression of positive secular thought and a powerful sign of the times, it defines the correct relationship between the civil sphere and the religious one, beginning with the acknowledgment of each person's fundamental right to religious freedom.

Article 18 of the Universal Declaration declares that:

> Everyone has the right to freedom of thought, conscience and religion: this right includes freedom to change his religion or belief, and freedom, either alone or in community with others and in public or private, to manifest his religion or belief in teaching, practice, worship and observance.

This right is recognised in the context of a norm dealing with the right to freedom of thought and freedom of conscience. It is part of the sacred triad of the universal code of human rights – it forms the heart, the strong axiological nucleus of rights inherent to the dignity of the human person.

Article 18 of the International Covenant on civil and political rights takes up the text quoted above, further defining the import in four paragraphs. The content of pertinent articles in other international legal instruments is essentially similar, in particular the European Convention of 1950 (article 9), the Inter-American Convention of 1969 (article 12), the African Charter of human rights and peoples' rights of 1989 (article 8), the International Convention on children's rights of 1989 (article 14), the European Union Charter of fundamental rights of 2000 (article 10), the Arab Charter of human rights of 2004 (article 30).

It is also useful to remember the detailed stipulation offered by the UN Declaration regarding the elimination of all forms of intolerance and discrimination based on religion or belief, endorsed by the General Assembly on 25 November 1981. Among other points, it specifies that:

> No one shall be subject to coercion which would impair his freedom to have a religion or belief of his choice [...] no one shall be subject to discrimination by any State, institution, group of persons, or person on the grounds of religion or other belief [...] all States shall take effective measures to prevent and eliminate discrimination [...] the parents or, as the case may be, the legal guardians of the child have the right to organise life in accordance with their religion or belief within the family and bearing in mind the moral education in which they believe the child should be brought up [...] every child shall enjoy the right to have access to education in the matter of religion or belief in accordance with the wishes of his parents or, as the case may be, legal guardians, and shall not be compelled to receive teaching on religion or belief against the wishes of his parents or legal guardians, the best interests of the child being the guiding principle.

The document then states that the child "shall be brought up in a spirit of understanding, tolerance, friendship among peoples, peace and universal brotherhood, respect for freedom of religion, or belief of others, and in full consciousness that his energy and talents should be devoted to the service of his fellow man."

Similarly, article 19 of the Italian Constitution is perfectly aligned with current International law, establishing that "anyone is entitled to freely profess their religious belief in any form, individually or with others, and to promote them and celebrate rites in public or in private, provided they are not offensive to public morality."

This universal concordance of norms is itself a significant sign of the times: it indicates that we are contemplating a fundamental right of the person, which is assigned the highest juridical and moral value, and whose exercise is not confined simply to the private sphere.

The Recommendation 1962 (2011) "The religious dimension of intercultural dialogue," endorsed by the Parliamentary Assembly of the Council of Europe on 12 April 2011, emphasises this very aspect, affirming that the right to freedom of thought, conscience and religion "represents one of the foundations of a 'democratic society' […] it is, in its religious dimension, one of the most vital elements of believers' identity and their conception of life, but is also a precious asset for atheists, agnostics, sceptics or the unconcerned."

In his Message for the World Day of Peace 2011, Pope Benedict XVI is substantially in accordance with the concept, recognising what I am calling the supra-constitutional value of article 18 of the Universal Declaration: he declares that "among the fundamental rights and freedoms rooted in the dignity of the person, religious freedom enjoys a special status." Referring to the contents of the Second Vatican Council's "Declaration on religious freedom *Dignitatis humanae*," he explains its profound *raison d'être*:

> The right to religious freedom is rooted in the very dignity of the human person, whose transcendent nature must not be ignored or overlooked […]. This dignity understood as a capacity to transcend one's own materiality and to seek truth, must be acknowledged as a universal good, indispensable for the building of a society directed to human fulfilment.

The Pope also declares:

> Religious freedom expresses what is unique about the human person, for it allows us to direct our personal and social life to God, in whose light the identity, meaning and purpose of the person are fully understood. To deny or arbitrarily restrict this freedom is to foster a reductive vision of the human person.

Religious freedom, then, is not a separate part of the person's identity; it permeates his whole being. We cannot concretely separate the person's religiosity from other roles and conditions regarding his sociality. We must remember that the internationally recognised human rights are civil and political as well as economic, social, and cultural. As expressly required by International human rights law, they must be realised according to the principle of their interdependence and indivisibility: a principle rooted in the ontological truth of the human being's integrity, made up of body and soul, spirit and matter: the human being cannot be torn in two. To this regard the Pope warns: "It is inconceivable that believers should have to suppress a part of themselves – their faith – in order to be active citizens. It should never be necessary to deny God in order to enjoy one's rights."

III. Religious Values for a Just and Peaceful Glocal Order

As regards the Catholic religion in particular, we must first point out that the Popes of the 20th century constantly refer to international rules "based on moral norms," in particular to universal human rights law, and to the United Nations. Like his predecessors, in the aforementioned Message for the World Day of Peace, Benedict XVI once again points out that:

> International law is a model and an essential point of reference for states, insofar as it allows no derogation from religious freedom, as long as the just requirements of public order are observed. The international order thus recognises that rights of a religious nature have the same status as the right to life and to personal freedom, as proof of the fact that they belong to the essential core of human rights, to those universal and natural rights which human law can never deny.

This truth implies:

> Fostering an unswerving commitment to base positive law on the principles of the natural law. All this is necessarily consistent with respect for the dignity and worth of the human person enshrined by the world's peoples in the 1945 Charter of the United Nations, which presents universal values and moral principles as a point of reference for the norms, institutions and systems governing co-existence on the national and international levels.

This orientation clearly reflects the doctrine, now consolidated, according to which the Universal Declaration is customary law, containing principles of *ius cogens*.

Sustained also by these norms of universal *ius positum*, the Pope admonishes:

> Whenever the legal system at any level, national or international, allows or tolerates religious or antireligious fanaticism, it fails in its mission, which is to protect and promote justice and the rights of all. These matters cannot be left to the discretion of the legislator or the majority since, as Cicero once pointed out, justice is something more than a mere act which produces and

> applies law. It entails acknowledging the dignity of each person, which, unless religious freedom is guaranteed and lived in its essence, ends up being curtailed and offended, exposed to the risk of falling under the sway of idols, of relative goods which then become absolute.

In light of this strong acknowledgment of the providential utility of International human rights law, based on the dignity and centrality of each member of the human family, we may also suggest that current international norms allow us to hold that all those who make up the "people of God" within the Church, have a right, based on their fundamental right to religious freedom, to demand that the freedom and independence of the Catholic Church as a trans-national institution, beginning with its governing bodies, be safeguarded throughout the world. In other words, it is the fundamental right to religious freedom of the person who accepts and professes the Christian-Catholic faith – more than any analogies with the sovereignty of states or with centuries-long customs involving diplomatic relations and "concordatory" – which *de iure* founded the independence of the Church, both in the single countries and in the wider context of international relations.

In interpreting this international normative reality according to the grammar of signs of the times (which is widely used in the Encyclical "Pacem in Terris" by John XXIII, 1963), we might say that Providence is working in history to produce the fruits of a truly infrastructural relevance *pro humana dignitate*. To quote Benedict XVI again:

> The world needs God. It needs universal, shared ethical and spiritual values, and religion can offer a precious contribution to their pursuit, for the building of a just and peaceful social order at the national and international levels.

It immediately comes to mind that article 28 of the Universal Declaration offers formal, almost literal, legitimation: "Everyone is entitled to a social and international order in which the rights and freedoms set forth in this Declaration can be fully realised." This implies peace founded on justice – *opus iustitiae pax* – proclaimed, indeed, as a fundamental human right: "a gift of God and at the same time a task which is never fully completed." The Pope then adds: "Religious freedom is an authentic weapon of peace, with a *historical* and *prophetic mission*."

For the realisation of this project, to be carried out with "moral weapons, those which give strength and prestige to international law," the Pope invokes several Beatitudes of the Gospel, such as: "Blessed are you when men revile you and persecute you and utter all kinds of evil against you falsely on my account." The reference to the Sermon harmonises well – even on the grounds of "positive secularity" – with the UN Declaration "on the right and responsibility of individuals, groups and organs of society to promote and protect universally recognized human rights and fundamental freedoms," adopted by General Assembly resolution 53/144 on December 9th, 1998. Throughout the world, this is considered as the Magna Carta of *human rights defenders*, the pioneers of universal citizenship. It seems appropriate here to quote two of the twenty articles that compose it. Article 1: "Everyone has the right, individually and in association with others, to promote and to strive for the protection and realisation of human rights and fundamental freedoms at the national and international levels." The sense of this statement, the commitment, even the non-violent struggle to build peace, is without borders.

Article 7 states: "Everyone has the right, individually and in association with others, to develop and discuss new human rights ideas and principles and to advocate their acceptance." This means that the "project" for peace in justice, needs courageous people – capable of contradicting and disarming the followers of *Realpolitik*, whether they are politicians without scruples, or arrogant, presumptuous intellectuals. The Beatitude specifically appropriate to this case is that of the poor in spirit: those who are not ashamed to think on a high level; those whose gaze falls near and travels far at the same time; those who actively exercise the virtue of hope; those who do not fear derision; those who do not mind being accused of utopianism, or of being goody-goodies.

The three great monotheistic religions immanently foster peace because they foster human dignity and therefore, the life of the human being as created by God in his image. The life of the human person is therefore sacred; who kills him/her commits a crime against his/her Creator. The death penalty, the killing of an individual, is a crime against God. Similarly, war – collective killing – is a crime against God: "Every act of war […] is a crime against God and against humanity itself; with firmness and without hesitation it must be condemned" (Council Constitution "Gaudium et Spes," 1965, n. 80). The condemnation of war is even more radical, if possible, in the above-mentioned "Pacem in Terris" by John XXIII (n. 67): "*Quare aetate hac nostra, quae vi atomica gloriatur, alienum est a ratione, bellum iam aptum esse ad violata iura sarcienda.*" We might translate: "In an era like ours, which glories in the power of the atom, it is crazy to believe that war is the suitable instrument for re-establishing violated rights." In other words, war is for madmen.

In 2003, John Paul II offered this heart-wringing testimony: "I belong to the generation that lived through world war two and survived. I have the duty to say to all young people that have not experienced this: no more war." This is the same cry – *jamais plus la guerre, jamais plus la guerre* – made by Paul VI in his memorable speech given before the General Assembly of the United Nations in 1965.

Any authentic religion cannot but profess the imperative: *si vis pacem, para pacem*. If you want peace, prepare peace. This finds juridical formulation in the above-mentioned article 28 of the Universal Declaration of human rights. In this dynamic sphere of positive peace, religious freedom operates fruitfully through inter-religious dialogue. It becomes an instrument capable of spiritualising intercultural dialogue and of creating synergies for strengthening thanksgiving and worship of the one God; strengthening respect for universal ethics in the system of international relations; building bridges and fostering acts of solidarity within this system, in particular, favouring multi-lateral co-operation and the democratic development of legitimate international institutions, beginning with the United Nations. In short, it is capable of making the world a "shared home" for all members of the human family – a "house of prayer" and for peace. We recall that on 27 October 1987, John Paul II said: "Peace is the result of a prayer that, even in the diversity of religions, expresses the relationship with a supreme being that surpasses our mere human capacities."

IV. The Principle of "Ethico-juridical Compatibility"

We need to point out here that the exercise of the specific right to religious freedom must be compatible with the general principles of the universal code of human rights. Any religion or credo of a different nature, which pretends to legitimate false values such as racial, religious or sexual discrimination, violence, intolerance, or social exclusion, openly contradicts the principles and norms of the current International law of human rights, which declares that all members of the human family "are born free and equal in dignity and right. They are endowed with reason and conscience and should act towards one another in a spirit of brotherhood" (article 1 of the Universal Declaration).

We should also cite the second paragraph of article 20 of the International Covenant on civil and political rights: "Any advocacy of national, racial or religious hatred that constitutes incitement to discrimination, hostility or violence shall be prohibited by law." Significantly, the first paragraph of this article firmly states: "Any propaganda for war shall be prohibited by law." In short, in order for the claim for religious freedom to be legitimate, it must take into account all the other internationally recognised fundamental rights and freedoms. This means that religions, like cultures, must refer to the universal paradigm of human rights, and deeply examine their conscience in order to reveal the negative part of their respective histories, and repudiate it.

In order to elucidate what we might call the "principle of ethico-juridical compatibility," we could profitably appeal to the above-mentioned Recommendation 1962 (2011) of the Parliamentary Assembly of the Council of Europe: "The religious dimension of intercultural dialogue." Its underlying concept is that in Europe, while "Churches and religious communities have the right to exist and to organise themselves independently [...] freedom of religion and freedom to have a philosophical or secular world view are inseparable from unreserved acceptance by all of the fundamental values enshrined in the Convention." Explicit reference is made here to the European Convention for the protection of human rights and fundamental freedoms of 1950, and implicitly, to International human rights law as a whole.

The Parliamentary Assembly of the Council of Europe's Recommendation clarifies the fact that "differences, as long as they are compatible with respect for human rights and the principles that underpin democracy, not only have every right to be there but also help determine the essence of our plural societies." It "considers it not only desirable, but necessary, that the various Churches and religious communities – in particular the Christians, Jews and Muslims – recognise each other's right to freedom of religion and belief."

Furthermore it affirms that:

> It is also indispensable that people of all beliefs and world views, religious or otherwise, accept to intensify dialogue building on the common assertion of all people's equal dignity and wholehearted commitment to democratic principles and human rights. These are two crucial conditions for developing a new culture of living together.

The Assembly "calls upon all religious communities and Churches to persevere in their endeavours for dialogue, including with humanist movements, in order to work in unison to attain the goal of effectively safeguarding these values everywhere, throughout Europe and worldwide."

We find special relevance in that part of the Strasbourg Recommendation that regards the teaching of religion in schools, and the formation of teachers of religion and persons having religious responsibilities. After affirming the importance and function of the education system relative to teaching about and understanding various cultures and religions, the Recommendation emphasises the need for religious communities and states to co-operate with one another in reviewing this sector together, "following a holistic approach."

The principle of "state neutrality" as regards religious education in schools is expressly invoked in urging the national authorities to commit themselves to preventing parents' religious and non-religious convictions from being "offended." The Recommendation affirms that the internal autonomy of religious institutions in forming persons assigned religious responsibilities, beginning with ministers of worship, is a principle intrinsic to religious freedom, but that it has a limit in fundamental rights, in the principles of democracy and in the rule of law. With this premise, the Parliamentary Assembly, while urging religious institutions to study together, within a context of inter-religious dialogue, how best to educate their own "cadres," at the same time gives indications as to method and substance: such religious formation must be carried out open-mindedly, through dialogue and co-operation among religious communities; it must transmit knowledge and understanding of other religions and faiths; and it must educate persons to respect human rights, the democratic principles, and the rule of law as a common basis for dialogue and co-operation amongst themselves.

The Strasburg Recommendation's insistence on the paradigm of human rights, the rule of law and democratic principles, must be interpreted in light of the concept of positive secularity. In affirming that human rights must be included even in the educational curricula of ecclesiastic persons (religious responsibles), the Council of Europe clearly has no intention of promoting the "secularisation" of religious practice. Human rights are universal ethical values, recognised as such by international *ius positum*: knowledge relating to them, being intrinsically value-driven, is in perfect accord with the universalistic, transcendent vocation of the great religions: in particular, with the three monotheistic religions present in Europe.

I might add that the duty of duties – shall we say – for anyone invoking respect for his/her right to religious freedom, is that of the believer towards his/her own religion: anyone asking for the respect of this very sensitive right, must first of all honour his/her own religion, that is, be consistent by word and deed with the creed professed, and participate actively in constructing dialogue and peace along a pathway leading from local levels to the great sanctuaries of international politics.

V. Inter- instead of Multi- for Cultural Dialogue and Inclusion in the European Space

> One thing no one should doubt: if we are to build a world where law prevails over the use of force, the rule of law shall need to be its bedrock [...] Where, after all, do universal human rights begin? In small places, close to home – so close and so small that they cannot be seen on any maps of the world. Yet they are the world of the individual person; the neighbourhood he lives in; the school or college he attends; the factory,

farm, or office where he works. Such are the places where every man, woman, and child seeks equal justice, equal opportunity, equal dignity without discrimination. Unless these rights have meaning there, they have little meaning anywhere. Without concerted citizen action to uphold them close to home, we shall look in vain for progress in the larger world. (Eleanor Roosevelt).

The effects of religious inspiration on the development of intercultural dialogue may well be of fundamental importance, especially as regards processes of inclusion where people live their daily lives, and the acceptance of the new concept of plural citizenship. What follows is an example of practical *infrastructural* implications at the local level.

The government of cities is conditioned by the effects of globalisation in various domains – starting with the economy – and by increasingly rapid migration and multi-culturalisation processes: cities need to equip themselves in order to actively adapt to these new dynamics and to take a pro-active role in global, multilevel governance. The model cannot be that of historical multi-ethnic cities, made up of sub-systems that draw their strength for co-existence from the mutual defence of different identities – that is, in a perspective in which multi- prevails over inter-.

The model for a sustainable city is an holistic model, based on the fundamental rights of the human person more than on a "minorities" approaches, within which the sub-systemic (ethnic, cultural, religious) dimensions are encouraged to actively interact, in compliance with the overarching systemic paradigms. Sustainability is expressed through the interaction of the different cultural components, pursuing the goals of the common good and good governance, in full respect of all diversities compatible with the systemic value system (or ethical-legal system).

The multicultural city is required to become essentially intercultural, stimulated to act as a laboratory for human security, human development, new (plural) citizenship, universal culture (or culture of the universal) and an active workshop of good governance. To use the language of cybernetics, our cities are called on to trigger active adaptation processes in view of the current world transformation: this involves abandoning those features of their original identity that contrast with the substance of the new paradigm provided by International human rights law.

The joint Council of Europe and European Commission Programme on Intercultural Cities provide a good indication:

The Intercultural City does not simply 'cope' with diversity but uses it as a source of dynamism, innovation, creativity and growth. It accepts diversity

> as a norm and helps people from all groups – minority as well as the majority – benefit from it. The intercultural city shapes its educational, social, housing, employment, cultural and related policies, and its public spaces, in ways which enable people from different cultural backgrounds to mix, exchange and interact for mutual benefit.

UNESCO is on the same wavelength, as we can see from its fundamental Convention on the "Protection and Promotion of the Diversities of Cultural Expressions," adopted in 2005, and which entered into force in 2007: it was ratified by the EU member states and by the European Union as well. The Preamble of this Convention states that "Cultural diversity, flourishing within a framework of democracy, tolerance, social justice and mutual respect between peoples and cultures, is indispensable for peace and security at the local, national and international levels," and that cultural diversity is important "for the full realisation of human rights and fundamental freedoms proclaimed in the Universal Declaration of Human Rights and other universally recognised instruments."

Among the many articles of this Convention, I would like to highlight the one that establishes eight guiding principles (article 2) and the one that provides the Convention's definitions (article 4). The first principle establishes that "Cultural diversity can be protected and promoted only if human rights and fundamental freedoms, such as freedom of expression, information and communication, as well as the ability of individuals to choose cultural expressions, are guaranteed." The definition of cultural diversity "refers to the manifold ways in which the cultures of groups and societies find expression. These expressions are passed on within and among groups and societies." Article 4 further states that:

> Cultural diversity is made manifest not only through the varied ways in which the cultural heritage of humanity is expressed, augmented and transmitted through the variety of cultural expressions, but also through diverse modes of artistic creation, production, dissemination, distribution and enjoyment, whatever the means and technologies used.

Especially useful in relation to cities as intercultural workshops is definition number 8: "Interculturality refers to the existence and equitable interaction of diverse cultures and the possibility of generating shared cultural expressions through dialogue and mutual respect."

Thus, the intercultural city is envisaged as a womb in which new and "shared" cultural expressions are nurtured, in other words where the development of a universal culture is fostered, a culture which holds as its central tenet the principle that "recognition of the inherent dignity and of the equal and inalienable rights of all members of the human family is the foundation of freedom, justice and peace in the world" (Preamble of the Universal Declaration of Human Rights).

From this perspective, intercultural dialogue is not merely an exchange of cognitive data on human beings' different identities: the exchange is needed in order to agree on a single transcultural-universal code and to pursue together, as already pointed out, the goals of the common good. In brief, the intercultural city does not accept and freeze cultural diversity as an absolute, static value; rather, it considers it as the means of cultural enrichment, as a driver for human development and human security and for social and territorial cohesion within a scheme of multi-level governance.

It is very important that there should be a shared code of rules, on which there is consensus, and which is used as the instrument for the construction of the inclusive city. These rules cannot but be rooted in the universal code of human rights and in democratic constitutions, and their content must become part of the culture of the city. This must also be carried out through formal means – being enshrined in its statutes and charters of principles. There is an increasing number of examples of this "glocalisation" (and "popularisation") of International human rights law: from the "European Charter for the safeguarding of human rights in the City" (2000), whose article 1 proclaims the "Right to the City" as a fundamental right, to the "Montreal Charter of Rights and Responsibilities" (2005).

The precursor to this highly innovative practice, is what happened in Italy, starting in 1991. In compliance with the law on local autonomies (in the sense of increasing self-government), Municipalities and Provinces drew up new statutes: hundreds of these statutes include rules recognising human rights, in particular peace as a fundamental right of the person and of the peoples, with explicit reference to the principles enshrined in the national Constitution and in the International law of human rights. Some of these statutes refer explicitly to the Universal Declaration, to the International Convention on the Rights of the Child, to the Charter of Fundamental Rights of the European Union and even to the United Nations Charter.

The deeper meaning of these legal developments at the sub-national level, is that local government institutions intend to affirm the real effectiveness of a Law that is intrinsically universal, since it brings together the legal systems at different levels by referring to a single and shared "fundamental norm." The intercultural city promotes and benefits from this link, and can thus proclaim – including through formal deeds – its primary "responsibility to protect" the fundamental rights of all those who live on its territory, thereby claiming also its right to participate in multilevel governance processes.

VI. The Intercultural City: an Identikit

The intercultural city is a workshop for the development of plural citizenship. The birth of International human rights law in 1945-1948 launched the age of *plenitudo iuris* for all legal systems and, by implication, *plenitudo civitatis* – fullness of citizenship. By virtue of the international legal recognition of human rights, the concept and status of citizenship should be redefined based on the notion that *ius humanae dignitatis* prevails over the traditional parameter of *ius sanguinis*. The international recognition of the human rights of any member of the human family, assigns pre-eminence to this universal citizenship; this requires that traditional forms of citizenship (national, regional, EU) comply fully with the overarching universal legal statute of the human person.

The intercultural city is an inclusive city, meaning that it shoulders the responsibility of establishing the conditions necessary for all the rights and duties of citizenship to be concretely exercisable by all those (autochthonous and immigrant) who live in it. Inclusion does not mean integration, but it is the necessary prerequisite for processes of voluntary integration. The inclusive city respects the multiple identities of persons and fosters the acquisition of a transcending civic identity, understood as a greater civic awareness, which is needed to develop interculturality and solidarity projects for pursuing goals of common good.

The intercultural city is secular by definition: it is a space open to the exercise of all human rights by all persons (including the right to freedom of religion and worship), according to the principle of the interdependence and indivisibility of all rights. It promotes positive secular values, in that it is open to enriching autochthonous values and cultural symbols with new values and symbols. As previously emphasised, religious belief is not a separate part of a person's identity: it permeates the person in his/her entirety. Faith cannot be separated – except in an abstract manner – from the roles and the status a person enjoys in society; from that person's civic commitment. It has been very aptly stated, that "it is inconceivable that believers should have to suppress a part of themselves – their faith – in order to be active citizens. It should never be necessary to deny God in order to enjoy one's rights" (Benedict XVI).

Based on a misguided interpretation of secularism, in some European contexts immigrants are expected to deny *in toto* their history and the religious symbols that has characterised the most deeply rooted part of their identity. There is a need to distinguish between negative and positive secularism. Positive secularism does not call for the eradication and cancellation of all cultural and religious symbols, of one's historical roots – provided that they are compatible with the universal code of human rights – on the contrary, it is a space of freedom, open to the exercise of all human rights for all, including freedom of religion.

In this age in which societies are becoming increasingly multicultural – especially in Europe – the lessons of a secularism that respects all rights pertaining to a person are fully in the spirit of bridge-building and of inclusion. Of course, this is on the condition that the cultural diversities are always compatible with the paradigms of these universal values, in other words as long as they cleanse themselves and drink at the common spring of universal values in order to engage in fertile dialogue. This means that there shall be no need to remove existing religious symbols, or other symbols of collective identity, from public places: if necessary, additional symbols can be added, as long as the message they convey is compatible with the Universal Declaration. Negative secularism is impoverishment; positive secularism enriches all.

The intercultural city is genuinely a "territory" but not a "boundary." It contributes to the redefinition of the category of territoriality, in that it mitigates the monopolistic use made of the term by States; it instead promotes forms of cross-border territorial co-operation for the purpose of strengthening social and territorial cohesion.

The intercultural city is the Human Rights City. As such, it establishes its own "human rights infrastructure," consisting essentially in a Statute recalling the principles enshrined in the national Constitution and in International human rights law, with, for example, a Human Rights Committee, a City Councillor responsible for human rights, peace and intercultural dialogue, and an Ombudsman. Finally, the intercultural city is a city committed to educating its citizens in human rights, dialogue, solidarity, beauty, artistic creativity and respect for nature and the environment. It is a laboratory for a new Humanism, open to transcendence and positive secularity.

PART II

VALUE-DRIVEN FOUNDATIONS OF EUROPE

A Value-Driven Foundation: Introduction

Léonce BEKEMANS

Part II analyses the value-driven foundations of Europe and the European integration process from different perspectives (historical, ethical and human rights), providing a solid base for reading, understanding and developing future developments. The various papers contribute to clarifying, exploring and identifying possible answers to the current European debate about its objectives and finality.

In "*Value-Driven Foundations of European Integration*" Thomas Jansen stresses that the need to recover the common historical and cultural origins of Europe is essential in order to address the challenges the European project is confronted with today. The classic principles underlying the European unification process – peace, reconciliation, solidarity, justice and freedom – are now integrated with new emerging values such as sustainable development, political and social subsidiary and social peace. These values and principles, representing all together the ethics of the European unification process, are at the same time substantially Christian ethics. In order to build a European common future, they have to be preserved, cultivated and applied to the world, changing realities as well as the interactions amongst European and non-Europeans.

The paper by Léonce Bekemans on "*The Idea of Europe: Identity-building from a Historical Perspective*" offers first a historical reading of the idea of Europe from its classical origin to today's cosmopolitan understanding. Secondly it proposes an overview of the building of a European identity, explaining concepts, models and paths in the EU framework. The author perceives Europe as a community of shared values evolving throughout history with a multiplicity of expressions and experiences. Today it is a political project with a legal framework that struggles to keep its identity in the interdependence and complexity of the global and European systems. The paper pleas for a value based foundation of Europe to inspire and commit its citizens to a value-driven European identity and citizenship.

In "*A Spiritual Foundation of Europe: a Future Oriented Perspective*," Luk Bouckaert, Emeritus Professor of Ethics at the Catholic University of Leuven, argues that the economic-driven logic at the heart of the European integration process is under pressure. While the European marked model is confronted with global, ecological and religious challenges, the author defends the case for a spiritual foundation of Europe. Starting from an analysis of the failures of a market driven process of European integration and the potential of a value-driven alternative, this paper first deals with the principle of universal responsibility as a foundational value commitment, creating unity in diversity. It then explores the meaning of spirituality and the nature of economics in a value-driven process of European integration.

Christoph Eberhard, researcher and visiting Professor in Anthropology and Theory of Law at the Saint Louis Faculties in Brussels, explores in "*Human Rights and Intercultural Dialogue: European Challenges and Perspectives*," the European originality of the question of human rights and intercultural dialogue from the perspective of legal anthropology. On the one hand, he highlights the major changes that have contributed to emancipating human rights thought and practice in the intercultural dialogue from a universal to a pluralist approach, on the other hand, he identifies the four poles delineating the pluralist horizon of living together: alterity, complexity, interculturality and humanity. The paper finally asserts that a dialogical awareness of these four poles may lead to the emergence of a responsible pluralism.

In the chapter "*The European Parliament as an Institutional Memory Entrepreneur*" Wolfram Kaiser, a historian and Professor of European Studies, analyses the role of the European Parliament in the politics of European memory. It focuses on the EP's promotion of a shared collective memory to strengthen notions of commonality and identity, to foster a commitment to shared values and norms, and to enhance its legitimacy in the eyes of its citizens. He argues that the more individualised character of memory means that a top-down approach to engineering new forms of collective memory is not likely to succeed because memory politics and cultural integration are shaped as much by initiatives from below, by citizens in localities, as from above, by state institutions.

A different approach in context and content to value-driven foundations in Europe is presented by Riccardo Scartezzini, in his paper "*The Champions of the Cultural Dialogue between Europe and China: Jesuit Missionaries and Scientists in China between the 17th and the 18th century.*" Some valid lessons can be drawn from the outcomes of two centuries of efforts to promote cultural understanding between two millenary societies: China and Europe. A very interesting intercultural encounter was that of the first China Jesuit missionaries with the Mandarins of the Ming and Qing dynasties, from the end of the 16th until the beginning of the 18th century. These Jesuits were both missionaries and scientists and presented a peculiar attitude towards Chinese culture, in the footsteps of Matteo Ricci. Ricci's strategy entailed an adaptation to Chinese customs. Furthermore, it involved the use of Western scientific and technological knowledge to support the propagation of the Christian faith, carrying out a top-to-bottom conversion of the Chinese people. Ricci was the pioneer of the mission and he was followed by many other less well known China Jesuits who, nevertheless, greatly contributed to the cultural encounters between China and the West: Adam Schall, Giulio Aleni, Ferdinand Verbiest, Martino Martini, Johann Schreck, Michael Boym, Prospero Intorcetta, Joachim Bouvet etc. Unfortunately, the "Chinese Rites controversy" deeply influenced the life and the work of these missionaries and eventually led to the suppression of the Society of Jesus in the late 18th century, thus ending their exceptional efforts.

Value-Driven Foundations of European Integration

Thomas JANSEN

European Movement

When speaking about the values which have driven the foundations of Europe, we have to consider a variety of different aspects and dimensions, dealing with the ideal, spiritual, cultural, political, historical and other elements of the European project as well as its realisation, i.e. the process of European unification.

Today we are looking back over six decades of the history of this European project. From the onset – from the European Coal and Steel Community in 1952 to its current shape as the European Union – the evolution of this project can be read as an extraordinary success story. This is all the more true, considering that Europe was torn apart by a terrible war which ended just a few years before the first efforts to initiate the process of European unification were undertaken. The psychological and moral ruins, caused by nationalist and racist ideologies that were put into practice during the war, continued to be widely experienced, even after the war, for quite a long time.

I. Historical Premises

The unification of Europe and the building of a Community embracing a significant number of peoples and states is a long and complex process that requires patience and understanding towards the partners and neighbours who are part of this process. The serious crisis that has hit the European Union in recent times has brought related difficulties to the fore. This crisis is marked by a lack of trust among member states, due to heavy indebtedness contracted by certain countries belonging to the Euro area and by the desperate efforts to safeguard the stability of the common currency, which represents the central nucleus of the European Union and is the solid expression of an ideal cohesion. This dramatic crisis is wearing out the solidarity between member states and is affecting trust relationships with national and

European institutions. It entails not only a risk for the integration and unification process, but also for democracy in Europe.

The risk of giving up and relinquishing all hopes that the endeavour will succeed is real and it is expressed in a growing diffidence on the part of the public opinion. To counter this temptation and convince others that it is worthwhile to persevere with faith and trust on what has been recognised as the right path, it is important to remember the value system underlying European unification, as expressed in the Founding Fathers' commitment in the 1950s and in the founding treaties of the European Communities and the EU.

No one could guarantee the success of European integration, which had been consolidated over past decades. It was, however, widely acknowledged that the enterprise, which had been launched on the solid grounds of the common interest of all Europeans, did not have to fail – because no better way existed for overcoming the moral and material ruins, ensuring peace across Europe, reconstructing its villages and towns, defending the freedom of European populations and promoting their welfare.

The history of integration and unification has always been marked by heavy ups and downs. The evolution of the European Union is characterised by an oscillation. Times of momentous changes, with new successes of integration and related, ensuing, optimism, were always followed by crises, retrocession, stagnation and phases of pessimistic forecasts. These changes express the dialectic dynamics referring to and aiming for the future, reinforcing finally the positive aspects of Europe's unification process. This seems to be a fundamental condition of that process. The ongoing crisis will probably trigger a renewed thrust that will go beyond the defeatist view that the monetary Union and the European Union have reached a dead end. In the past, the European Union has always grown through its crises. Crises stir those forces aimed at their resolution, giving them the necessary energy to dare and overcome the status quo, contributing to the development of the European government system, strengthening its democratic and federal structures.

In other words, the European unification project will not fail under this crisis. An important reason for this lies indeed in the "value-driven foundations of Europe." Therefore it is highly opportune and even necessary to speak today – when Europe seems to be reduced to the deficits of its member states and to the problems of its banking system – about these foundations, and to recall the ideal, spiritual and cultural roots of the European project.

II. Classic Principles of European Unification Building

Examining the establishment of the European Community at the beginning of the 1950s, it is easy to identify the desire for peace, reconciliation, solidarity, justice and freedom as determining values and principles; values recovered after the terrible war waged by unrestrained nationalism and by a totalitarian ideology that scorned human dignity. These principles represent the backbone of the ethical consensus on which reposes the European unification building and its most significant concretisation, i.e. the European Union.

Peace was a prerequisite for the rebirth and evolution of the nations of Europe as well as for the healing of its societies. This peace was to be anchored in action and fact and given enduring expression in the shape of institutionalised, transnational co-operation.

There could be no lasting peace without Reconciliation between former enemies. Considerable efforts were needed if the various sides were to understand each other and accept each other's differences. This learning process was made possible by working together in the service of a common project for the future.

Solidarity between the nations was a necessary precondition for the promotion and accomplishment of that joint project for the future, namely the creation of a European Community. This solidarity was to be sought in the joint action and joint solution of common problems and it had to be given practical and concrete expression in the shaping of common policies.

Justice was a necessary prerequisite for a living form of solidarity, supported and accepted by all partners. It had to be based on treaties organising the relations between the parties and setting out rules for a co-existence transcending the borders.

Lastly, Freedom was a necessary precondition for the fulfilment of human dignity and for the application of all these values and principles in political action as well as in its manifestations in society and in people's private lives.

Indeed, as points of reference, these classic values are, and will remain, just as indispensable to the European Union as they have been to the European Community throughout the decades since it was founded. They are comprised, in one way or another, in the founding Treaties – as rules, rights, obligations or guiding principles. However, the new challenges confronting us call for a measure of revitalisation – and perhaps of reappraisal.

More precisely, given the success of the reconciliation process so far, it is no longer primarily a matter of peace between the European peoples and states, but one of social peace in Europe, which is under threat from poverty, exclusion and the loss of social cohesion and – because of globalisation and its consequences – of world peace, which is threatened by the glaring differences between the rich and poor continents.

Thus, today, reconciliation is strongly needed, along with the recovery of solidarity within European societies and within our world society. In order to overcome social injustice and the related fragmentation of society, it is necessary to reaffirm the rule of law as the foundation of peaceful co-existence at all levels, and in particular, at the level of "our one world."

III. Emerging Values of European Integration

Beyond these classic principles which underlie the European unification process, new values arising from a new conception of transnational political and social accountability, are now gaining ground as guiding principles for the Union – for example that of "sustainable development" as an expression of solidarity with subsequent generations. Another example is "subsidiarity." It concerns us as "political subsidiarity," in the shape of autonomy for parliaments and governments at the different levels of governance, including local and regional authorities, in matters falling within their respective fields of responsibility, in parallel with co-responsibility for the solution of problems in all other fields. But it concerns us as well as "social subsidiarity," which finds expression in the autonomy of the active forces of civil society in those areas of responsibility in which they have chosen to work or to be involved.

Altogether these values represent the ethics of the European Unification process. Derived from the long history of European nations sharing the same destiny, they are substantially Christian ethics. They must be defended, cultivated and applied to the changing realities, particularly in times of crises.

IV. Christian Legacy and Beyond

Europe's centuries-long history engendered, indeed, a community of interdependent and intertwined destinies. Vicinity, along with collective experiences, has led to the establishment of special relationships linking European populations, whether or not explicitly acknowledged. Also in those cases where co-existence has turned into confrontation, where vicinity prompted the erection of boundaries, and whereby cohabitation has been transformed into conflicts that ultimately led to the outburst of war – the community experience has deeply shaped Europeans, originating their very identity.

The common historical experience is strengthened by considerable cultural unity, for which paradoxically, multiplicity represents a constitutive element. That multiplicity has a common root, namely, the combination of Greek-Roman Mediterranean culture and continental Slav-Germanic culture. In this synthesis, Christianity played a decisive, catalysing role. In the Middle Ages, the European world that was born of this synthesis always acknowledged its unity. In modern times, and in contemporary societies, this awareness never ceased to exist, despite fierce armed conflicts, waged under the banner of the differentiation of nations and nationalistic and/or ideological antagonisms.

Certainly, today this unitary awareness is no longer based on a declared and lived adherence to the Church or to a Christian religious community. But even Europe is no longer the "Christian Europe" that was taken for granted a century ago, dear to European populations after World War Two and notably in the aftermath of the Holocaust, as it was dear to the Founding Fathers of the European Community, who considered it their hope and their project. European Christianity presents itself today with differentiated facets, and so does Europe. Catholicism, Orthodoxy, along with Protestantism – a product of the Reformation – with their diverse expressions, contributed to the establishment of the multifarious cultural richness of our continent. On the other hand, the various confessions, for too long viewed as opposing ways of Salvation, mutually excluding one other, implied a considerable potential for conflicts and divisions.

But if Christianity, with its numerous manifestations and tensions, marked by wrong paths and divisions, is considered co-responsible for Europe's divisions, then the extent to which Christianity has always been exploited by political leadership – falling victim to territorial, hegemonic and social divisions – should not be overlooked. In a complex way, the history of Christianity is reflected in the destiny of Europe – and vice versa.

Even the Enlightenment, which from many angles questioned ecclesiastic traditions and doctrines, could only flourish on Christian grounds. For this reason, the claim that Christianity – an exception is made for Orthodoxy – has internalised the Enlightenment in its proclamation and, in particular, within its very own social doctrine, is not contradictory. On the other hand, it can be said that even atheistic humanism, born of the Enlightenment, cannot deny its Christian roots, even when marked by evident anticlerical and antireligious stands.

Despite numerous attempts at erasing the forming role of Christianity, its contribution to Europe remains; perceivable across European nations and cultures. European populations' cultural consensus, made possible by Christianity, has been a fundamental prerequisite of the astonishing success of the European unification process of past decades. Such consensus is not obvious; it must be healed and recreated, over and over again. It is the condition *sine qua non* for European cohesion, which encompasses the future development of the European Union.

Whenever emphasis is placed on the strong, determining influence of Christianity on European culture, along with its close ties with the history of our Continent, the fact that Europe's spiritual, cultural, and social imprint is owed exclusively to Christianity, fails to be mentioned. Also those traditions that Christianity absorbed and confronted, or which are the result of Europe's encounter with Christianity – such as the Enlightenment – left significant vestiges which contributed to the shaping of Europe and to the European populations' "formation."

This is true especially in the case of Judaism, which Christianity stems from. Europe's Jewish-Christian heritage is thus a truthful concept. Indeed Judaism – with Christianity – was present in Europe for centuries, in the form of important communities that contributed to noteworthy expressions of European identity in a number of sectors, notably in the artistic, literary and scientific realms as well as in the economy, industry and trade sectors, also owing to the activity of the Jewish communities and to that of their eminent personalities.

Also Islam, the third religious tradition born in the Mediterranean, whose doctrine stems from the Bible, the Book of Books, has exerted its influence on European culture and consciousness. The transmission into Europe of a large part of the philosophical and literary production of ancient Greece was made possible thanks to Islamic scholars, whose scientific knowledge exceeded by far that which characterised the early Latin Middle-Ages. Moreover, their contribution was critical to the achievement of a synthesis encompassing the rationality of ancient texts and Christian spirituality.

It is equally necessary not to underestimate the political, religious and civilisation challenges that Europe was called to address for centuries in its relations with Islam and the Muslim world, and especially in the Balkans, which in the 19th century were still under the Turkish Ottoman rule, which had extended its dominion to Vienna in the 17th century. Also in Spain, where the Arab Moors ruled until the 15th century, the encounter between Christianity and Islam was significantly fruitful, with traces that are visible still today.

This must be remembered. In fact, when the populations of Northern, Southern, Eastern and Western Europe convene to address decisive issues, they must also necessarily address the question of their historical and cultural origins. Efforts aimed at a common future imply the need to recover these common origins. Remembering the influence that contributed – alongside and in conjunction with Christianity – to the shaping of the spiritual profile and of the cultural identity of Europe, is a necessity, because simultaneously with the unification process, we are experiencing new encounters with other religions and faith communities.

At present these encounters are especially evident in the ongoing, massive integration of Islam, from Turkey and from the Arab countries, a phenomenon that constitutes a challenge for the Europeans, Christian believers or not, bearers of European "leading culture," marked primarily by Christianity. Referring to the sense and purpose of the European unification movement, this challenge can be addressed and met only by means of ongoing dialogue. Indeed, historical experience has taught us that encounters with the "Other" and with the "Stranger" can be a source of enrichment if they are aimed at mutual understanding, conscious of the tragic consequences of policies based on an a-priori refusal and opposition.

A dialogue tending towards peace and reconciliation can succeed only if it emanates from deep-grounded beliefs and if it rejects all attempts to relativise European values and principles. If we take our faith or convictions – and therefore ourselves – seriously we will be capable of taking others seriously too. It is the condition sine qua non for successful mutual understanding among Europeans and with Non-Europeans.

The Idea of Europe:
Identity-building from a Historical Perspective[1]

Léonce BEKEMANS

Jean Monnet Chair "Globalisation, Intercultural Dialogue and Inclusiveness in the EU," Academic co-ordinator of the Jean Monnet Centre of Excellence "Intercultural Dialogue, Human Rights and Multi-level Governance," University of Padua

Introduction

History illustrates that Europe is a dynamic and evolving entity with many faces, multiple identities, multiple expressions and experiences and diversified co-operation forms.[2] Europe is a two thousand year old civilisation with a multiplicity of cultures; it is also a socio-economic model and a unique integration process. The whole European history is characterised by forms of and attempts at economic, political, military and cultural co-operation to find an equilibrium between integration and diversity within certain contours. Europe is however, in the first place a community of shared values, based on values such as the centrality of the human being, freedom, equality, respect for human rights, and acceptance of diversity as an asset, tolerance, justice and solidarity. Europe is also a political project trying to unite people while respecting their diversity. Today however Europe is struggling to keep this diversified societal model alive in the midst of complex and interconnected issues of globalisation vs. europeanisation.[3]

Identity and identity-building have been treated by numerous scholars from various disciplines and perspectives. Many have contributed to understanding the complexity and the dynamism of these terms and offered theoretical instruments to deal with changing realities.

---

1 Parts of this contribution have benefitted from Chiarello, A., *European Identity beyond the Nation State. Plurality and Inclusion for a new Democratic Space*, Thesis, June 2012, University of Padua.

2 An innovative analysis of ideas about Europe from an interdisciplinary perspective is given by Dainotto, R., *Europe (in Theory)*, Durham, Duke University Press, 2007.

3 Giddens, A., *Europe in the Global Age*, Cambridge, Polity Press, 2007.

However, identity remains an open concept, increasingly shaped by growing interdependencies and transformations in the current international system. "*The globalising world is characterised by some asymmetry between the growing extra-territorial nature of much power and the continuing territoriality of the ways in which people live their everyday lives.*"[4]

The European Union can be perceived as a unique but complex system of governance with a policy mix of supranational and intergovernmental elements. After many centuries of rivalries and wars among European countries, the end of the Second World War paved the way for a peace-building process of integration. This process has followed a "neo-functionalist" step-by-step approach very much embodied by Jean Monnet, envisaging spill-over effects from the economy to the political arena and beyond. We are convinced that the only way of making people identify with Europe and build a sense of belonging without trying to replace national affiliations or marginalise regional or national identities, is the development of a community driven political project, embodied in a set of shared values and common principles. Such a political consensus might give coherence to its actions, legitimacy to its institutions and inspiration to the citizens of Europe.[5]

I. The Idea of Europe

The French poet and philosopher Paul Valéry described the common characteristics of Europe in his "*Homo Europaeus.*" He focussed on the Europe of the spirit, shaped by the legacies of Rome, Athens and Jerusalem. This means that Europe is a world of historical references, memories and experiences shared by people. In his book "*The Origins of European civilisation*"[6] Hendrik Brugmans identified two major elements of European civilisation: active participation in its many spiritual heritages and a series of historical experiences from the Roman Empire onwards. He distinguished three phases: the Empire of Constantine or a Mediterranean Europe, Medieval or Christian Europe and the Europe of the Nation-State. It is in the broader space of today's

---

4 Bekemans, L., "A Cosmopolitan Perspective of Multi-level Governance in Europe," in *Pace Diritti Umani/Peace Human Rights*, 2/2010. p. 46.

5 Jansen, T. (ed.), *Reflections on European Identity*, European Commission, Forward Studies Unit, Working Paper, 1999; Bekemans, L., "The Idea and Practice of Europe in a Globalising World: Reality and Responsibility," in *Pace Diritti Umani/Peace Human Rights*, 1/2005, pp. 121-133.

6 Brugmans, H., "Europe: One Civilization, One Destiny, One Vocation," in H. Brugmans (ed.), *Dream, Adventure, Reality*, New York, Greenwood, 1987, pp. 11-39.

Europe that the original virtue of the spirit of Europe – namely democracy, dialogue, respect for rights and harmonious development – should be understood, sharing a common heritage and rooted in Christian values.

A. Classical Origin

The term "Europe" has many origins and interpretations. For some authors it derives from the Greek word "*eurus*" meaning "wide." Some others refer to the dualism in the Acadian language between "*asu/acu*" and "*erib/erebu*," where the first means "to rise" and would indicate the dawn, i.e. the East and Asia in particular, while the second means "to enter" and stands for the sunset, so the West and specifically Europe.[7]

In Greek mythology "Europa" was the daughter of Agenor, the Phoenician king of Tyre. Zeus felt in love with her, transformed himself into a bull, brought her to Crete, assumed human form and had three sons with her. It can be argued that the opposition between West and East was illustrated in the Classical Age by the Greek and the Persian world: the former was the symbol of democracy and freedom, opposed to the absolutism and despotism of the latter. According to Herodotus, the geographical boundaries of Europe were defined by the Mediterranean Sea in the South, the Sea of Azov and the River Don in the East, and the Pillars of Hercules in Gibraltar in the West – also considered the limit of the human civilisation.

Following the historical track of the origin of Europe, authors such as Mikkeli and Braque argue that the Roman Empire cannot be defined as the first European superpower.[8] According to Mikkeli the principal aim of the Roman Empire was to control the main commercial routes, extending its territorial power to the southern coast of the Mediterranean and a part of Asia. However the impact of various philosophical and religious currents made it difficult to define Europe ideologically. Brague follows the same of line of reasoning, asserting that the constant confrontation with "the Other" during the Roman Era represented the most significant element on which a European common cultural heritage can be understood.[9] This perspective conceives the European culture not as a fixed set of values, but in terms of a "cultural transmission." The myth of the "abduction of Europa" underlines the fact that its origins

---

7 Mikkeli, H., *Europe as an Idea and an Identity*, Basingstoke, Palgrave Publishers, 1998.

8 *Ibidem*, p. 18.

9 Brague, R., *Eccentric Culture: A Theory of Western Civilization*, South Bend, Ind., St. Augustine's Press, 2002.

were constructed from an appropriation of what belonged to others, moving from the East to the West.[10]

It is clear that in the Ancient Age, Europe was not perceived as a political community with unifying characteristics, but rather as a geographical area with unstable borders. In spite of some mythological common origin, none of the citizens of the Roman Empire defined himself/herself as a European, preferring instead the image of Rome as *caput mundi*. After the schism in 395 AD, the term "Europe" became more and more used to identify the western part of the Empire, whose identity was strongly shaped by Christianity.[11]

B. A Res Publica Christiana in the Middle Ages

The period after the fall of the Western Roman Empire, which coincides with the enormous Arab expansion, was characterised by cultural fragmentation. The Frankish attempt to build a united political community is considered by many authors as the very origin of Europe. This term was used in the Middle Ages to create a sense of solidarity in addressing a common enemy; the struggle against Islam to preserve Christianity as the religion of Europe.

During the battle of Poitiers (732 AD) the word "*Europeenses*" (meaning "Europeans") was used to refer to Charles Martel's coalition army against the Arabs.[12] However, there are some critiques to the alleged unifying role of the Frankish Empire, as it did not cover the whole of Europe and it co-existed with the remaining Roman territories in the East. For some authors, the Carolingian period cannot be defined as the starting point of the European integration process and would be better termed as the end of a specific historical era, characterised by the attempt of Charlemagne to combine the Roman classical heritage with Christianity.[13] The Crusades need to be understood in this historical context. The beginning of the crusading period is generally attributed to Pope Urban II's calling of the First Crusade at the Council of Clermont in 1095 to an armed pilgrimage to the Holy Land, to defend Europe from the Muslim invasion.

An important contribution by Christianity to European unity has been given by the Catholic Church. Its aim was the creation of a community of independent states under the spiritual guidance of the

---

10 Boon, V. and Delanty, G., "Europe and its Histories," in H. Persson and B. Strath, *Reflections on Europe*, Brussels, P.I.E. Peter Lang, 2007, pp. 159-182.

11 Delanty, G., *Inventing Europe. Idea, Identity, Reality*, London, MacMillan Press UTD, 1995.

12 Wilson, K. and Van der Dussen, J. (eds.), *The History of the Idea of Europe*, London, Routlege, 1995, p. 26.

13 See for example Mikkeli, H., *Europe as an Idea*, *op. cit.*, p. 27.

Pope. It promoted a policy of international mobility of students and lecturers, with Latin as the vehicular language. In the 9th century the term "*christianitas*" stood for the whole territory inhabited by Christian people, however with a focal attention towards universalism. Pope Innocent III (1198-1216), one of the most powerful and influential popes of the Middle Ages, affirmed the existence of a Christian territory ("*terrae Christianorum*"), with specific borders ("*fines Christianorum*") and one single "*populus christianus*," though under different political communities, but with the need to defend its identity against non-believers.

A crucial historical moment in the identification of Europe with Christendom was the fall of Constantinople to the Ottomans in 1453. It resulted in a clear separation between Christian Europe and Muslim Asia. Although the fragmentation caused by the schism between the Orthodox and the Catholic Church was reduced, a sense of unity of the continent was not yet present. The crusaders went fighting for Christendom and not for Europe.

Still the importance of Christianity in Europe needs to be put into its proper perspective. It was an Asian religion, born in the Middle East, with a universal message that transcended European borders. Nonetheless it gave Europe its territorial grounding and became the symbol of European unity against the Islamic East.[14] In Pagden's words, it means that "*an abducted Asian woman gave Europe her name, a vagrant Asian exile gave Europe its political and finally its cultural identity; and an Asian prophet gave Europe its religion.*"[15]

To summarise, it is difficult to state that the idea of Europe in the Middle Ages assumed a strong political connotation; it was instead used as a vague geographical expression which covered the cultural and religious common heritage of Christianity and the Classical Roman Age. The unification of the continent was therefore a mere answer to external threats and internal common interests were not strong enough to favour a process of actual integration.[16]

C. A Process of Secularisation towards a European Civilisation

History shows that the idea of Europe assumed many different connotations throughout the centuries, according to political and cultural contexts. In the humanistic culture of the Renaissance 14th and 15th century, the word "Europe" regained a strong meaning, recognised as a

---

[14] Delanty, G., *Inventing Europe*, *op. cit*.

[15] Pagden, A. (ed.), *The Idea of Europe from Antiquity to the European Union*, Cambridge, Cambridge UP, 2002.

[16] Mikkeli, H., *Europe as an Idea*, *op. cit.*, p. 36.

common reference by the intellectual classes in most European countries.[17] From the beginning of the 16th century, Christianity gradually lost its central role in the conception of Europe. Both the outbreak of religious conflicts with the Protestant Reformation challenging the role of the Catholic Church as European cultural unifier and the discovery of the New World with the colonisation of American territories, led to a process of secularisation. The ties with Christianity were loosened and the affirmation of a European civilisation emerged, exhibiting a high level of knowledge and a differentiated culture.[18] The Protestant Sebastian Münster describes Europe in *Cosmographia Universalis* as the most fertile and cultivated area despite its relatively small dimensions. The actual conceptualisation of a "European civilisation," however, was made during the Enlightenment (17th-18th century).

From the political point of view, the Peace of Westphalia in 1648 marked the beginning of a new European era, where the balance of power between sovereign states came to be a central element. The term "Europe," detached from its religious connotations, gained common usage among political decision-makers. Moreover, it constituted the base of political projects that aimed at achieving an internal peaceful organisation of the continent.

On the cultural side, Europeans believed in the universal value and superiority of their civilisation. It was seen as a process leading towards a virtuous and ideal state[19] and finally to eternal peace.[20] The highest expression of civilisation was represented by the nation-state, which was to be legitimised in the context of "methodological nationalism."[21] The idea of different and equally valuable forms of society was not taken into consideration so that other populations were labelled as "barbarians" who needed to be civilised by having European values imposed on them. This concept of civilisation is thought to be the secular substitute of Christendom as the unifying element for the continent. Norman Davies notes that in the early phase of the Enlightenment "*it became an embarrassment for the divided community of nations to be reminded of their common Christian identity; and 'Europe' filled the need for a designation with more neutral connotations.*"[22]

---

17 Wilson, K. and Van der Dussen, J. (eds.), *The History of the Idea*, *op. cit.*, p. 36.

18 Mikkeli, H., *Europe as an Idea, op cit*, p. 44.

19 Wilson, K. and Van der Dussen, J. (eds.), *The History of the Idea*, *op. cit.*, p. 64.

20 Kant, I., *Perpetual Peace: A Philosophical Sketch*, 1795.

21 Beck, U. and Grande, E., *Cosmopolitan Europe*, Cambridge, Polity, 2007, pp. 94-97.

22 Davies, N., *Europe: a History*, London, Oxford University Press, 1996.

Another contribution recognising the European common culture came from the French philosopher Voltaire. He argued that, in spite of political fragmentations, Europeans share the same religious background and the same civil principles. Strong focus was put on arts and natural sciences, which create close ties among nations and result in a "*République littéraire*." This was in his view the decisive element that made Europe the most civilised continent in the world. It should however, be mentioned, that the feeling of belonging to the same cultural community was shared only by the closed circles of intellectuals with the same classical education, without much influence on ordinary people; for them, the privileged reference was their closer local community and the idea of Europe was seen as abstract.[23]

D. A Cosmopolitan Perspective of European identity

As was said earlier, the idea of Europe has mainly emerged from a constant confrontation with otherness. However, this process is more complex and cannot be reduced to a mere clash or rigid distinction from the "Other." Hobson argues that Europeans have always had intense interaction and exchanges with the Eastern countries. In fact, some elements of European culture originate in and are borrowed from outside Europe. It is worth being reminded that the mathematical models used by Copernicus were invented by Ibn al-Shatir and that the typical British tea-drinking comes from the Chinese tradition.[24] The distinctive features of European culture are often the appropriation, acculturation and reworking of elements of other cultures.

The fundamental ambiguity accompanying European identity-building throughout the centuries, has been the constant effort to provide its identity with a kind of substance,[25] referring to an alleged common geographical belonging, ethnic origins, or to a common cultural heritage. This effort has often implied the demonisation of the "Other" and the refusal to build constructive forms of dialogue; looking instead for unity as common opposition to an enemy. History shows however that every attempt to purify Europe from the presence of an alleged hostile "Other" has always ended in tragedy.

Understanding the historical trajectory of how the idea of Europe evolved and how its identity was built over the years to a common cultural heritage, is fundamental to interpreting today's scenarios and

---

23 Burke, P., "Did Europe Exist Before 1700?," in *History of European Idea*, vol. I, 1980, pp. 21-29.

24 Hobson, J., "Revealing the Cosmopolitan Side of Europe: the Eastern Origins of European Civilisation," in G. Delanty (ed.), *Europe and Asia Beyond East and West: Towards a New Cosmopolitanism*, London, Routledge, 2006.

25 *Ibidem*, p. 180.

making policy assessments for Europe's future. Some of the cultural specificities of Europe can therefore be related to: 1) the rescue of history from memory to focus on ideas which travel irrespective of borders; 2) the move beyond assimilation and multiculturalism towards interculturalism to management of diversity and living with differences; 3) the acceptance of change so that dialogue and mutual listening becomes the driving social force and 4) the learning from humility so that Europe can draw from its religious and non-religious traditions and from its Christian roots in learning how to practice humility. We consider these characteristics major components of the European spirit.

In order to valorise these components, a cosmopolitan perspective of the European integration process might be helpful in recognising plural and multifaceted identities in Europe, accepting its constitutive otherness and benefiting from its diversity. Stimulating intercultural dialogue[26] as the instrument and objective of building cohesive and sustainable societies, might therefore create new forms of relationship between the Self and the "Other," leading towards a democratic and inclusive Europe.

II. European Identity-building

A. Concept and Models

Identity is related to the way individuals reach certain self-awareness, in relation to their family, social or ethnic group, language, culture, religious affiliation and political commitment. It is often expressed by the idea of "belonging." Therefore psychological and social factors play an important role in creating that awareness. As identity always implies both a strong interaction between the individual and the group and an affirmation of a group as distinct from others groups, its political implications are fundamental. This is especially the case in the different ways identity can be experienced or exploited.

However, identity determination is not a constant invariable process; it changes over time according to criteria such as birth, family, language, religion, territory, etc. Nowadays this has become more complex with the heightened mobility of people and the trespassing of visual and virtual borders; it has also become more disturbed by the growing individualisation and vagueness of the moral norms within society. In short, given the growing interdependent globalisation trends in today's world, a shift has taken place from a more static definition to a more contextual and dynamic understanding of identity.

---

26 See Bekemans, L. (ed.), *Intercultural Dialogue and Multi-level Governance. A Human Rights Based Approach*, Brussels, P.I.E. Peter Lang, 2012.

Such a relational identity requires an open attitude towards "the Other"; listening to them and inducing comprehension and benefitting from dialogue with them. However, many people are still afraid that intercultural encounters result in a loss of identity and create insecurity. Therefore, to overcome the perception of "the Other" as a potential threat, it is necessary to build the sense of belonging as close as possible to the citizen and to valorise local communities and cities as living places of intercultural conviviality. Subsequently, a spill-over effect can support the building up of identities, characterised as belonging to a group differentiated but sharing a basic set of common values and interests.

Literature presents different models of European identity-building with various policy consequences. The Communitarian view stresses the Europe of culture as a family of nations anchored in a common history and culture. It emphasises that European identity has emerged from common movements in religion and philosophy, politics, science and the arts and argues for a stronger awareness of the Christian (or Judeo-Christian) tradition. On the contrary, the Liberal and Republican view argues for a common political culture, i.e. a civic identity, based on universal principles of democracy, human rights, the rule of law, etc. that are expressed in the framework of a common public sphere and political participation (or "constitutional patriotism").[27] It is said that cultural identities, religious beliefs, etc. should be confined to the private sphere. According to this view European identity will emerge from the common political and civic practices of citizens sharing the same political and civic values, while at the same time adhering to different cultural practices. Finally, Constructivists argue that a European identity can only emerge as a consequence of intensified civic, political and cultural exchanges and co-operation. As identities undergo constant change, European identity encompasses multiple meanings and identifications and is constantly redefined through relationships with others. According to this view, Europe is a place of encounters and the participation of citizens in collective political and cultural practices.

The point of departure of most discussions on European identity is the idea that a political community needs a common set of values and references to ensure its coherence, to guide its actions and to endow it with legitimacy and meaningfulness. However, despite fundamental differences, preconditions for the emergence of a European identity are linked to the strengthening of democratic participation at all levels of

---

27 Habermas, J., "The European Nation State. Its Achievements and Its Limitations. On the Past and Future of Sovereignty and Citizenship," in *Ratio Juris*, vol. 9, Issue 2, June 1996, pp. 125-137.

decision-making, the valorising of the European dimension in education and culture and achieving social and economic sustainable cohesion.

As far as the European political identity is concerned, the nation-state continues to be the predominant reference for European citizens despite the growing Europeanisation of identity-building. The Eurobarometer surveys show that EU citizens continue to identify first of all with their own country. The relatively low political participation and weak attachment, poses a legitimacy problem for the EU.[28] Moreover, in this current period of dramatic transformations of societies within the globalising context, new (and different) political actors are shaping the world scene, undermining traditional forms of national statehood.[29]

Prospecting a sustainable European future today requires more advanced forms of supranational and multi-level governance, capable of managing complex and interconnected economic and political issues while strengthening a common sense of belonging. It is therefore important to understand the necessity for European identities to be inclusive and intrinsically plural, far from the exclusive national patterns of identity, nationality and citizenship.

It would be undesirable, and rather impossible for the EU to return to the historical path of nation-state building. Europe does not represent an actual European "demos," its borders are not fixed and it contains many different peoples and cultures. That's why the "Unity in Diversity" motto represents institutional and political challenges in today's Europe.

B. European Identity-building in the EU Treaties

The identity of the European Union has so far predominantly been defined politically. The EU is founded "*on the principles of liberty, democracy, respect for human rights and fundamental freedoms, and the rule of law*" (Art. 6 TEU). Fundamental disagreements emerged in the work on the EU Constitutional Treaty about a reference to "God" or "Christianity," in the preamble. It now only refers to the "religious heritance" of Europe. The Copenhagen criteria of stable and democratic institutions, functioning market economy and adequate administrative structures, are to be interpreted in this process of European identity-building.

The recent developments in European identity-building very much refer to the EU legal context. The treaties from 1951 onwards, up to the Treaty of Lisbon, highlight the different contexted approaches that were

28 Eurobarometer 71, *The Future of Europe*, January 2010.

29 Papisca, A., "Dallo Stato Confinario allo Stato Sostenibile," in *Pace, Diritti dell'Uomo, Diritti dei Popoli*, Anno VI, numero 3, 1992 (1994).

used to strengthen the idea of Europe and European identity. During the first decades of the European integration process, the only reference to the identity issue was connected to distinguishing Europe from other international political actors. From the second half of the eighties, Europe has been more and more conceived as a community of shared values and a political space for active citizens, embodied in the Treaty of Lisbon and implemented in various EU programmes.

1) The Early Years of European Integration

The end of the Second World War paved the way for the process of European integration. The French Foreign Minister Robert Schuman stressed in his Declaration on May 9, 1950 that durable peace in Europe could only be achieved if the age-old rivalry between France and Germany could be eliminated. The first period of an economic driven integration was thus characterised by a strong pragmatism and a "step-by-step" strategy aimed at building up a common economic space.

In this context, little space existed for debating identity. The preamble of the Treaty establishing the ECSC in 1951, expressed the conviction that "*the contribution which an organised and vital Europe can make to civilisation is indispensable to the maintenance of peaceful relations*." The pursuit of common economic interests would create "*the basis for a broader and deeper community among peoples long divided by bloody conflicts*," or, as the Treaties of Rome suggest, "*lay the foundations of an ever-closer union among the peoples of Europe.*"

The idea of Europe emerging from the first treaties is deeply influenced by the historical tragedy of the World Wars. Economic areas were privileged for co-operation in accordance to the neo-functional approach. It was nevertheless always the objective to develop the process of integration beyond the European Economic Community. However, most attempts to go beyond the mere economic orientation of the European integration process failed in their early years.

2) The Declaration on European Identity (1973)

The concept of European identity was introduced for the first time in the European political agenda with the "Declaration on European Identity" (Copenhagen 14th December 1973). It was said that co-operation among European peoples represented a real need to effectively face the current global threats. The action proposed was oriented to "*defend the principles of representative democracy, of the rule of law, of social justice – which is the ultimate goal of economic progress – and of respect for human rights [...].*" All of these are fundamental elements of the European identity. A number of articles of the Copenhagen Declaration are illustrative for this changed (at least rhetoric) focus on

European identity-building. Very interesting in this perspective is Article 3:

> The diversity of cultures within the framework of a common European civilization, the attachment to common values and principles, the increasing convergence of attitudes to life, the awareness of having specific interests in common and the determination to take part in the construction of a United Europe, all give the European Identity its originality and its own dynamism.

Article 4 reaffirms the open nature of the Community, leaving space for further enlargement to peoples who share its same ideals. Another important aspect is the external dimension of identity, i.e. Europe's place and responsibility in the international landscape. Article 6 recognises that global problems cannot any longer be solved at a national level and consequently that Europe is to "*speak increasingly with one voice*" with other countries and regional areas.[30]

It has already been said that in the first decades of integration, the issue of European identity was raised mainly in its external dimension, as an attempt to collocate the new supranational actor within the world context, or as a common project, founded on the search for "*l'intérêt communautaire*" in the co-ordination of national policies. There is however, another aspect, which has to be taken into consideration from the Single European Act onwards, i.e. the existence of a community of citizens.[31]

3) Europe as a Community of Citizens

The first attempt to push European integration beyond the notion of a common market dates back to 1976 with the Tindemans Report. In the chapter, "Europe of the Citizens," a community of citizens was proposed by raising the European awareness through visible (symbolic) measures (e.g. unification of passports, the vanishing of border controls, the common use of the benefits of social security systems, the accreditation of academic courses and degrees, etc). In 1984, the European Council of Fontainebleau set up the Adonnino Committee, to address issues related to a "people's Europe." In spite of its ambitious goals only some (modest) proposals were adopted to increase the sense of belonging to the European Community (e.g. the European flag, a unified passport and the anthem.[32] In the same year Altiero Spinelli

---

30 Strath, B., "A European Identity: To the Historical Limits of a Concept," in *European Journal of Social Theory*, Sage Publications, 2002.

31 Jouen, M. and Chambon, N., "L'identité Européenne dans les Textes et les Politiques Communautaires," in www.notre-europe.eu, 2006.

32 Panebianco, S., *European Citizenship and European Identity: from the Treaty of Maastricht to Public Opinion Attitudes*, Jean Monnet Working Papers in Comparative and International Politics, no. 03/96, December, 1996.

advocated a more ambitious idea of the establishment of a political union, which was, however, not translated into a more political commitment.

A milestone in the European integration process, is represented by the Treaty of Maastricht (1993). It instituted the establishment of a "European citizenship," a legal status that guarantees a set of rights to individuals possessing the nationality of one of the member states. At last, the Treaty of Maastricht started a path towards an ever closer relationship between the European institutions and citizens. European identity was no longer exclusively addressed to the external dimension, but acquired a more specific internal meaning. In fact, it was not reduced to an instrumental usage for co-ordinating national policies, but created a constitutional and founding value for the concept of the "Europe of citizens."[33]

The debate on the existence of a European demos, often referring to "the peoples of Europe," remains open to various interpretations. The construction of a single European subject is an ongoing process thanks to the direct application of EU norms to the citizens. The democratic base is no longer the representation of "*the peoples of the European States brought together in the Community*" (art. 189 TEC); in fact "*Citizens are directly represented at Union level in the European Parliament*" (art.10.2 TEU).

The Convention on the Future of Europe produced a draft for a Constitutional Treaty which expressed an intention to increase the level of participation from European citizens in the decision-making process.[34] Despite its failure following the negative outcomes of the French and Dutch referenda in 2005, the Treaty of Lisbon (2009) has finally followed the same, focused line on citizenship. Next to the principle of representative democracy, which is the base of the functioning of the Union (Art. 10.1 TEU), Article 11(1) states that "*the institutions shall, by appropriate means, give citizens and representative associations the opportunity to make known and publicly exchange their views in all areas of Union action.*" The method chosen to put this general principle into practice is the "Citizens' Initiative," as formulated in article 11(4):

> Not less than one million citizens who are nationals of a significant number of Member States may take the initiative of inviting the European Commission, within the framework of its powers, to submit any appropriate

33 Mangiameli, S., *L'Identità dell'Europa: Laicità e Libertà Religiosa*, paper from www.forumcostituzionale.it.

34 Dauvergne, A., "The Treaty of Lisbon: Assessments and Prospects as of Summer 2011," in *Notre Europe*, Studies & Researches, 2011.

proposal on matters where citizens consider that a legal act of the Union is required for the purpose of implementing the Treaties [...].

According to Article 24 of the Lisbon Treaty, the details of and the conditions for an effective implementation of the Citizens' Initiative, have been discussed by the Council and the European Parliament within the so-called "ordinary legislative procedure" and a specific regulation has been adopted.[35] The ECI was finally launched on May 9th, 2012 with the registration of *Fraternité 2020*.

4) European Citizenship in a Cosmopolitan Perspective

European citizenship not only includes a set of rights and responsibilities, but also contains an important symbolic value. Even if the concept remains linked to national belongingness, the existence of a "common citizenship" applying to many nationalities and covering multiple identities, establishes a fundamental shift in the relation between identity, nationality and citizenship. This innovative legal status produces political implications as it favours "trans-national democracy" and the development of a European public sphere.[36]

Moreover, the recognition of a multiplicity of identities can be simultaneously envisaged under the traditional notion of nationality, as well as under the notion of European citizenship. Amartya Sen's argument on the multiplicity of identities[37] finds in this context the possibility of implementation, even if European citizenship is only addressed to the member states' nationals. However, if European identity could be based on the principle of inclusiveness, EU citizenship should also be obtained by legal, long-term, third country nationals. Papisca argues that the sense of belongingness to a European political community can be achieved if individuals and peoples will be its principal actors.[38] Sharing projects and participating in the decision-making process is the only way for Europeans to be inspired, motivated and committed to Europe.

In the cosmopolitan view,[39] European citizenship is a step towards a global citizenship. Europe is conceived as a political laboratory for a new supranational and transcendental democracy, but the outcome of

---

35 Regulation (EU) no. 211/2011 of the European Parliament and of the Council on the Citizens' Initiative, 16 February 2011.

36 Morganti, L. and Bekemans. L., *The European Public Sphere. From Critical Thinking to Responsible Action,* Brussels, P.I.E. Peter Lang, 2012.

37 Sen, A., *Identity and Violence: The Illusion of Destiny*, Cambridge, Polity Press, London, 2007.

38 Papisca, A., "Riflessioni in Tema di Cittadinanza Europea e Diritti Umani," in *Pace Diritti Umani/Peace Human Rights*, 1/2004.

39 Beck, U. and Grande, E., *Cosmopolitan Europe*, *op. cit.*

this process cannot be a mere translation of functions from the national to the European level. The horizon for active citizenship is the European and world space of internationally recognised human rights. The EU provides the evolutionary context and spatial horizon in which plural citizenship and inclusion practices can be implemented. Citizenship rights therefore must be exercised in a broader constitutional space, expressing both legitimisation of decision-making and citizen's participation in the formation of a global civil society.

With this approach, the universal human rights paradigm is the fundamental point of departure for conceiving a citizenship "*ad omnes includendosi.*"[40] It is therefore worthwhile to focus both on the set of values adopted in the Treaties as constitutive of European identity and on the process of codifying human rights.

5) The Role of Cultures and EU Founding Values

The aspect of the cultural and religious heritage of the European peoples is introduced in the Treaties as an element of differentiation rather than unification.[41] However, to imagine Europe beyond the beaten track of institutional, economic and political integration requires a value-driven foundation for the search for European identity.[42] This is underscored by the words of Karel Verleye, one of the founders of the College of Europe in Bruges:

> It is excluded that a European citizenship or a European commitment will be stimulated with the population, when no ample consideration will be given to a number of forgotten or undervalued factors in the construction of the new Europe, such as the cultural, regional, ethical, historical and spiritual dimensions.[43]

European identity-building within the EU legal context is not based on a common linguistic, cultural or religious origin; the focus is instead on the necessity for EU institutions to "respect the equality of member states before the Treaties as well as their national identities" (Art. 4.2 TEU). The Treaty of Lisbon includes the Title XIII on culture and clearly defines the role of the Union in cultural matters in its Article 167. It affirms that "*[t]he Union shall contribute to the flowering of the*

40 Papisca, A., "Citizenship and Citizenships Ad Omnes Includendos: A Human Rights Approach," in L. Bekemans *et al.* (eds.), *Intercultural Dialogue and Citizenship. Translating Values into Actions. A Common Project for Europeans and Their Partners*, Venezia, Marsilio, 2007.

41 Mangiameli, S., *L'Identità dell'Europa, op. cit.*, pp. 7-8.

42 Bouckaert, L. and Eynikel, J. (eds.), *Imagine Europe: The Search for European Identity and Spirituality*, Leuven, Garant, 2009.

43 Bekemans, L., "The Idea and Practice of Europe in a Globalising World: Reality and Responsibility," in *Pace Diritti Umani/Peace Human Rights*, 1/2005, p. 131.

cultures of the Member States, while respecting their national and regional diversity and at the same time bringing the common cultural heritage to the fore" (Art 167.1). Furthermore, "*[t]he Union shall take cultural aspects into account in its action under other provisions of the Treaties, in particular in order to respect and to promote the diversity of its cultures*" (Art 167.4).

A clear signal of the EU attitude has been the refusal of making any reference to Europe's Christian roots in the Constitutional Treaty. Despite a strong opposition from the Catholic Church, the Preamble reads as follows:

> Drawing inspiration from the cultural, religious and humanist inheritance of Europe, from which have developed the universal values of the inviolable and inalienable rights of the human person, freedom, democracy, equality and the rule of law, [...].

The same formulation has been adopted within the Treaty of Lisbon, adding the intention "to deepen the solidarity between their peoples while respecting their history, their culture and their traditions."

In recent years, significant progress has been made to recognise the importance of fundamental rights within the European Union. The Amsterdam Treaty (1997) introduced for the first time a specific reference to human rights. The Treaty of Lisbon reinforced this perspective: "*The Union is founded on the values of respect for human dignity, freedom, democracy, equality, the rule of law and respect for human rights, including the rights of persons belonging to minorities. These values are common to the Member States in a society in which pluralism, non-discrimination, tolerance, justice, solidarity and equality between women and men prevail*" (Art. 2).

It also stipulates that "*the Union shall respect fundamental rights, as guaranteed by the European Convention for the Protection of Human Rights and Fundamental Freedoms signed in Rome on 4 November 1950 and as they result from the constitutional traditions common to the Member States, as principles of Community law*" (Art. 6.2). Moreover the Charter of Fundamental Rights of the European Union has been given the same legal value as the Treaties. Its binding value commits the EU to building a political community within which human rights have the utmost importance as the ultimate reference.[44] It illustrates a relevant qualitative shift in European integration, leading towards an inclusive community where the citizens can be the real protagonists.

---

[44] Papisca, A., "'Europe 2020': What Compass, What Soul, Which Kind of Architecture for the EU Governance? The Need for Human Rights Mainstreaming," in *Pace Diritti Umani/Peace Human Rights*, 3/2010.

Conclusion

The historical path of the idea of Europe shows that European identity-building is the result of a mixture of elements coming from different contexts, set in a process of cultural appropriation and a continuous reworking of a dialogue of civilisations. The evolution of the European identity issue within the main European Treaties highlights the fact that only in the eighties – when the importance of the political legitimisation of EU institutions was clearly perceived – did the European Commission start engaging in the cultural sphere. It defined EU founding values and officially embraced the universal human rights paradigm. The relative failure of the EU in the attempt to make people identify with the European project is partly due to the state-like "top-down" strategy and the lack of a genuine post-national identity.

Cosmopolitanism as a new way of conceiving cultural otherness opposes both hierarchical subordination and universal equality, recognising instead the existing (and undeniable) differences between peoples and giving them a positive value. Territorial boundaries, social groups and cultural barriers are transcended. The ultimate reference remains "*the worldwide community of human beings*"[45] where everyone is seen as both equal and different in order to expand "*the concept of the public beyond its national borders and opening it up to an emerging European space.*"[46]

[45] Nussbaum, M. *et al.*, *For love of Country. Debating the Limits of Patriotism*, Boston, Beacon Press, 1996.

[46] Bekemans, L., "A Cosmopolitan Perspective of Multi-level Governance in Europe," in *Pace Diritti Umani /Peace Human Rights*, 2/2010, p. 58.

A Spiritual Foundation for Europe: a Future Oriented Perspective

Luk BOUCKAERT

Professor Emeritus of Ethics, Catholic University of Leuven, Belgium

The post-war integration of Europe was driven by the incentive of expanding economic markets and the promise of more economic growth, generating personal as well as social welfare. Political integration has always followed the imperatives of globalising markets and economic growth – not a path of spiritual progress. Would it not be more accurate to speak about a materialistic foundation of Europe? How could spiritual values play a *foundational* role in such an economic-driven process of integration?

There is a second puzzle: if we believe that Christian and humanistic values are deeply embedded in Europe's social and cultural past and that new spiritual practices coming from Buddhism, Islam and other global religious movements will play a role in the future fabric of European values; how could such a melting pot of different spiritualities be a founding source for the future of Europe?

In my contribution I will start by analysing some of the failures of a market driven process of European integration, along with the potential for a value-driven alternative. Next, I will deal with the principle of universal responsibility as a foundational value commitment creating unity in diversity. The last sections of my paper will explore the meaning of spirituality and the nature of economics in a value-driven process of European integration.

I. Two Ideas of Integration

The idea of the European Union originated from the post-war shared will to secure an everlasting peace across the continent. The founding fathers of post-war Europe were deeply committed to peace but their strategy for peace was not based on spiritual ideas and practices but on economic integration and co-operation. Using this method of economic integration, they hoped to create an area of shared interest beyond nationalism. In retrospect it is fair to say that the European concept of peace through economic co-operation and solidarity mechanisms has been a very successful model for guaranteeing an enduring period of peace for our continent.

Nevertheless, the European model is under pressure because some of its post-war assumptions are challenged by at least three new facts:

1) The global challenge. The globalisation process deconstructs not only the national but the European boundaries as well. The recent financial crisis, which originated in the US housing markets, rapidly spread its effects all over the world. In this context of globalisation, the European concept of peace must be globalised as well. While the post-war European concept of peace was an effort to avoid nationalistic wars, the global concept of peace must be an answer to the sources of world conflict today (e.g. the intercontinental competition for energy and other resources).

2) The ecological challenge. Economic growth as a way to solve social and political problems – and to guarantee welfare and peace for future generations – has lost some of its evidence. The impact of unrestricted economic growth on the planet is unsustainable. A steady economic growth rate of 2% will again double the European GNP in a period of less than 50 years. Added to the explosive growth rates of China and other fast growing countries, this will create an unprecedented battle for scarce resources and generate a lot of ecological problems. Although we know this and are taking some measures to avoid the disasters, the logic of economic growth remains dominant. Who is willing to accept the principle of frugality as an economic device?

3) The religious challenge. The assumption that we can reduce religion to the private sphere and run the world by a religion-free rationality, may have some plausibility in Europe, but not on a global scale. In many countries religion, politics and economics are deeply intermingled. Even within Europe the new migrants re-introduce religion as a factor of social identity and social polarisation. This polarisation is much more than a clash between faith-based radicalism and secular Western liberalism. In most of the religious families today, we find a strong polarisation between the more moderate and the more fundamentalist groups. To overcome this conflict, the European integration model has to offer ways of coping with deep-rooted value conflicts. Europe has to offer a model of tolerant humanism that gives religion its due place.

So far three challenges that deconstruct the post-war European logic that a market-driven integration will trigger political integration, which, in its turn, will generate a context of peace and a common European cultural identity. What seems necessary in today's context is a reversed sequence where the process starts from a vision of Europe's mission and values in the global world orienting our political strategies and economic choices. Of course, reality always offers a more complex picture with many positive and negative feedbacks at work between economics, politics and cultural values. But the point here is to stress the *priority* of self-reflection and vision for the future, in order to orient political and economic life. Without a *foundational value commitment*, no individuals or communities can make consistent choices; they will be swayed by the issues of the day, by volatile market expectations or short time political opportunism. Europe is missing a strong, value-based leadership that enables people to envision its future role in the globalising world.

However, a value-driven integration project for Europe creates its own problems. If we accept "diversity of values" as a bottom line for Europe's cultural identity, how do we cope with the problem of opposite value claims? If every value-driven group claims more recognition and support, how do we make a fair evaluation? In this context, it seems very helpful to remind ourselves of E.F. Schumacher's distinction between *convergent and divergent* problems. E.F. Schumacher is the well-known author of *Small is Beautiful*,[1] a cult book in the seventies. At the end of his life, he wrote a small but beautiful book, A *Guide for the Perplexed*,[2] and made in his last chapter the distinction between divergent and convergent problems.

Convergent problems are problems that can be designed and solved as technical or rational problems. In the end there is one optimal solution. Divergent problems, on the other hand, are problems that cannot be solved by technical or rational modelling, leading to one optimal solution. Schumacher illustrates this with the case of education where those who are primarily committed to *freedom* will defend non-authoritarian answers to all educational problems while people primarily committed to *order* will always call for discipline and obedience on the part of pupils. Such divergent value commitments lead to different and often opposite positions. They cannot be solved on logical grounds. To quote Schumacher:

> Divergent problems cannot be solved in the sense of establishing a 'correct formula'; they can, however, be transcended. A pair of opposites – like freedom and order – are opposites at the level of ordinary life, but they cease to be opposites at the higher level, the really *human* level, where self-awareness plays its proper role. It is then that such higher forces as love and

---

1 Schumacher, E. F., *Small is Beautiful. Economics as if People Mattered*, London, Harper Perennial, 2010 (first edition 1973).

2 *Id.*, *A Guide for the Perplexed*, London, Harper Perennial, 2004 (first edition 1977).

> compassion, understanding and empathy, become available, not simply as occasional impulses (which they are at the lower level) but as a regular and reliable resource.[3]

Applying Schumacher to the European case, this means that to integrate diversity in Europe we must cultivate a higher level of self-reflection and a higher level of value commitment.[4] But saying that a deeper value commitment is needed, is not yet saying what *kind* of value commitment is involved. I believe that the *principle of universal responsibility* is the key factor in this value commitment. The characteristic of *universality* stresses the fact that the principle of responsibility is not confined to national or international borderlines. Neither is it confined to existing persons. It involves all persons including future and past generations, marginalised groups or embryonic human beings.

Why focusing on responsibility? Because responsibility as a spiritual commitment has the potential to stimulate self-reflection, to mobilise our higher capacities such as empathy and compassion and to "transcend" blocked polarisations between values such as freedom versus order, freedom versus equality, growth versus frugality, individualism versus community, etc. It would be interesting to disclose how the notion of responsibility has developed throughout Europe's cultural history, but this would take us too far. I will restrict myself to an elucidation of the distinction between a spiritual and a political interpretation of the principle of universal responsibility.

II. Responsibility as a Spiritual Commitment

Basic references for international politics such as the Universal Declaration of Human Rights or the principles of the *ius gentium*, do not speak in terms of responsibilities but in terms of rights. They consider rights as prior to responsibilities, which are interpreted as duties derived from rights. However some progressive movements today are pleading for a "charter of universal responsibilities." Their plea is based on a common observation. People do claim their rights as much as they can but they are less keen to realise that every right implies a duty or responsibility to protect the rights of other people as well. We prefer people defending their own legitimate rights instead of helping them to realise their rights and to be involved in paternalistic do-good practices. Although responsibilities are recognised as the other side of the coin of

3 *Ibidem*, p. 126.

4 Therefore Schumacher pleaded in his *Guide* to introduce wisdom and methods of spiritual knowledge such as introspection, intuition, reflection and contemplation in the field of social science and in educational programs.

rights, they are not our prime concern. Many social workers call attention to this imbalance between claiming rights and being committed to our responsibilities. In order to restore balance, they want a charter of universal responsibilities.

However, a charter of universal responsibilities runs the risk of remaining a cosmetic operation if we don't succeed in changing our basic attitude towards rights and responsibilities. If we don't succeed in substituting the *symmetry* thesis with a claim that responsibilities are *prior* to rights, we will not overcome the imbalance between rights and responsibilities. But the problem is that the priority claim of responsibilities over rights doesn't mesh with the dominant paradigm in political philosophy. This cannot be argued within the framework of liberal political philosophy, which supports the symmetry thesis. Hence, the priority claim in the context of today, can only be articulated as a spiritual commitment that generates important political consequences – without being a political claim.

The *political* claim for universal responsibilities looks at responsibilities as derivative principles reflecting the rights of people. Rights are not "physical things," there as a kind of real object; they are "moral things," i.e. things that exist as ideal objects and must be realised through free human commitment. If we claim rights as *universal* moral principles, we assume a commitment to apply them to every one, everywhere. We are accountable for their realisation and application. Therefore universal rights and universal responsibilities are two sides of the same coin. They are symmetrical in their reciprocity. It sounds theoretically perfect but in practice, this view results in the previously mentioned imbalance of claiming rights first and implementing responsibilities as a secondary, derivative duty.

The philosophical foundation for the *political* claim of symmetry between rights and responsibilities is the liberal and egalitarian concept of the human person ("all persons are equally free") extended by the idea that equal freedom requires a minimum of social and cultural conditions to be implemented. These minimum conditions are defined as social rights, enabling people to fulfil their basic needs. The liberal-egalitarian foundation of rights and responsibilities can be strengthened by the utilitarian and rational argument that the implementation of universal rights/duties is also beneficial to every person. Being unable to foresee and control my future, I will be better protected if I accept minimum standards for everyone. This is the well-known Rawlsian argument to promote universal rights/duties "under the veil of ignorance."

In contrast to this political view, a spiritual approach views the foundation of rights and responsibilities as non-symmetrical, non-egalitarian and non-rational. *Non-symmetrical*: duties have priority over rights; *non-egalitarian*: the rights of the other precede my rights; and *non-rational*: gratuity has precedence over utility maximisation. We find one of the most powerful expressions of this approach in the works of the French-Jewish philosopher Emmanuel Levinas.[5] In contrast to the egocentric approach to freedom and responsibility, he develops an other-centric notion of freedom and responsibility. More generally, we can refer to the tradition of spiritual humanism, or in terms of Levinas, to the *Humanism of the Other* as the philosophical base for claiming the priority of responsibilities over rights.[6]

The basic assumption of the other-centric humanism is the idea that the ego/self is always preceded by the presence of the other (eventually perceived as an absence which is a particular modus of being present). My life, my education, my freedom, my capabilities and my rights are always given before I can appropriate them as part of myself. Gift is prior to ownership. Before being a legal right, autonomy exists as a gift from others eliciting me to give, in turn, real freedom to other people. Being respected as a free and creative person, I am invited to respond to this gift by respecting other people's freedom and creativity.

But the experience of gift and its appeal to reciprocity is not the only way to become aware of the priority of the other over the self. In Levinas view, there is a more radical or traumatic infusion of the presence of the other in the self. The more radical intrigue of the other coincides with the experience of being claimed by the other before I can claim my own rights. Being claimed by the other is not based on a physical, emotional or other external superiority of the other. It is an ethical and spiritual claim expressed through the vulnerability of the human face. Only a powerless, naked human face calling for understanding and respect can infuse in my consciousness an immediate, deep and concrete sense of responsibility that precedes my own goodwill or free choice. Accepting my non-chosen responsibility makes it possible to transform my freedom into a mission at the service of the other. It liberates my freedom from egocentrism and opens a space for servant leadership or servant entrepreneurship. It makes me capable of doing things *for* the other without paternalism because the ethical priority of the other implies that I am first of all accountable to the other, before being responsible *for* the other.

---

5 Levinas, E., *Totalité et Infini*, Den Haag, Martinus Nijhoff, 1961; Peperzak, A. T., Critchley, S. and Bernasconi, R. (eds.), *Emmanuel Levinas: Basic Philosophical Writings*, Bloomingtom and Indianapolis, Indiana University Press, 1996.

6 Levinas, E., *Humanisme de l'Autre Homme,* Montpellier, Fata Morgana, 1972.

The difference between being responsible *to* and *for* the other looks subtle but is crucial for a non-paternalistic reading of the charter of universal responsibilities. A paternalist will appeal to feelings of goodwill and compassion to support the rights of other people, while a non-paternalistic reading will appeal to the ethical claims of other people. A paternalist will focus on my responsibility *for* the other while a democrat will prioritise the idea of being responsible *to* the other. Caring for the other without being accountable *to* him runs the risk of reducing the other to an object of my care instead of respecting him as the subject of caring activities.

Another important experience revealing the priority of responsibilities over rights is our relation to future generations.[7] We often speak about the rights of future generations. Actually non-existent beings cannot claim rights. Of course, we can imagine them as virtual beings and give them virtual rights. But this is only possible because there is already an intuition of our responsibility to non-existent future generations. Our gift of rights to them is founded on a primary intuition of responsibility *for* future life and *to* the other as the subject of future life. The example of caring for future generations illustrates very well that on the one hand, a spiritual commitment is prior to every declaration of rights (and makes such a declaration possible), but, on the other hand, this commitment must be implemented by giving people political rights and the instruments to realise them.

To conclude this section let me give an example of how different readings of human responsibilities are possible and assume a different value commitment. Take e.g. art. 3 of the Universal Declaration of Human Rights, which explains that: "Everyone has the right to life, liberty and security." Reading this article in the political-liberal modus means: "I have a right to life, liberty and security and nobody can deny me this right." Reading the article in the spiritual-ethical modus sounds different: "I have to respect and protect everybody's right to life, liberty and security especially those who cannot defend their rights." From a logical point of view both claims can be deduced on equal grounds from the general statement that everyone has the right to life, liberty and security. The point however, is that it makes a lot of ethical and practical difference which of both readings we give priority and commit ourselves to.

---

7 Jonas, H., *The Imperative of Responsibility: in Search of an Ethics for the Tchnological Age*, Chicago, University of Chicago Press, 1984.

III. The Re-emergence of Spirituality as a Public Good

As far as true religion makes people aware of the priority of the Other over the self and, hence, of the priority of responsibilities over rights; religion is a strong ally in supporting an ethic of universal responsibility. In a pluralistic Europe this openness for the Other cannot be monopolised by one particular religion or philosophical tradition. In its history of religious wars, Europe has solved the problem of religious intolerance by crowding out religion from the political sphere. However, Europe's strong secular humanism and its crowding out of religion from the public space is felt today by many European citizens as a form of spiritual impoverishment. This may explain a renewed interest in spirituality as a public and pluriform good and a discourse that can foster an other-centric practice of universal responsibility.[8]

Today a growing stream of deep ecologists, new age adherents, religious and non-religious people exploring non-rational sources of knowledge such as traditional wisdom, emotional intelligence, intuition and meditation, try to find new perspectives for meaning and purpose in life. Some call it a "spiritual revolution," shaping a new type of human civilisation.[9] It is important to remember that spirituality in this new context does not coincide with a particular, institutionalised form of religion. Spiritual humanism is a post-secular forum for religious and non-religious people in search of a deep, personal and transcendent meaning in life. It is committed to a pluralist and interreligious dialogue and is very sensitive to non-rational sources of knowledge and ethics. The rise of spirituality is remarkable since it contradicts the classic thesis of secularisation, which, though it predicted the decline of religion, failed to notice the diffuse emergence of spirituality.

Where modern humanists believe that the human ratio is the measure of all things, spiritual humanists explore new ways of self-transcendence and mysticism in history and cosmology.[10] Early philosophical expressions of this new sense of transcendence can be found in Bergson's idea of *L'Evolution Créatrice*,[11] Heidegger's philosophy of

---

8 Bouckaert, L. and Zsolnai, L. (eds.), *Spirituality as a Public Good,* Antwerp, Garant, 2007.

9 Heelas, P. and Woodhead, L., *The Spiritual Revolution. Why religion is Giving Way to Spirituality*, Oxford, Blackwell Publishing, 2005; Tacey, D., *The Spirituality Revolution. The Emergence of Contemporary Spirituality*, Hove/New York, Brunner-Routledge, 2004.

10 Capra, F., *The Tao of Physics*, Boston, Shambhala, 1975; Wilber, K., *A Brief History of Everything,* Boston, Shambhala, 1996.

11 Bergson, H., *L'Évolution Creatrice*, Paris, Presses Universitaires de France, 1907 (translated: *Creative Evolutions*, London, MacMillan, 1911).

Sein und Zeit[12] and Whitehead's *Process Philosophy*.[13] Buddhism and Taoism opened Western people to a perspective of spiritual, non-theistic enlightenment that fitted very well with some aspirations of the deep ecology movement. What seems to be the core element in this spiritual eco-humanism is the experience of deep interconnectedness with all beings and with Being itself. This experience, which discloses the human subject as a receptive and interconnected self, fundamentally differs from modern perceptions of the subject as a rational and self-defining ego. Spiritual humanism must not be reduced to its ecological and cosmological expression. As we have seen in the previous section, there is also a social experience of interconnectedness articulated by personalists, who define human freedom as a gift from and a responsibility to the other.

The experience of universal interconnectedness is not derived from empirical observation or conceptual representation. It is based on an intuitive, pre-conceptual awareness revealing interconnectedness as an *ontological condition*. The disclosure of the interconnected self enables us to take some distance from our self-constructed and active egos and to live in touch with our deeper intuitions. It generates a space of inner freedom, which allows new meaning and purpose in life. It coincides with the experience of the *Spirit* as the ultimate driver of meaning in every being and in the cosmos as a whole. Believers will interpret the Spirit as the manifestation of the creative love of God, whilst non-believers will see it as a non-material source of creativity in the evolutionary process. What these different interpretations may be and what unites them is (1) a rejection of scientific materialism reducing nature to a complex chain of causal and mechanistic relations, (2) a respect for the non-instrumental value of all living beings and (3) a sense of responsibility for the cosmos as a whole. This emergent wave of spiritual humanism may be one of the strongest incentives for people to limit their growth obsessions and to balance material welfare with spiritual values.[14]

To regain the European openness for religion as a public and pluriform good, a re-appraisal of renaissance humanism could be very helpful. The renaissance (from the 14th to the 16th century) was a period in Europe where antique wisdom, Christian spirituality, modern science and art, came together in a very productive way. Humanists wanted to create a new sense of *humanitas*, enabling people to participate fully in

12 Heidegger, M., *Sein und Zeit*, Tübingen, Max Niemeyer Verlag, 1927.

13 Whitehead, A., *Process and Reality: an Essay in Cosmology*, 1929. Corrected edition edited by D. R. Griffin and D. W. Sherburne, Free Press, 1979.

14 Bouckaert, L., Opdebeeck, H., Zsolnai, L. (eds.), *Frugality. Rebalancing Material and Spiritual Values in Economic Life*, Oxford, Peter Lang, 2008.

public and cultural life. Familiarity with the cultural and moral legacy of antiquity was seen as the way to shape a culturally literate and emancipated citizenship. The movement started in Italy (Florence and Naples) but spread across Europe. It was not an anti-clerical or anti-religious movement; many humanists worked for the organised Church and were in holy orders like Petrarch or Erasmus, "the prince of humanists." It was a period of tolerance, critical debate and cultural creativity, which, according to Stephen Toulmin, was substituted in the 17th century under pressure of religious conflicts by the modern and rational agendas of Newton, Descartes and Leibnitz.[15]

"*Refaire la renaissance*" (remaking the renaissance) was one of the first motto's of the personalist movement of Emmanuel Mounier in France during the 1930s. What had to be awakened, according to the personalists, was a type of profane spirituality. In *Humanisme Intégral*[16] Jacques Maritain explained why modern humanism's shortcomings would lead to a renewed interest in spirituality, not as a return to the sacred spirituality of medieval society but as a quest for a *profane spirituality* that does not segregate the spiritual but integrates it as a component of our political, social, economic and scientific activities. This sounds fine but how do we integrate this spiritual dimension in the European context of today, where economics is still the prime mover of the future but, simultaneously, is deeply challenged by its failures?

IV. The Challenge of a Post-capitalist, Value-based Economy

The agenda of responsibility as a spiritual commitment does not end with a new declaration of universal responsibilities. If we want to make a real difference, we have to change the economy. This is an old Marxist adagio but it is also the way Europe started its post-war process of integration. But how do we change an economy? Listen again to Marx's advice: economic and other changes will never be the mere result of voluntarism and good intentions – they only occur if people (or at least some of their leaders) become aware of the underlying contradictions in the political and economic system. Deep changes do not happen without a strong awareness and analysis of systemic crisis. Only then will voluntarism lead to effective change. In this sense, our current financial and economic crisis, complemented by the awareness of a deep ecological and climate crisis, is an opportunity to transform the economy – but it is up to us to see the *kairos* and to reflect on what we really want for future generations.

---

15 Toulmin, S., *Cosmopolis. The Hidden Agenda of Modernity*, New York, The Free Press, 1990.

16 Maritain, J., *Humanisme Intégral*, Paris, Aubier, 1936.

The way we look at this crisis will qualify the way we respond to it. If we analyse the current crisis merely in terms of market or governance failures, we will respond to the crisis by creating new measures of market regulation and increasing control over national debt management and budget discipline. Because these measures imply a substantial loss of welfare and freedom, a lot of discussion will concentrate on the fair distribution of these losses. Who has to pay what? But the point here is that this type of discussion does not question the post-war framework. They do not question the assumptions of economic growth, consumerism and the over-exploitation of natural and human resources.[17]

To initiate a higher level of European self-reflection we have to question the assumptions of the post-war economic model of economic growth and consumerism. We have to look at the crisis from a broader perspective beyond conventional market and government regulations. Only if we perceive the crisis as the result of a disordered set of values in our individual and collective lives, will we be interested in a process of self-reflection and value transformation. Just to enumerate some of the relevant questions: To what extent are we as individuals or as civil organisations part of and co-responsible for a system of disordered values? What are the symptoms and effects of this imbalance? Why are we blind to this imbalance? To what extent do we as Europeans want to change it? Are we able to transform the capitalist social market economy from the inside out into a post-capitalist value-based economy? What do we mean by a post-capitalist value-based economy?

Undoubtedly, what a post-capitalist economy is or will be is not yet fully visible, nor is there any certainty that it will be completely realised. But as an opportunity for a better and more sustainable world, the idea is already present in the mindset of progressive organisations and leaders. They are already aware of the limits of our planetary resources and the conditions of a sustainable world. They realise that it will not suffice to replace the existing technology with "green technology" without changing the incessant underlying drive towards "more and bigger." Green capitalism may be a step in the right direction, but it is not a sufficient one. The transformation of means must be embedded in a transformation of values and preferences. If we build green cars but, at the same time, stimulate the production and consumption of more cars, we will not stop the over-exploitation of our planet.

17 Bouckaert, L., "Doing Business Ethics in Europe. Before and After the Financial Crisis," in L. Bouckaert and J. Eynikel (eds.), *Imagine Europe. The Search for European Identity and Spirituality*, Antwerp, Garant, 2009, pp. 79-89.

The challenge of sustainability requires both the greening of our technology and the self-restricting of our needs. Therefore we use the term "post-capitalism." Whereas capitalist economies are ultimately driven by the highest return on financial capital and may support "green capitalism" as a profit opportunity, post-capitalist economies are driven by a complex function of value creation that balances spiritual and material values and respects the human condition of future generations.

A post-capitalist economy requires an institutional environment that corrects unregulated market competition and promotes a more frugal and responsible ethic of consumption. I believe that religions and wisdom-based philosophies have a lot to say about motivations for self-restriction and voluntary simplicity. Recent economics, revealing the *happiness paradox*, discloses in a contemporary and utilitarian language the old wisdom that more welfare does not correlate with more happiness.

Our obsessive need for more sophisticated material goods obstructs relational and spiritual needs such as friendship, a meaningful life, artistic self-expression, communing with nature, time for silence and meditation. The over-production and consumption of material goods at the cost of relational and spiritual goods explains the happiness paradox.[18] It is up to us to restore the balance. In my view, the problems of money, climate and happiness are linked. All three are the result of an over-materialistic and competitive way of life that undermines our quality of life. If this is true, we will not solve the crisis without changing our lifestyle and our way of looking at the common good. Therefore, inspired by a foundational commitment to the principle of universal responsibility, we need a new perception and management of the common good. Let me end by making a brief remark on this new perception of global common goods.[19]

Planetary resources (as space, oceans, rivers, forests, climate, etc) are perceived and managed today as competitive goods with an expected high return on (national) investment and not as global, common goods with a high degree of vulnerability. The lack of appropriate management of those global goods leads to the tragedy of the planetary commons, which is already visible today in the form of climate change and other symptoms of ecological deterioration.

18 Bruni, L. and Zamagni, S., *Civil Economy. Efficiency, Equity, Public Happiness*, Oxford, Peter Lang, 2007, chapter 9.

19 Bouckaert, L., "Business Spirituality and the Common Good," in H.-C. De Bettignies and J. Thompson Mike (eds.), *Leadership, Spirituality and the Common Good*, European SPES Cahier 4, Garant, Antwerp, 2009, pp. 13-27.

There is however another area of common goods that deserve our particular interest: the area of *nonmaterial or spiritual* goods such as silence, trust, respect, beauty, moral values, wisdom, etc. All these goods share the characteristics of common goods. They are not excludable. Silence and trust, for example, are values and practices open to everyone. They are free, not regulated by markets and cannot be enforced by law. But at the same time, they are vulnerable goods. Silence can only be maintained if others share it as a public good. If some people do not respect it, silence will diminish. Trust is another example of a common good with a high degree of vulnerability. One's trust is dependent on other people's trust and implies a reciprocal commitment to be realised. Hence, as a common good, trust can only exist when it is carefully managed as a vulnerable and shared good. The ongoing worldwide financial crisis clearly illustrates the importance of trust as a common and vulnerable good that needs more than market regulation.

It is important to define the new values of the post-capitalist economy – frugality, deep ecology, trust, reciprocity, responsibility for future generations, and authenticity – as vulnerable, common goods. Within this value-based economy, profit and growth are no longer ultimate aims but elements in a wider set of values. In a similar way cost-benefit calculations are part of a broader concept of wisdom in leadership.

V. Conclusion

Let me conclude by paraphrasing a well-known quote by Antoine de Saint Exupéry (where he explains what is needed to build a ship). It may put succinctly my reflection on a spiritual foundation for Europe.

If you want to build a European Union
Do not start with organising a referendum
or setting up a new commission
or writing a new treaty
But rather teach people
to long for a sustainable world
that feeds every child
For sure Europe will be built
as a responsible part of this planet
and we will find the right leaders as well

Bibliography

Bouckaert, L., "The Search for a 'Profane Spirituality'," in *Spiritus. Journal for Christian Spirituality*, 2011, vol 11, pp. 24-38.

Opdebeeck, H. and Zsolnai, L. (eds), *Spiritual Humanism and Economic Wisdom*, Garant, Antwerp, 2011.

Human Rights and Intercultural Dialogue: European Challenges and Perspectives

Christoph EBERHARD

Researcher and invited Professor in Anthropology and Theory of Law at the Facultés universitaires Saint Louis, Brussels

I. Introduction

"What are the cultural and value roots for intercultural dialogue in a European context?" This deep and important question, raised by the Jean Monnet Centre of Excellence "Intercultural Dialogue, Human Rights and Multi-level Governance" and the Interdepartmental Centre on Human Rights and the Rights of Peoples of the University of Padua, constitutes the red thread of an ongoing exploration that has already resulted in a previous publication "*Intercultural Dialogue and Citizenship. Translating Values into Actions. A Common Project for Europeans and their Partners*."[1]

In the introduction to the fourth part of this publication, which dealt with "Intercultural Dialogue and Human Rights, Civil Society and World Order Issues," Marco Mascia[2] pointed out that "analysis on intercultural dialogue was extended to comprise dialogue that is internal and external to the European Union, to find a common thread to enable and enhance its orientation towards 'dialogue' and its vocation to be a 'civil' actor, endowed with soft power within the world system." In his concluding remarks, Léonce Bekemans[3] summed up a few important points to keep in mind for that orientation, so that from a multi and interdisciplinary perspective, the human rights paradigm may assume the role of a "powerful trans-cultural facilitator to move from the (increasingly) conflicting stage of multi-culturality to the dialogic stage of interculturality." This affirmation has various consequences:

1 Bekemans, L. *et al.* (eds.), *Intercultural Dialogue and Citizenship. Translating Values into Actions. A Common Project for Europeans and their Partners*, Venice, Marsilio, 2007.

2 *Ibidem*, p. 447.

3 *Ibidem*, pp. 654-655.

1) Intercultural dialogue is a very complex process knotting together political, anthropological and psychological aspects and having implications in Europe as well as *vis-à-vis* other cultures; 2) Intercultural dialogue is becoming a major issue in contemporary political debates in Europe, urging clarification of what its stakes and challenges are; and 3) Intercultural dialogue requires a redefinition and practical reinvention of terms such as identity, citizenship, democracy and responsibility from the most local to the most global levels.[4]

II. Premises

Tackling the question of human rights and intercultural dialogue from the perspective of legal anthropology[5] allows us to take these reflections even further. Indeed, through its emphasis on the comparison of human experiences, it allows us to gain awareness of the European originality by contrasting it with other cultural traditions, while at the same time opening up the European window to invite a welcome intercultural dialogue within Europe and also with the broader world.[6] Through its focus on fieldwork, and thus not only dwelling on theories or systemic approaches, it brings into the picture the nexus between theories and practices and sheds an original light on the interactions between diverse global and local fields, such as the global fields of transnational human rights institutions and advocacy groups and the more local, regional, national or infra-national field realities.[7]

The question of human rights and intercultural dialogue crystallises challenges that Europe is currently facing, while offering an interesting and original perspective on our global living together and on what the specific European contribution to it may be. It plunges into the depths of European thinking and experience of living together between the unity of humankind and the diversity of its manifestations. It invites a glocal approach that articulates the European perspective with other cultural perspectives within the broader global horizon.

The *problématique* also reveals the complexity of the current world situation. It highlights the paradigmatic shifts we are experiencing. The postmodern transition is said to challenge modern assumptions on law,

---

4 See in this context Foblets, M.-C., Gaudreault-Desbiens, J.-F., Dundes Renteln, A. (dir.), *Cultural Diversity and the Law. State Responses from Around the World*, Brussels, Bruylant/Éditions Yvon Blais, 2010.

5 Eberhard, C., *Droits de l'Homme et Dialogue Interculturel*, Paris, Connaissances et savoirs, 2011.

6 *Id.*, *Le Droit au Miroir des Cultures. Pour une Autre Mondialisation*, Paris, LGDJ/Lextenso, Col. Droit et Société Classics, 2010.

7 *Id.*, "Law and Anthropology in a 'Glocal' World. The Challenge of Dialogue," in *Current Legal Issues 2009 – Law and Anthropology*, vol. 12, 2009, pp. 67-88.

politics, social sciences and their relationships. Central concepts that shaped modern perceptions of the world and its organisation are being redefined: "governance" replaces or at least complements the notion of "government"; "good governance" complements the "rule of law," "accountability" complements "human rights." The state loses its centrality and its monopoly on politics and regulation; citizenship emerges as a pluralist concept.[8] Analyses bridging the distance between the diverse local and global fields, as defined above, are on the rise.[9] Inclusive notions such as participation, inclusion and dialogue become cornerstones of an emerging pluralist and intercultural horizon of living together. The challenges are multiple as approaches emancipate themselves from monodisciplinarity and increasingly embrace multi-, inter- and even trans-disciplinarity,[10] not to forget the timid opening up to more intercultural approaches to our contemporary human predicament.

This paper will explore the European originality of the question of human rights and intercultural dialogue. It will highlight the major changes that have occurred over the last decade and which contribute to emancipating human rights thought and practice in the intercultural dialogue, from a universe familiar to us, to a pluriverse that we are still struggling to understand.[11] Four poles will delineate the pluralist horizon of living together: alterity, complexity, interculturality and humanity.[12] These four sensitivities, or landmarks, that I call "poles," also constitute four "cultural disarmaments,"[13] i.e. four ways to become aware and go beyond our ethnocentrism. Walking the path outlined between these four poles will avoid the pitfalls of oppressive universalism or the ghetto of particularisms and may lead to a pluralist horizon of responsibility.

---

8 See Arnaud, A.-J., *Critique de la Raison Juridique 2. Gouvernants sans Frontières. Entre Mondialisation et Post-mondialisation*, Paris, LGDJ, 2003.

9 See Goodale, M., Merry, S. E., *The Practice of Human Rights. Tracking Law Between the Global and the Local*, New York, Cambridge University Press, 2007; Merry, S. E., *Human Rights and Gender Violence. Translating International Law into Local Contexts*, Chicago and London, University of Chicago Press, 2006.

10 Ost, F., van de Kerchove, M., *Jalons pour une Théorie Critique du Droit*, Brussels, Publications des Facultés universitaires Saint-Louis, 1987.

11 Eberhard, C., "De l'Univers au Plurivers. Fatalité, Utopie, Alternative?," in A.-M. Dillens (dir.), *La Mondialisation: Utopie, Fatalité, Alternatives*, Brussels, Publications des Facultés universitaires Saint Louis, 2008, pp. 67-104; Eberhard, C., *Oser le Plurivers. Pour une Globalisation Interculutrelle et Responsable*, Paris, LGDJ/Lextenso, forthcoming.

12 For an introduction to the "path" of the legal anthropologist between these poles see Eberhard, C., *Le Droit au Miroir des Cultures*, *op. cit.*, pp. 23 *et seq*.

13 See Panikkar, R., *Cultural Disarmament – The Way to Peace*, USA, Westminster John Knox Press, 1995; Vachon, R., "Le Désarmement Culturel et la Paix," *Interculture*, 1985, vol. XVIII, no. 4, Cahier 89, pp. 37-43.

III. Law and Anthropology: Universalism and Relativism

The question of human rights and intercultural dialogue draws on two important streams of European thinking: the law tradition and the social sciences tradition, especially anthropology. Although these two approaches appear quite different, they draw on European humanistic core questions: how to make sense out of unity and diversity? How to organise a living together between unity and diversity? How to reach a universal understanding of humanity that necessarily has to take into account the diversity of its expressions and has to start from the observation of this diversity in order to distillate what is the same? How to build legal systems based on equality, which entails simultaneously a recognition of what binds us as well as what distinguishes us?

It has become perfectly clear that it is not enough to refer to the other as formally equal: we must open up to his or her self-understanding. The objective claim to universality, which is deeply embedded in the European's quest for Reason, paradoxically compels us to deal with the subjectivities of human beings. It is by observing the differences that one can understand the commonalities, as Rousseau remarked in a famous quote that anthropologists like to use as a credo for their research.[14] This tension between unity and diversity, implicitly resting on the horizon of the universality of the human nature, is central to European thinking.

Generally speaking lawyers have emphasised the pole of unity in this equation and have embraced a universalistic approach. Anthropologists on the other hand have favoured more relativistic positions. Partly, this difference can be understood as the result of two different aims: law is about *Sollen*, it is about how things should be, how they need to be organised. The perspective is a top-down perspective, a perspective that is meant to see the world in a certain way – through legal glasses – in order to be able to deal with it, to impact on it and to organise it. Anthropology is about *Sein*, about how things are. The main aim is understanding, not acting. It is about looking beyond the accepted perspectives, putting on different glasses to reveal the reality of human beings living together. The approach is thus more a bottom-up approach: it starts from the actors, their actions, perceptions, worldviews, and not from the point of view of a system. It is quite destabilising and disruptive to any existing system that looks at the world in one given

---

14 "Quand on veut étudier les hommes, il faut regarder près de soi; mais pour étudier l'homme, il faut apprendre à porter sa vue au loin; il faut d'abord observer les différences pour découvrir les propriétés." *Essai sur l'Origine des Langues*, Ch. VIII quoted in C. Lévi-Strauss, *Anthropologie Structurale*, Paris, Plon, 1995 (1958), p. 413.

way. In short, both approaches have their legitimacy and hold part of the truth. Universalism points to the important insight that we do share a common destiny. Relativism reminds us of the irreducible originality of every living being.

However, both the universalistic and the relativistic approach are incomplete. The universalistic position is highly ethnocentric. It turns values and conceptions of the society of belonging into universal ones in an undue manner.[15] A monologue arises instead of a necessary "duologue."[16] It is potentially oppressive to those who do not share our values and conceptions. The lack of clear awareness of this predicament makes intercultural dialogue difficult if not impossible. The universalistic position leads to the imposition of a "globalised Western localism" on others.[17]

Such an ethnocentric view is undoubtedly counterproductive in the search for true universality, or for an interculturally shared outlook on human rights. First, by negating the voice of the other, it does not allow for a mutual enrichment between our and other cultures. The recognition of the other is the cornerstone of sharing. No consensus can be reached nor a common future built without such a sharing. Second, the universalistic position paves the way to a logic of exclusion and of power instead of a much needed logic of complementarity of differences and of exchange. Particularistic withdrawals can partly be seen as defensive reactions against the "Western steam-roller."[18] It appears that instead of strengthening the universality of human rights, the universalistic position may turn out to weaken it, especially when core global players are seen as instrumentalising human rights to further their own interests, as is reflected in a selective awareness of human rights issues in the world. The building of a human rights' community becomes difficult, if not impossible.

The relativistic position absolutises differences and forgets about the common human nature and condition. It is so fascinated by the differences that the similarities become invisible. It emphasises the different perspectives so much that it loses sight of the common horizon.

---

15 Todorov, T., *Nous et les Autres – La Réflexion Française sur la Diversité Humaine*, Paris, Seuil, 1992, pp. 21-22 *et seq.*

16 Panikkar, R., *Myth, Faith and Hermeneutics – Cross-cultural studies*, USA, Paulist Press, 1979, p. 346.

17 de Sousa Santos, B., *Toward a New Commnon Sense – Law, Science and Politics in the Paradigmatic Transition*, New York-London, Routledge, After the Law Series, 1995, pp. 262 *et seq.*

18 Latouche, S., *La Planète des Naufragés – Essai sur l'Après-développement*, Paris, La Découverte, 1991, p. 8; Abou, S., *Cultures et Droits de l'Homme*, Paris, Hachette, 1992, p. 16.

Universality of any kind, therefore appears impossible. The values, conceptions and worldviews of different cultures cannot be challenged, understood or even questioned by other cultures. The picture is that of a fundamental "Other" with whom no dialogue is conceivable and with whom no mutual enrichment is possible. No mutual understanding, no sharing, no building of a common future, no real living together, seems possible. The best to be expected is a more or less harmonious co-existence. In the words of Sélim Abou,[19] such a relativistic outlook can lead, in the case of an acknowledgement of an absolute right, to difference, to a "right to confinement," or even to a "right to oppression" or to a "right to death."

These two views as well as the related distinction between universalism and particularism reflecting the gap between a general, idealistic, view and the pragmatic realities on the "grass root levels," constitute two opposite and nevertheless inseparable realities, of the European modern worldview.[20] As we will see further, they refer to the modern principle of the "encompassing of the contrary" (*englobement du contraire*) highlighted by Louis Dumont.[21] Lately, these two sensitivities, complementary rather than contradictory, have been reinterpreted through the lenses of the global/local nexus, thus revealing a new emerging reality – replacing the universe with the pluriverse.

IV. From Universe to Pluriverse: Towards a Pluralist Approach

The legal anthropologist's position is one in between law and anthropology, universalism and relativism, theories and practices, top-down and bottom-up, between global and local, and even between these in-betweens. Interestingly enough, although still quite at the margins a decade ago, current mainstream approaches to law, cultures and human rights seem increasingly to echo this view. Attention is increasingly drawn to this field of study, which nevertheless still remains on the edges of political and legal thought and action.[22]

The current developments of "globalisation" or rather the dynamics of "glocalisation" and of the mutual reinterpretation of local and global

19 Abou, S., *Cultures et Droits*, *op. cit.*, pp. 34-35.

20 Berthoud, G., *Vers une Anthropologie Générale. Modernité et Altérité*, Geneva, Librairie Droz S. A., 1992, p. 142.

21 Dumont, L., *Essais sur l'Individualisme – Une Perspective Anthropologique sur l'Idéologie Moderne*, Paris, Seuil, 1991 (1983), pp. 140-141.

22 See for example *Current Legal Issues 2009 – Law and Anthropology*, vol. 12, edited by M. Freeman and more especially on human rights: Goodale, M., *Surrendering to Utopia. An Anthropology of Human Rights*, Stanford, Stanford University Press, 2009.

realities on the factual and ideological levels, raise awareness of pluralism. They force us to deal with the universal *and* the particular, the global *and* the local. The classical universality/relativity distinction is reinterpreted into the unity/diversity nexus of the "global-local paradigm."[23] The disillusions of universalist approaches as well as the clear need to go beyond relativist approaches provide fertile ground to take the challenges of pluralism – and of the related interculturalism – seriously. There is a felt need to organise this living together in a responsible and culturally sensitive way. From a social science perspective, this entails understanding diverse normative organisations; from a legal perspective, this implies mapping out new ways to articulate them.[24]

This trend is illustrated in the recent Report of the International Council on Human Rights Policy "*When Legal Worlds Overlap. Human Rights, State and Non-State Law*." It addresses the burning question of human rights confronted by normative pluralism. In the chapter "Going Beyond Common Presumptions about Law, Culture and Human Rights" we read:

> The way we think about human rights changes the way we 'do' human rights: this point can be applied to many of the ideas that are central to this report. For example, if human rights in the context of plural legal orders are presumably trapped in binaries (such as modern and traditional, or universalism and cultural relativism), then discussion will fail to reflect the complexity of human rights practice or the ways in which plural legal orders are experienced on the ground, and rights protection may be weakened as a result. [...] Many presumptions about concepts associated with plural legal orders need to be interrogated. This chapter starts by discussing the centrality and power of law. Then, since the report prioritises plural legal orders in the context of cultural diversity, it discusses the relationship between law and culture and whether presumed cultural differences, such as those based on religion and ethnicity, necessarily generates plural legal

23 See for example: Kilani, M., *Introduction à l'Anthropologie*, Lausanne, Payot, 1992. For recent work on human rights in the context of globalisation see: Merry, S. E., *Human Rights and Gender Violence. Translating International Law into Local Contexts*, Chicago and London, University of Chicago Press, 2006; Goodale, M., and Merry, S. E., *The Practice of Human Rights. Tracking Law Between the Global and the Local*, New York, Cambridge University Press, 2007.

24 For an illustration of the stakes of translation and of dialogue between disciplines, cultures, different levels of "globality" and of "locality" in the current socio-legal-political-economic transition see: Eberhard, C. (ed.), *Traduire nos Responsabilités Planétaires. Recomposer nos Paysages Juridiques*, Brussels, Bruylant, 2008.

orders. Finally, it considers some constructive ways of thinking about human rights in the context of cultural differences.[25]

Some insights from legal anthropology help in the current deconstruction and reconstruction process of the modalities of our living together between unity and diversity. The four "poles/cultural disarmaments" defined above, which will now be explained further, may delineate the rising pluriverse. They are alterity, complexity, inter-culturality and humanity.

V. Alterity

Three decades ago, Raimon Panikkar asked in a very influential article[26] if human rights were a Western concept. In his comparisons with classical Indian thought, he came to the conclusion that they were – which in his view did not entail that they are useless or may not have a legitimate claim to universality. But he emphasised that it is a bad question to ask if other cultures have the same institutions as we have. We may miss the mark by assuming that all cultures necessarily share our outlooks and questions. It may be more rewarding to dig down to similar existential problematics and to try to understand how they are played out in diverse cultural contexts.

Panikkar pleads for a search for homeomorphic equivalences, or existential functional analogies from one culture to another.[27] In his dialogue with India, he remarked that the Indian notion of Dharma is an equivalent to the Western notion of human rights. However, it does not correspond exactly because the notion seems to be much more "cosmic" in outlook and "relational" in structure than the Western human rights' approach. Moreover, it focuses heavily on responsibilities and duties. Still it embraces a similar concern for human dignity and an organisation of living together based on the recognition of this dignity.

Searching for homeomorphic equivalences is always rooted in concrete explorations. Thus, if Dharma appears as a homeomorphic equivalent to human rights when one puts the question from a Western point of view, starting from the Indian context and the notion of Dharma, religion may appear as the European counterpart. It is important to be aware that there are no perfect translations or

---

[25] International Council on Human Rights Policy (ICHRP), *When Legal Worlds Overlap Human Rights, State and Non-State Law*, Geneva, Switzerland, 2009, p. 17.

[26] Panikkar, R., "Is the Notion of Human Rights a Western Concept?," in *Interculture*, vol. XVII, no. 1, Cahier 82, 1984, pp. 28-47.

[27] *Ibidem*, pp. 29 *et seq*.

equivalences from one culture to another as all cultural elements are part of a broader cultural complex, which endows them with meaning.[28]

European conceptions of what it is to be human and what law is about, are not universal. European culture is not the only existing culture. It is not the benchmark to which all human experience must be compared to, nor is it the ultimate horizon of civilisation that eventually all other cultures have to reach.

The recognition of alterity represents a first "cultural disarmament": the realisation that our culture, although being wrapped in a universalistic vision, is but one perspective, among others, to apprehend our existence and to live. This is not only an ethical wake-up call. It also entails an epistemological shift. Indeed, in its search for universality, the modern European tradition may have – in all good faith – missed the mark in genuinely understanding and recognising the other, embedded as it was, to use Raimon Panikkar's terms, in a dialectical horizon.

Within this horizon, Reason plays a predominant role and the world is seen as a puzzle to be solved. It mainly appears as an object that can be entirely known through the light of Reason, putting within reach the underlying unity and order of the plurality of life's manifestations. As it is objective, two different claims cannot be true simultaneously – in other words, the principle of non-contradiction rules.

Raimon Panikkar recognises the importance and the usefulness of the dialectical horizon, but stresses an often ignored precondition for its validity: a shared framework of reference. Anthropological research has shown, that although human beings do share the faculty of reasoning, it is nevertheless used in very different ways according to the different worldviews that people hold. Michel Alliot,[29] a founding father of French legal anthropology, expresses this variety with an inspiring aphorism: *Dis-moi comment tu penses le monde*; *je te dirai comment tu penses le Droit*, implying that our ways of perceiving the world influence our understanding of it and our organisation of it. Our subjectivities do count. Henceforth, the subjective experience of human beings should not be overlooked in European history. The rise of Reason was concomitant with the Romantic Movement. Often, especially in the political and legal domain, it is the more objective

28 Further reading in Eberhard, C., *Droits de l'Homme et Dialogue Interculturel*, *op. cit.* An overview in English in *id.*, "Towards an Intercultural Legal Theory – The Dialogical Challenge," in *Social & Legal Studies. An International Journal*, no. 10 (2), 2001, pp. 171-201; *id.*, "Human Rights and Intercultural Dialogue. An Anthropological Perspective," in *Indian Socio-Legal Journal*, vol. XXVII, 2001, pp. 99-120.

29 Alliot, M., *Le Droit et le Service Public au Miroir de l'Anthropologie. Textes choisis et édités par Camille Kuyu*, Paris, Karthala, 2003, p. 87.

pillar of regulation that tends to come to mind, overshadowing the complementary pillar of emancipation, which always counterbalanced it with its emphasis on subjectivity, creativity and poetry.[30]

As long as we remain exclusively dependent on the rhetoric of the dialectical dialogue and on the pillar of regulation, the danger of falling into the trap of "encompassing of the contrary" (*englobement du contraire*) as explained by Louis Dumont, is always present.[31] Although explicitly including the other into the category of humanity, we implicitly remain the reference point for what this humanity is. The other, although encompassed in the general category of humanity, is nevertheless constructed as the inverted image, often an inferior image of ourselves. This vision has shaped the European understanding of other legal cultures, thus failing to discover the Other behind the other, and to understand him/her in his/her originality.

If European researchers recognised *Ubi societas, ibi jus* (where there is a society, there is law), the law of traditional African societies for example was perceived as an inferior and inverted image of our own, i.e. a law still on a lower step of evolution. In the interpretation of Western law, real law is written, but theirs is oral; real law is abstract from other domains of life such as morals, religion, politics, but theirs is mixed up with these aspects; law is linked to the state, but they do not even have a state. Following this line of thought, these so-called primitive forms of life and sociability needed to be "civilised," according to the colonial terminology. They required "a translation" into a more contemporary wording, the degree of civilisation or development being measured by their likeness to the Western model.

For Europeans, there is a tendency to assume that the ultimate horizon of globalisation is given by Western "modernity" and its constructs: human rights, state, democracy, market, development, science, etc. This view is underpinned by the myth of a teleological move towards unity through a uniformisation of our ways of living together, of constructing meaning for our lives, of relating to our environment. Even though we observe differences, we assume – and even may wish – that they will slowly move to a universal culture that is identifiable with "Western" culture. The majority of the discourses promoting respect for cultural diversity and intercultural dialogue, are in fact, embedded in this paradigm.

Diversity is usually perceived as only a secondary aspect in our living together: it enriches us once our social cohesion is already secured by a uniform framework, providing unity. Cultural diversity is

30 de Sousa Santos, B., *Toward a New Commnon Sense, op. cit.*, pp. 2 *et seq.*.

31 Dumont, L., *op. cit.*

accepted only as long as it conforms and integrates in the broader, seemingly universal, modern and secular frame. The problem is that this frame and the world vision underlying it, are far from being universal and do only appear so from a "Western" or at least "Westernised" point of view.[32]

We may not live in a "universe" but in a "pluriverse," a world where differences are as constitutive of our world as unity. This pluriverse is not only a pluriverse of contents but, more fundamentally, a pluriverse in the ways we construct meaning and organise our living together[33] in relation to the others, to the cosmos, to the divine. Raimon Panikkar has elaborated this notion in his cross-cultural exploration of cosmotheandric intuition.[34] Anthropology of Law helps us to become aware of this pluralist view when it sees "Law" not as a set of rules (linked or not to the state) but as that which "puts forms and puts into forms the reproduction of humanity in the domains a society considers as being vital."

As a consequence, the dialectical dialogue needs to be complemented by another form of dialogue, i.e. the dialogical dialogue.[35] The dialogical dialogue cares less about the object to be discussed than about the subjects discussing it. Its aim is to unveil the hidden assumptions or "myths" of the partners in the dialogue. These myths only become apparent when confronted with a different myth and a different ultimate horizon of intelligibility. Consequently completely different perspectives on life and the world may emerge: for the Buddhists, human beings have no special status amongst all other sentient beings, or for the Hindu, human beings follow an endless path of reincarnation within universes that are part of cycles of creation and destruction and where the notion of right is much less present than that of duty.

The dialogical dialogue is a dialogue that recognises that the world is not only an objective reality, but is also made up of the self-understanding and subjectivity of the human beings living in it. The world appears as being fundamentally pluralistic: there are as many subjectivities as human beings. Logos or Reason is not the sole centre of

32 See Vachon, R., "Beyond the Universalisation and Interculturalisation of Human Rights, the Law and Negotiated Order," in *Interculture*, 2004, no. 146, pp. 15-30.

33 Eberhard, C., "De l'Univers au Plurivers. Fatalité, Utopie, Alternative?," *op. cit.*; *id.*, *Oser le Plurivers. Pour une Globalisation Interculutrelle et Responsable*, *op. cit.*

34 Panikkar, R., *The Cosmotheandric Experience – Emerging Religious Consciousness*, New York, Orbis Books, 1993.

35 *Id.*, "The Dialogical Dialogue," in F. Whaling (ed.), *The World's Religious Traditions*, Edinburgh, T. & T. Clark, 1984, pp. 201-221.

intelligibility – there is also mythos.[36] In short, the universe turns into a pluriverse. This does not only entail a move from the one to the many, but also results in a shift from a static to a dynamic perception of reality, from a simple to a complex view.

VI. Complexity

In recent years, notions such as "governance," "sustainable development," and "participation" are increasingly used to understand the emerging socio-legal-economic-political world. They reflect a change of perception that may be assessed in two opposite directions. A closed approach may lead to more "oppressing universalisms" than the former concepts of "government," "state" and "growth," while a more open-ended view may result in a more emancipatory approach to normative organisation,[37] to use de Sousa Santos' terminology.[38] Indeed, contrary to the former universalisms, these new "universalisms" explicitly point to the necessity of taking into account "particularisms," and of replacing more segmentary by more holistic approaches.

Taking participation seriously implies the recognition of the role of the state, the official law, the market, etc., while *simultaneously* realising that these are not exclusive realities. Legal anthropology may be of help in trying to tackle these delicate agendas and for rethinking contemporary legal issues in more holistic and pluralistic ways. The current political, legal and economic situation of the "glocalising" world indeed invites us to engage in what de Sousa Santos called "heterotopia,"[39] "a displacement in the very world we live in – from the centre to the margins," or in what Panikkar calls a "healthy pluralism."[40]

This second "cultural disarmament" of complexity, focuses on the totality and the dynamics of experience. The first "cultural disarmament" consisted in revealing alterity by unveiling the structural differences between cultures. Although a very important step in the process, the tendency exists to "freeze" realities in pictures. The consequence may result in a relativistic or culturalist outlook where one may not be able to perceive the film of life as it unfolds and to look beyond the pictures.

---

36 See Panikkar, R., *Myth, Faith and Hermeneutics, op. cit.*

37 For further reading, see for example, Eberhard, C., "Préliminaires pour des Approches Participatives du Droit, de la Gouvernance et du Développement Durable," in *Revue Interdisciplinaire d'Études Juridiques* 2009, n. 62, pp. 125-151.

38 de Sousa Santos, B., *Toward a New Commnon Sense, op. cit.*

39 *Ibidem.*

40 Panikkar, R., "Is the Notion of Human Rights," *op. cit.*

Pluralism goes beyond the recognition of otherness. The awareness of pluralism triggered by an encounter with the other, ultimately leads to the discovery of the pluralist nature of oneself. This can be illustrated by Le Roy's theory of *multijuridisme* and of a tripodic law.[41] Building on Michel Alliot's insights of the existence of diverse legal archetypes in different societies,[42] Etienne Le Roy argued that different mechanisms for shaping the organisation of societies and the organisation of living together as well as for solving conflicts in relation to each legal archetype, actually are present in all societies. These mechanisms are: general and impersonal norms linked to an imposed ordering; models of conduct and behaviour related to a negotiated ordering; and systems of lasting dispositions for action, or a "habitus," related to an accepted ordering. These mechanisms constitute the "three feet" of Law.

The articulation of these mechanisms varies from one society to another, and what is valued in one may be much neglected or even obscured in others.[43] Raimon Panikkar[44] points to a similar insight into the perception of Life. He argues that some cultures seem to value a more anthropocentric outlook; others are more cosmocentric and still others put much weight on the divine and the underlying mystery of existence. However, according to Panikkar, it appears that all cultures and human beings share a cosmotheandric experience, containing aspects of all three but actualising and articulating them in their own original way.

Seen in its dynamic framework, the second "cultural disarmament" also invites us to de-absolutise the notion of culture, being sometimes invoked as a monolithical excuse for not entering into dialogue, with the excuse that "it is cultural," implying that it is "sacred and non negotiable." However, historical, social, economic, political and geographical factors do play a role in shaping societies. From the acknowledgement of cultural differences, we need to emancipate ourselves from the purely culturalist framework.[45] In short, the Law is a complex and plural phenomenon. As Etienne Le Roy illustrates in his

---

41 Le Roy, É., "L'Hypothese du Multijuridisme dans un Contexte de Sortie de Modernité," in A. Lajoie *et al.*, *Théories et Émergence du Droit: Pluralisme, Surdetermination et Effectivité*, Brussels, Bruylant/Thémis, 1998, pp. 29-43.

42 Alliot, M., "Anthropologie et Juristique. Sur les Conditions de l'Élaboration d'une Science du Droit," in M. Alliot, *Le Droit et le Service Public*, *op. cit.*, pp. 283-305.

43 To deepen the presentation of this tripodic approach to Law and its cultural variations see: Le Roy, E., *Le Jeu des Lois. Une Anthropologie "Dynamique" du Droit*, Paris, LGDJ, p. 203.

44 Panikkar, R., *The Cosmotheandric Experience, op. cit.*

45 See in this context: Merry, S. E., *Human Rights and Gender Violence, op. cit.*, pp. 10 *et seq*; Sen, A., *Identity & Violence. The Illusion of Destiny*, London, Penguin Books, 2007.

dynamic approach to Law, the Game of Laws or *Jeu des Lois*,[46] we need to understand how the three feet of Law presented above actually "walk." However the challenges do not stop with this recognition of dynamic complexity. Indeed pluralism is not only a problem of the *logos*, it also reaches into our existential realities, our *mythos*.

VII. Interculturality

Recognising *alterity* is like widening our own window to the world, after having looked at it through other cultural windows, in order to enrich and broaden our outlook. *Interculturality* gives credit to the fact that even opening up one's window to the world from another cultural window is nevertheless not to be equated with looking at the world through that other cultural window.

The translation of a different culture's perspective into one's own necessarily translates the latter. For example, the recognition of indigenous people's rights by the predominant Western worldview transforms their claims into anthropocentric claims on collective rights. It does not deal with the cosmic aspect of these approaches to Life and to "Law."

The main question that has to be addressed, beyond the opening up of socio-legal sciences to alterity and complexity, is how to deal with the more radical intercultural pluralism, which can never be unified in any system.[47] In other words, what happens between windows? A dialogue between Chinese and European partners may happen in English. But once the dialogue is over, how does each of the partners take home what they shared? How do they fit it into their language and worldvision? We can know various languages, but we cannot speak them all at the same time. Our general perception may have been increased by knowing different linguistic and cultural universes, but as soon as we speak, we enter one of the existing windows – though opening it up more – while other windows continue to co-exist.

Robert Vachon rightly remarks in his reflections of intercultural approaches to Peace that:

> No one culture, religion, wisdom – no matter how modern, traditional or even intercultural it may be, is self-sufficient, even to properly ask the question (of Peace). To deepen as much as possible the various cultures of Man is a prerequisite. But it is not enough. […] Peace is not simply a matter of preserving our traditional cultures, of opening up to modernity or to post-modernity, or even of accepting our different ways of living, and co-existing

---

46 Le Roy, E., *Le Jeu des Lois, op. cit.*

47 Panikkar, R., "The Pluralism of Truth," in H. J. Carger (ed.), *Invisible Harmony. Essays on Contemplation and Responsibility*, USA, Fortress Press, 1990, pp. 92-101.

> in mutual indifference or resigned tolerance. It requires meeting, understanding ('standing under'...), a common horizon, new vision. But this requires that we acknowledge together a centre – a circle – which transcends the intelligence that we have or can have of it, at a particular moment of space and time. In short, in order to be at peace, we cannot start with the presupposition that we know what peace is. Neither before, during, nor after, our peace attempt. [...] Peace requires that we overcome our individualisms, sociocentrisms and monoculturalisms; that we relativise not only the convictions, beliefs, 'myths' that we are aware of (assumptions), but even the presuppositions that we are not aware of. [...] Strictly speaking, nothing is purely cultural; we are always within a transcultural reality. Yet, nothing is purely transcultural: we are always in a concrete culture. To speak thus of the radical relativity [...] of peace, is not to fall into the relativism of agnosticism and skepticism. We are dealing here with a wisdom of peace that is constitutively in search of itself. [...] What we are proposing is to approach peace together in an intercultural way, which involves a cultural disarmament, but is accorded the greatest cultural authenticity and fidelity. It is the way of non-duality, in a world which is ripped apart by the tyranny of monism and the cancer of dualism. It is a path of homeostatic balance between cultural authenticity, interculturalism, cultural disarmament and Peace.[48]

VIII. Humanity and the Emergence of a Horizon of Responsible Pluralism

The "cultural disarmament" *of interculturality* leads to a fourth existential "cultural disarmament": the recognition that we are humans. This "cultural disarmament" of *humanity* is closely related to an attitude of humility. We are not Gods, we are not perfect, we are not immortal, and we are not beyond suffering. We are incomplete, fragile and open-minded beings. By carrying its interpretation of universalism to the world through its former colonial endeavours and the Westernised process of globalisation, the European tradition is perceived as a Western steamroller in the eyes of many cultures. Its emphasis on knowledge building through Reason in order to master and rationally organise the world, has remained the main focus of attention and has become increasingly a target for criticism. However, the European tradition is also a tradition that hints to the fundamental fragility of the human condition and invites a very humble approach to life.

In comparison with other cultures, the European culture seems to put much focus on doubt, on the recognition that actually we do not really know who we are and what we are, but that we have to try to find out.

---

48 Vachon, R., "Guswenta or the Intercultural Imperative. Part 2: A Common Horizon," in *Interculture*, no. 128, 1995, pp. 38-40.

This is destabilising and is perceived by many cultures as being destructive. It should therefore be criticised and deconstructed in order to find its true validity. This approach actually also is a particular way of being, a tradition in itself. The European tradition has emphasised the freedom of choice of the individual. It centres on the individual and on the tool of Reason and has derived its approaches to rights and responsibilities from there.[49]

A humble approach of critical self-awareness, individual and collective, coupled with a sense of the ensuing responsibilities, may be what the European tradition could contribute to the intercultural dialogue not only on human rights but also on the underlying question of human dignity. By opening up to the positive insights of other cultures – although they may seem strange or disturbing at first sight[50] – we may achieve a more complete, responsible, maybe cosmotheandric, horizon of pluralism and interculturalism.[51] By furthering the European tradition of dialogue and debate through a genuine dialogical awareness of alterity, complexity, interculturality and humanity, it may be possible to unveil parts of the mystery that we are in relationship with others and share it in peace?

---

49 Eberhard, C., "Responsibility in France. A Juridical Approach in the Face of the Complexity of the World," in E. Sizoo (ed.), *Responsibility and Cultures of the World: Dialogue Around a Collective Challenge*, Brussels, P.I.E. Peter Lang, 2010, pp. 113-134.

50 For an example of an unsettling but enriching dialogue with the Buddhist world see *id.*, *Vers une Société Éveillée. Une Approche Bouddhiste d'un Vivre-ensemble Responsable et Solidaire*, Paris, Connaissances et savoirs, 2012.

51 Eberhard, C., "Au-delà de l'Universalisme et du Relativisme: L'Horizon d'un Pluralisme Responsable," in *Anthropologie et Sociétés – De l'anthropologie des moralités à l'éthnoéthique*, vol. 33, no. 3, pp. 79-100.

The European Parliament as an Institutional Memory Entrepreneur

Wolfram KAISER

Professor of European Studies, University of Portsmouth and Visiting Professor, College of Europe, Bruges

I. Introduction

Values and norms can be derived from abstract rational reasoning. In the present-day European Union (EU) with its growing cross-border connections and ties, at least at the elite level, they can be debated and agreed in dialogical forms of intercultural communication. Thus, they can become embedded in transnational communities and propagated by common institutions. In the EU these institutions would include the European Commission and the European Parliament (EP), for example.

But societies, like individuals, have a past. If this past is regarded as shared, or if it was not shared and rather divisive, but its interpretation and memory is nevertheless largely shared, then such collective memory has the potential to legitimise a particular set of values and norms. Thus, the EU, its member-states and the vast majority of European citizens will hopefully regard the collective memory of the industrial extermination of European Jewry during World War II, which continues to be promoted in political discourse, education and cultural institutions beyond the lifespan of the last survivors of the Holocaust, as an effective warning to vigorously protect basic human values and legal and political norms. This attitude of "never again" has become culturally embedded in the societal legitimation of present-day values and norms as they are enshrined in national constitutions and the EU's Charter on Fundamental Rights, for example.

More often than not, however, the past proves to be very divisive within and across national borders. Different historical experiences, and their fragmented and possibly opposed collective memory, can make it very difficult if not impossible for societies to develop shared identities, to see common institutions and their policies as legitimate, and to agree on the most desirable future. This is precisely why central political institutions – which were created or strengthened by processes of national integration and nation state-building in 19th century Europe – prioritised the cultivation of collective memory alongside education as a means to foster collective identity and allegiance to newly created states like the German Reich and the Kingdom of Italy, or to new political systems like the Third Republic in France. At the time, these strategies of cultural integration went hand in hand with those of economic and political integration.

Policies of European integration since 1945 have differed from these processes of national integration and nation-state formation in various ways. Most importantly for the purpose of this chapter, some institutions did promote cultural integration, but this remained completely marginal to "core Europe" integration in the present-day EU for a long time.

Of all the European institutions set up after 1945, it was the Council of Europe with its much larger and more heterogeneous membership and limited ambitions for political integration, which invested most resources into fostering cultural co-operation and integration across borders.[1] In contrast, "core Europe" integration was strongly dominated by the (neo-) functionalist paradigm and associated assumptions about the beneficial economic effects of market integration and its long-term "spill-over" into political integration.[2] Alternative visions of European integration prioritised the development of a political system akin to those of the member-states by emphasising in particular the need for a strong and directly elected European parliament that would eventually acquire legislative and budgetary powers comparable to those enjoyed by national parliaments.[3]

More recently, however, the potential contribution of culture (including collective memory) to strengthening European identity and the legitimacy of the EU has been emphasised much more by EU institutions. The limited research on cultural policy-making to date has mostly studied the Commission's role and initiatives in the cultural

1 Cf. Haigh, A., *Cultural Diplomacy in Europe*, Strasbourg, Council of Europe, 1974.

2 See Haas, E. B., *The Uniting of Europe. Political, Social, and Economic Forces, 1950-1958*, Stanford/Cal., Stanford University Press, 1958. For an introduction to the historiography of European integration see Kaiser, W., Varsori, A. (eds.), *European Union History. Themes and Debates*, Basingstoke, Palgrave, 2010.

3 Cf. Kaiser, W., *Christian Democracy and the Origins of European Union*, Cambridge, Cambridge University Press, 2007; Jachtenfuchs, M., *Die Konstruktion Europas. Verfassungsideen und institutionelle Entwicklung*, Baden-Baden, Nomos, 2002.

field, where the EU enjoys only very limited and strictly subsidiary competences.[4]

This chapter, in contrast, will analyse the role of the EP in the politics of memory. In fact, the EP has already played an important role in promoting EU action for strengthening its symbolic power in the run-up to the adoption of the European flag and anthem in 1985 and beyond.[5] Here, the focus will be on the EP's more recent promotion of a shared collective memory as a cultural foundation for the EU. As an institutional memory entrepreneur, the EP has passed normative resolutions with strong historical connotations and supported plans for the creation of a House of European History (HEH) in Brussels, which would narrate the history of Europe in the 20th century from a European perspective of some kind.

After briefly discussing these initiatives, this chapter will analyse the reasons for the EP's new interest in shaping European memory politics. It will also draw out some initial conclusions about the potential contribution of such memory politics by supranational institutions to fostering a greater sense of shared values, norms and community among EU citizens.

II. Victimising Europeans: Resolutions on the Past

Passing resolutions is an established method that parliaments traditionally use to stir up or influence public debates. The EP has done so from early "core Europe" integration onwards precisely because its powers were so limited until the Maastricht Treaty introduced the co-decision procedure in 1992-93. For a long time, however, the focus was on enhancing its own institutional visibility and supporting its demands for greater power.

In contrast, using this parliamentary tool for memory politics is a more recent trend.[6] It reached a first high point with the EP's resolution on *European conscience and totalitarianism* of 2nd April 2009, which was passed by 553 votes for and 44 against. Building on a previous

4 See e.g. Littoz-Monnet, A., *The European Union and Culture. Between Economic Regulation and European Cultural Policy*, Manchester, Manchester University Press, 2007; Theiler, T., *Political Symbolism and European Integration*, Manchester, Manchester University Press, 2005; Shore, C., *Building Europe. The Cultural Politics of European Integration*, London, Routledge, 2000.

5 Cf. Foret, F., *Légitimer l'Europe. Pouvoir et Symbolique à l'Ère de la Gouvernance*, Paris, Sciences Po, Les Presses, 2008, pp. 175-214.

6 Cf. Troebst, S., "„Gedächtnis und Gewissen Europas"? Die Geschichtspolitik der Europäischen Union seit der Osterweiterung," in E. François, K. Kończal, R. Traba, S. Troebst (eds.), *Strategien der Geschichtspolitik in Europa seit 1989. Deutschland, Frankreich und Polen im internationalen Vergleich*, Göttingen, Wallstein, 2012.

resolution of 23rd September 2008, it also led to the institutionalisation of 23rd August as a European-wide so-called Remembrance Day "for victims of all totalitarian and authoritarian regimes, to be commemorated with dignity and impartiality."[7] This Remembrance Day marks the signing of the Molotov-Ribbentrop Pact on 23rd August 1939, when the Soviet Union and Nazi Germany divided East-Central Europe between them in what Jerzy Buzek, the Polish EP President, has called "the collusion of the two worst forms of totalitarianism in the history of humanity."[8] The Day of Remembrance has been observed annually by the EU since 2009.

In terms of its structure and content, the 2009 resolution is a compromise document. First, it combines references to previous declarations by the EP with appeals for the respect of European values and norms and a shared understanding of the most recent European past, very general references to how to understand such a shared European past and calls for action by EU institutions to assist with research into this recent past and with its commemoration. The resolution refers to the United Nations' Universal Declaration of Human Rights and to the EU's Charter of Fundamental Rights. More concretely, it mentions "the values of respect for human dignity, freedom, democracy, equality, the rule of law and respect for human rights" – values that have been violated by various forms of "totalitarian rule" in the 20th century. Crucially, the resolution stresses that: "From the perspective of the victims it is immaterial which regime deprived them of their liberty or tortured or murdered them for whatever reason."

Secondly, the 2009 resolution explicitly rejects a positivist understanding of history with explanations that do not go beyond the intellectual level of high school teaching. It claims that: "Historians agree that fully objective interpretations of historical facts are not possible and objective historical narratives do not exist." At the same time, EU citizens are informed that: "Professional historians use scientific tools to study the past, and try to be as impartial as possible." The EP also admits that it can hardly impose one understanding of the allegedly shared past (whether objective or subjective) "by means of majority decisions of parliaments, whereas parliament cannot legislate on the past." Nevertheless, the MEPs actually advance their preferred interpretation of the past. Their understanding combines the strong preference for the totalitarian paradigm with a subsidiary reference to the Holocaust.

---

7 European Parliament resolution of 2 April 2009 on European conscience and totalitarianism, P6_TA(2009)0213.

8 http://www.europarl.europa.eu/president/view/en/press/press_release/2010/2010-August/press_release-2010-August-10.html (accessed 15 December 2011).

The totalitarian paradigm has its origins in the works of Hannah Arendt.[9] As an explanatory framework for understanding the history of the 20th century, it strongly emphasises the structural similarities in the regimes of oppression between National Socialist, fascist and authoritarian military dictatorships on one side and Stalinist and communist regimes on the other. At the same time, it downplays differences in terms of the social roots of the movements behind the rise and the consolidation of these regimes, their ideologies or the motives among sections of the population for supporting them, for example. Crucially, in the context of the EP debates over the contemporary history of Europe, the legitimate focus of the totalitarian paradigm on the similarities among the different regimes of oppression, facilitates a strong emphasis on the victims of this oppression in the vast majority of European countries – with the exceptions of cases such as the United Kingdom, Sweden and Switzerland, for example. This perspective is very strong in the EP resolution.

In contrast, the thesis of the singularity of the Holocaust, or the extermination of European Jewry, highlights differences. It emphasises the allegedly unique nature of the National Socialist regime in Germany, especially in terms of the industrialised mass murder of one (religious) social group. This issue of the singularity (or not) of the Holocaust was hotly debated in the so-called *Historikerstreit* in Germany in the 1980s.[10] At the time, the public battle between historians and intellectuals was clearly decided in favour of the singularity thesis – at least in societal and political terms, if not necessarily in academic terms. Subsequently, this thesis became what Timothy Garton Ash first called sarcastically (referring to the German technical norms) the "German DIN norm" for collective memory.[11]

German and social democratic and other left-wing movements and political parties in particular, sought to Europeanise and globalise this "DIN norm," especially in the context of the Holocaust conference in Stockholm in 2000.[12] The networks formed at this conference were also

---

9 Arendt, H., *The Origins of Totalitarianism*, New York, Harcourt, Brace & Co., 1951.

10 Cf. Wolfrum, E., *Geschichtspolitik in der Bundesrepublik Deutschland. Der Weg zur bundesrepublikanischen Erinnerung 1948-1990*, Darmstadt, Wissenschaftliche Buchgesellschaft, 1999; Kailitz, S. (ed.), *Die Vergangenheit der Gegenwart: der „Historikerstreit" und die deutsche Geschichtspolitik*, Wiesbaden, VS Verlag, 2008.

11 Garton Ash, T., "Mesomnesie. Plädoyer für ein mittleres Erinnern," in *Transit*, vol. 22, pp. 32-48.

12 Cf. Eckel, J., Moisel, C. (eds.), *Universalisierung des Holocaust? Erinnerungskultur und Geschichtspolitik in internationaler Perspektive*, Göttingen, Wallstein, 2008; Kansteiner, W., "Losing the War, Winning the Memory Battle: The Legacy of Nazism, World War II, and the Holocaust in the Federal Republic of Germany," in

instrumental in the temporary shunning of the newly formed Austrian government in 2002, which included the right-wing so-called Freedom Party alongside the Austrian People's Party – a short-lived policy directed at the symbolic cultivation of European values and norms and the domestic control of right-wing populist parties in other member-states like Denmark and the Netherlands, for example.[13]

Since then the memorialisation of the Holocaust has continued to grow, for example through the creation of museums exclusively devoted to Jewish life and the extermination of European Jewry. The EU has also fostered this memorialisation. For example, it devotes the largest part of its *Active Remembrance* programme to the Holocaust. This programme is designed to bring individuals and local groups from different member-states together to develop shared ways of understanding and commemorating the most recent past.[14]

Importantly, however, the totalitarian paradigm has become much stronger and now clearly overshadows the competing thesis of the singularity of the Holocaust in the 2009 resolution, as in other statements by the EP. Rather bizarrely, the resolution states that "millions of victims were deported, imprisoned, tortured and murdered by totalitarian and authoritarian regimes [...] in Europe," only to add directly afterwards that "the uniqueness of the Holocaust must nevertheless [!] be acknowledged."

Paradoxically, both perspectives on the contemporary history of Europe claim to draw the same lessons for the need to respect human rights and shared values and norms. As historical interpretations they are clearly incompatible, however. Crucially, the totalitarian paradigm, with its emphasis on all Europeans as the victims of similar totalitarian regimes, leads more naturally to a potentially shared understanding of the past. Perpetrators do not become "nationalised" any more, that is,

---

R. N. Lebow, W. Kansteiner, C. Fogu (eds.), *The Politics of Memory in Postwar Europe*, Durham/N.C., Duke University Press, 2006, pp. 102-146.

13 Kaiser, W., "„Warum lernen Sie nicht aus der Geschichte?" Deutschland und die Sanktionen der EU-14 gegen Österreich," in M. Gehler, I. Böhler (eds.), *Verschiedene europäische Wege im Vergleich. Österreich und die Bundesrepublik Deutschland 1945/49 bis zur Gegenwart*, Innsbruck, Studienverlag, 2007, pp. 531-547; Gehler, M., "Präventivschlag als Fehlschlag: Motive, Intentionen und Konsequenzen der EU-14-Sanktionsmaßnahmen gegen Österreich im Jahre 2000," in W. Loth (ed.), *Das europäische Projekt zu Beginn des 21. Jahrhunderts*, Opladen, Leske & Budrich, 2001, pp. 325-382.

14 Littoz-Monnet, A., "The EU Politics of Commemoration Post-Eastern Enlargement," in B. Arcidiacono, K. Milzow, A. Marion, P.-E. Bourneuf (eds.), *Europe Twenty Years After the End of the Cold War: The New Europe, New Europes? L'Europe vingt ans après la fin de la Guerre Froide: Nouvelle Europe, nouvelles Europes?*, Brussels, P.I.E. Peter Lang, 2012.

they were not exclusively or even mainly German, but had many nationalities. Moreover, perpetrators as distinctive individuals or social groups disappear from the historical narrative altogether, which prioritises a general victimisation of Europeans.[15] This trend is also visible in museums that showcase the most recent past – and a possible scenario for the EP's own planned museum, the House of European History.

III. Musealising Europeans: the House of European History

The EP's memory politics also extends to musealising Europeans and their allegedly shared past. Drawing upon its own institutional budget, the EP, under its liberal French President Simone Veil, first bought Jean Monnet's house in Houjarray near Paris in 1982. Since 1987, the house as a "memory site" has been accessible to visitors, and in 2010 the European Commission began to use it to carry out basic historical training in European integration for newly recruited officials.[16] More recently, the EP has built its own visitor centre, the so-called Parlamentarium, which opened in October 2011.[17] Originally proposed by Josep Borrell, the Spanish socialist EP President, the visitor centre also includes a section on the history of European integration and the EP itself, which starts with "Europe's visionaries" and the Schuman Plan of 9th May 1950. The Parlamentarium's overall objective is to demonstrate to the visitors "what the EP does for them."[18]

The second large EP project, the House of European History (HEH), is scheduled to open in 2014. The EP Bureau first supported the proposal by Hans-Gert Pöttering, the German Christian democratic EP President, on 12th December 2007. At the time of writing, in late 2011, the long-term financing of the HEH appeared to be largely secure. The plan for the museum and its overarching historical narratives was much less clear, however. Proposing the HEH in his inaugural address as EP president on 13 February 2007, Pöttering described the future museum as "a place that cultivates our memory of European history and European integration."[19] Addressing the expert committee, which had the task of developing an outline plan for the future museum, he

[15] Cf. Jureit, U., Schneider, C., *Gefühlte Opfer. Illusionen der Vergangenheitsbewältigung*, Stuttgart, Klett-Cotta, 2010.

[16] Interview J. Gascard, Conférencier, Maison de Jean Monnet, Houjarray, 9.6.2010.

[17] "Europa gucken," *Die Zeit*, 13 October 2011.

[18] Interviews A. Kleinig, Director, Parlamentarium, European Parliament, Brussels, 19.10.2011; 29.10.2009.

[19] http://www.hieronymi.de/PDF%20Dokumente/Programmrede.13.2.2007.DE.pdf (accessed 15 December 2011).

emphasised in particular that the HEH should "give a fresh boost to the spiritual dimension for the EU."[20]

In its report, the expert committee, which was chaired by Hans-Walter Hütter, the director of the House of History of the Federal Republic of Germany in Bonn, proposed that the HEH should concentrate on the history of Europe in the 20th century and devote 70 per cent of the permanent exhibition to the post-war history of European integration.[21] Two key assumptions characterise the report's emphasis on the *courte durée* of the present-day EU's history. First, in this perspective the post-war East-West conflict conceptualised as a battle between democracy and communist dictatorship, had already started with the Bolshevist "putsch" of 1917. Second, the report postulated that the end of World War II on 8-9th May 1945 was "without doubt a day of liberation." This was clearly a normative claim derived from the predominant western European experience of the end of the war and from West German memory politics of the 1970s.[22] According to the latter view, many Germans possibly experienced the end of the war as defeat and catastrophe. However, they should have experienced it as liberation and must definitely remember it as such. Crucially, however, the liberation thesis never really applied to East-Central European member-states, which made the transition during 1944 to 1948 from the Nazi German occupation to Stalinist rule.

The expert committee's report still reflected Pöttering's view of the EU as a highly institutionalised trans- and supranational "community of values."[23] As a result, Harald Rømer, the EP's Danish Secretary-General, noted in an internal document on the HEH plan for the EP Bureau that "specific emphasis should be put on the values of integration."[24] In this perspective the history of European integration appeared as a process of institutionalisation leading towards a

---

20 Committee of Experts, House of European History, *Minutes of the Constituent Meeting of 3 March 2008*, 6 March 2008.

21 Committee of Experts, House of European History, *Conceptual Basis for a House of European History,* Brussels, European Parliament, 2008: http://www.europarl.europa.eu/meetdocs/2004_2009/documents/dv/745/745721/745721_en.pdf (accessed 15 December 2011).

22 See in comparative perspective, Berger, S., "Remembering the Second World War in Western Europe, 1945-2005," in M. Pakier, B. Stråth (eds.), *A European Memory? Contested Histories and the Politics of Remembrance*, New York, Berghahn, 2010, pp. 119-136.

23 Interview Prof. Dr. L. Kühnhardt, Director, Center for European Integration Studies, Bonn University of Bonn, 30.4.2010.

24 Rømer, H., *Note for the Attention of the Bureau, Subject: Project Aiming at Founding of 'House of European History'*, no date [2007]; building on Kühnhardt to Pöttering, Subject: House of European History, 18 September 2007.

supranational constitutional order of sorts, which guaranteed its citizens political, social and economic rights as well as peace in Europe. This is a view that is close to the western German concept of constitutional patriotism initially developed by the political scientist Dolf Sternberger[25] which in turn is strongly influenced by the French Republican notion of allegiance to a particular (national Republican) constitutional order.

At the time of writing, however, a team of 13 historians and museologists, under the leadership of the Slovene Taja Vovk van Gaal, were working on an entirely new concept for the HEH, which would deviate substantially from the initial expert committee report. The majority of the exhibition space would still be devoted to the post-war period.[26] However, the western European experience of integration would be narrated much less extensively. Instead, the eastern European experience of life under communism would feature much more prominently, and it would be embedded in the same narrative of totalitarian rule and victimhood which also characterised the 2009 EP resolution discussed above – a shift influenced by general factors discussed in the conclusion below, but also by the now much more prominent role of politicians, historians and museologists from East-Central European member-states in driving the project: the new Polish EP President Jerzy Buzek; the Polish historian Włodzimierz Borodziej, who heads the new scientific committee of the HEH, and Vovk van Gaal, whose main professional experience was as director of the City Museum of Ljubljana between 1997 and 2006.

In part, the prominent role of these East-Central European actors was a response to severe criticism of the originally proposed, more western European narrative.[27] This occurred especially in Poland, where historians and commentators from the nationalist Right, advocated for inclusion in the HEH narrative of the entire canon of the allegedly heroic Polish history; from the defeat of the German knights in 1410 through to the role of the trade union movement, Solidarność, in ending the Cold War.[28] Crucially, this criticism was also linked to the aggressive

---

25 Sternberger, D., *Verfassungspatriotismus*, Frankfurt am Main, Insel, 1990.

26 *Explore, Engage, Enjoy – Europe!* The House of European History Project Team, Brussels, European Parliament, 2011.

27 Trüpel, H., "Haus der europäischen Geschichte," in *Jahrbuch für Kulturgeschichte*, vol. 9, 2009, pp. 185-191, here p. 187.

28 http://www.ipn.gov.pl/portal/en/35/1/Brief_history.html (accessed 15 December 2011).

propagation of the totalitarian paradigm so deeply engrained in the memory politics of Poland and the Baltic countries, among others.[29]

IV. The European Parliament as a Memory Entrepreneur

The EP has been developing and expanding its role as an institutional memory entrepreneur since around 2005, particularly prioritising resolutions on contemporary European history and the museum plan. Three reasons largely account for this new activism. First, like the other EU institutions, the EP has been affected by the debate about the (alleged) "democratic deficit" since the early 1990s, as well as the linked legitimacy crisis. The continuous decline in voter turnout for EP elections since the first direct elections in 1979 has aggravated this crisis for the EP as an institution. The EP is now as concerned, if not more so, about how to improve the legitimacy of the EU and its governance, as the Commission and the member states.

Second, it appears that established forms of legitimising the EU are (at least currently) not very effective. This concerns both "output" legitimacy, i.e. the quality of EU legislation and its actual and perceived positive impact on citizens' lives, and "input" legitimacy, i.e. the possibility of participation in the supranational democratic process either directly or via organised so-called "stakeholders" like non-governmental organisations. In these circumstances, which have been aggravated by the economic and financial crisis since 2007, the EP seeks to enhance what might be dubbed the cultural legitimacy of the EU, i.e. the allegiance of its citizens based on common values and norms and feelings of commonalities and shared identity – something that the EP wishes to strengthen by communicating an understanding of the contemporary history of Europe and the EU as shared and unifying.

Third, the Eastern enlargements of 2004-07 have actually made it much more difficult to agree on such a shared understanding of contemporary European history. Memory politics and discourses in East-Central Europe are dominated by the totalitarian paradigm, which is not easily compatible with the established "core Europe" narrative of integration and the originally western German narrative of the singularity of the National Socialist regime and the Holocaust. Within the EP, MEPs from the new member-states have strongly pushed a memory agenda drawing on the totalitarian paradigm. Not only have individual actors from the new member-states succeeded in occupying key positions of influence in the EP's internal debate over European

---

[29] Cf. Mälksoo, M., "The Memory Politics of Becoming European: The East European Subalterns and the Collective Memory of Europe," in *European Journal of International Relations*, vol. 15, no. 4, 2009, pp. 653-680.

memory, but as we have seen above, they have also been quite successful at inserting their agenda into the EP's political discourses and practices. Needless to say that the victimisation of Europeans, which largely writes its perpetrators as anonymous instruments of totalitarian regimes out of the history of Europe and its commemoration, in turn has huge normative implications.[30]

The question remains of how successful the EP can be as a memory entrepreneur. It is of course too early to tell. For a long time, historians of the 19th century tended to see processes of cultural integration in the national context as having been effective. Thus, Eugen Weber argued that the Third Republic's policies of national integration, including the cultural cultivation of a Republican interpretation of the past by means of political discourses, monuments and public events like the world exhibitions in Paris, for example, were very largely successful in turning "peasants into Frenchmen" until the start of World War I.[31]

More recent research has shown, however, that strong regional identities persisted not only in states like Germany and Italy – where the Risorgimento myth imposed a very superficial idea of Italy onto the newly created, highly fragmented state – but even in France.[32] Moreover, collective memory can remain highly contested even in the national context for a long time, as the example of France in the inter-war period demonstrates. Actually, the stronger politicisation of EU politics, which some authors have argued would mark a normalisation of the EU as a political system and could increase its legitimacy in the eyes if the citizens, could also fuel conflicts over European memory on what the German sociologist Claus Leggewie has recently and somewhat martially called a memory "battlefield."[33]

The limits of cultural integration, memory alignment and national identity politics in the 19th century, already point to one first important issue for the EP and its new role as a European memory entrepreneur: collective memory, like collective identity, changes very slowly. In

30 For these normative implications and for a much more detailed discussion of evolving transnational and European narratives in museums beyond the HEH plan see also Kaiser, W., Krankenhagen, S., Poehls, K., *Europa ausstellen. Das Museum als Praxisfeld der Europäisierung*, Cologne, Böhlau, 2012, chapter 6.

31 Weber, E., *Peasants into Frenchmen. The Modernization of Rural France 1870-1914*, Stanford/Cal., Stanford University Press, 1976.

32 Cf. e.g. Green, A., *Fatherlands. State-building and Nationhood in Nineteenth Century Germany*, Cambridge, Cambridge University Press, 2011; Ford, C., *Creating the Nation in Provincial France. Religion and Political Identity in Brittany*, Princeton/N.Y., Princeton University Press, 1993.

33 Leggewie, C., *Der Kampf um die europäische Erinnerung. Ein Schlachtfeld wird besichtigt*, Munich, Beck, 2011.

other words, even if the EP's initiatives were to show impact on the sentiments and attitudes of EU citizens, they are no panacea for the concerns over the EU's legitimacy in the short and medium term. Second, the EU as a multi-level governance system is a highly fragmented polity with only subsidiary competences in the cultural field, so that neither the EP nor any other EU institution will ever be able to penetrate the member-states deeply enough to influence memory politics on the ground. Memory politics in the EU is characterised by multiple institutional actors working alongside or competing with each other at different governance levels. The highly pluralistic nature of European memory politics constrains the EP further in its role as a memory entrepreneur. And third, memory in modern societies has become more individual and fragmented even at the national level. Arguably, it is also becoming more transnational (again), but this does not lead automatically to a kind of EUisation of memory. The more individualised character of memory also means that a top-down approach to engineering new forms of collective memory is anyway much less likely to be effective than in centralised states, like France in its 19th century period of intense nationalism and national conflict. Even then, however, memory politics and cultural integration were shaped as much by initiatives from below, by citizens in localities, as from above, by state institutions – something that for the moment is definitely not a widespread phenomenon in the EU.

The Champions of the Cultural Dialogue between Europe and China: Jesuit Missionaries and Scientists in China between the 17th and the 18th Century

Riccardo SCARTEZZINI

Jean Monnet Chair ad personam, University of Trento

Following the maritime explorations and discoveries of the 15th and 16th centuries, Europe began to interact with parts of the world that were previously completely unknown. European attitudes towards these newly encountered cultures, was not the same everywhere. The most interesting and culturally stimulating experience was the encounter of the first Jesuit missionaries with the Chinese Mandarins of the Ming and Qing dynasties, from the end of the 16th until the beginning of the 18th century. Their cultural interchange was carried out on an equal basis and largely contributed to the knowledge of China in Europe and, vice-versa.

G. H. Dunne's words at the end of the prologue of *Generation of Giants* provide a vivid portrait, despite its brevity, of the main characters of the early Jesuit China mission:

> This is the story of a small group of men who, breaking with the dominant spirit of their times and recalling a distant past, restored the concept of cultural adaptation to a central position in the world mission of Christianity. [...] Their story is worth telling not simply as an important segment of world history, but because it has much to say [...] to a world which has not yet learned to break down the barriers of cultural, racial and national pride.[1]

The Italian sinologist G. Bertuccioli, in *Italia e Cina*, defines the first China missionaries in this way:

> [...] those missionaries proved incredibly endowed both physically and mentally. This is witnessed by their resistance to endless hardships, including those of the long and dangerous journey from Europe to China; by their accommodation abilities and, above all, by the way they were able to support

1 Dunne, G., *Generation of Giants*, Notre Dame, Indiana, University of Notre Dame Press, 1962, p. 14.

> themselves and the mission [...]; by their remarkable, sometimes phenomenal, cultural production. Astronomers, mathematicians, geographers, theologicians, painters, musicians, experts in hydraulics and ballistics: the European Jesuits in China of that time were definitely ad omnia parati.[2]

"Missionaries and Scientists," this seemingly unusual combination aims to underline the importance of the innovative approach that the great Jesuit Matteo Ricci[3] used in his missionary work and in his understanding of the Chinese culture. His method, first of all, entailed an adaptation to Chinese customs, talking and dressing like a Chinese native and behaving like an intellectual or "Mandarin" in order to obtain their respect. Secondly, his strategy involved the use of Western scientific and technological knowledge to support the propagation of the Christian faith, carrying on the conversion of the upper classes and, possibly, of the Emperor himself, and then trying to convert the common people.[4]

It was thanks to their cultural preparation that the Jesuits could overcome the distrust and hostility towards foreigners displayed by the Ming society of that time, which was believed to be the richest and most advanced in a world of barbarians. China regarded other countries merely as vassals of the only, real Emperor living in Beijing; its civilisation did not need to learn anything from anyone else, aside from some technological innovations, which could be used to solve daily problems. This proud and haughty attitude could be partially justifiable until the 16th century, when the Chinese civilisation reached the apex of its development. However, in the 17th and 18th centuries, the West had largely surpassed China in several fields of human knowledge. The turning point in Europe was the Scientific Revolution of the 17th century, which called into question the traditional knowledge coming from medieval empiricism or transmitted from the Classical Age and rediscovered during the Renaissance. The "Revolution" was centred on Galileo's experimental method, which highlighted the importance of the results of sense experience, as Leonardo had already taught, and of the mathematisation and generalisation of natural laws.

---

2 Bertuccioli, G. and Masini, F., *Italia e Cina*, Bari, Laterza, 1996, p. 121.

3 Dehergne, D., *Repertoire de Jesuites de Chine de 1552 à 1800*, Rome, Institutuum Historicum S. I, 1973, pp. 219-220; Pfister, L., *Notices Biographiques et Bibliographiques sur le Jésuites de l'Ancienne Mission de Chine, 1552-1773*, Shanghai, Imprimerie de la Mission Catholique, 1932, pp. 22-42. Ricci's Opera omnia has been published in Pasquale, M., D'Elia, S., Fonti Ricciane, 3 vols., Roma, La Libreria dello Stato, 1942.

4 Mungello, D. E., *Curious Land: Jesuit Accommodation and the Origins of Sinology*, Honolulu, University of Hawaii Press, 1989, pp. 44-72.

Front-ranking mathematicians, astronomers and geographers – thanks to the teachings they had received in the Roman College by some of the most eminent European scholars, like Christopher Clavius and Athanasius Kircher – the Jesuit missionaries proved immediately perfect for the great task they had been called for. Most famous was Matteo Ricci, who became so well known for drawing maps, making clocks, optical prisms and other mechanic devices, that he was summoned to the court to explain how they worked and to inform the Emperor of what was beyond the borders of the Celestial Empire. Other Jesuits also became well known: Adam Schall[5] as mathematician, tutor and reformer of the official calendar; Martino Martini[6] as geographer, historian and reporter of the dynastic change between the Ming and Qing; Ferdinand Verbiest[7] as astronomer, geographer, cannon and instrument builder. However, all of those few but carefully chosen missionaries – who made it to Macao, on the Guandong coast of China, after a long and dangerous journey on Portuguese ships, facing pirate attacks as well as tempests – proved to be in possession of uncommon accommodation abilities, diplomacy and tolerance. Thanks to their efforts, the cultural dialogue between Europe and China was grounded on a new, deep and lasting foundation, especially when compared to contact during previous centuries. This marked an important success in the field of transmitting and sharing knowledge.

Furthermore, the Jesuits arrived in China when the local Ming dynasty had begun its decadence and was about to fall under the power of the Manchu dynasty of the Qing, which would rule until the end of the empire (1912). This caused a fluctuating attitude towards the European missionaries, who often had to face violence and persecution, since the authorities feared their involvement in the anti-government uprisings that were erupting in many provinces. The reason for these suspicions lay in the new vision of the world brought by the missionaries, which was very different from the Chinese one and thus revolutionary and dangerous. It was a comparison – and sometimes a collision – between two opposite conceptions: the Chinese one, extremely pragmatic, and the European one, which believed that the conscious theorisation of principles would lead to a real scientific and

5 Dehergne, D., *Repertoire de Jesuites*, *op. cit.*, pp. 66-67; Pfister, L., *Notices Biographiques et Bibliographiques*, *op. cit.*, pp. 307-314.

6 Dehergne, D., *Repertoire de Jesuites, op. cit.,* pp. 166-167; Pfister, L., *Notices Biographiques et Bibliographiques*, *op. cit.*, pp. 256-262; Bertuccioli, G. (ed.), *Martino Martini S.J., Opera Omnia, vol. I, Lettere e documenti*, Trento, Università degli Studi di Trento, 1998, pp. 511-533.

7 Dehergne, D., *Repertoire de Jesuites*, *op. cit.*, pp. 88-90; Pfister, L., *Notices Biographiques et Bibliographiques*, *op. cit.*, pp. 338-362.

technological progress. Therefore, it is not surprising that the Chinese particularly liked some of the products of Western technology, such as clocks, automations, weapons and astronomical instruments. They could see their effective practical application but had no interest in the theoretical elaborations behind them. This shortsightedness would eventually enlarge the gap between the West, launching towards a "magnificent and advanced" destiny, and China, stiffening in the sterile repetition of ancient rituals that were legitimated by their immutability. The collision of these two civilisations would eventually have a dramatic epilogue, when the Europeans felt strong enough, by both land and sea, to venture in a military expedition against China (around the middle of the 19th century), which had seemed an impossible enterprise until then. The leader of the expedition was the greatest European power on its way to becoming the World's greatest: Great Britain.

The Jesuit approach to Chinese civilisation was on the one hand based on a sincere admiration for the East and its culture, with a mixture of missionary spirit and curiosity for the exotic. On the other hand, it was grounded on the need to please the court and the Mandarins, without the approval of whom they could have not preached or even lived on Chinese land. It was thanks to this attitude, together with their great eloquence and writing skill, that the Jesuits became the heralds of the Chinese civilisation's grandeur in the West. They exalted China and its best aspects and sometimes hid its defects, even proposing it as a model to imitate for its millenary historical evolution. This caused the European infatuation of the Enlightenment period towards anything Chinese: from porcelain, to imperial bureaucracy or field cultivation systems. This passion for "the other" could not be simply satisfied by the letters and reports written by the missionaries for propaganda purposes, but it required new nourishment from fantasy and escapist literature.

We must remember that the conversion of the Celestial Empire was in some ways a failure; however, it was one of the greatest successes of human history in establishing a cultural dialogue based on the sharing of knowledge. These people, these "giants" in the true sense of the word, were able, in different epochs and in different ways, to become part of Chinese society, of its dominant class, befriending some of the highest authorities of the country and obtaining extraordinary fame and approval, especially if we think how sinocentric the world view of the majority of the Chinese people was.

Matteo Ricci is certainly one of the most known and esteemed Westerners in China, together with Marco Polo; moreover, his biography is a scientific and cultural adventure, which attracts the interest of Europeans as well. He was able to fully reflect the culture that was hosting him. Because of this, the formal, refined and proud Chinese society was able to accept the "scholar coming from the West." We know almost everything about Ricci and his Chinese experience. The road he paved relied on pillars which were innovations in the missionary practice: a policy of accommodation to Chinese culture; a top-to-bottom conversion strategy; use of European science and technology to attract the attention of the Chinese learned men; and tolerance and openness towards Chinese values.

We know less of the other missionaries, but recent studies on this generation, forgotten for over two centuries, are now revealing important information that allows us to understand the basis of the intercultural dialogue between the two main civilisations of the planet.[8] After Ricci, following his footsteps, a multitude of other Jesuit fathers coming from different European countries stepped and worked on Chinese ground, largely contributing to the mutual knowledge of the two extremities of the Eurasiatic continent. These men shared the passion and the desire to travel to the East. They were versed in the many subjects taught in the Jesuit schools all over Europe and especially at the *Collegio Romano* in Rome. Here we remember some of them: Giulio Aleni, the Confucius of the West, according to his Chinese admirers; Johann Schreck, who left Europe looking for a better place for the development of scientific thought; Michael Boym, who brought copious material from China to Europe concerning Chinese flora and fauna; Prospero Intorcetta, who engaged in the hard task of translating the Confucian classics into Latin; Tomás Pereira, musician for the Kangxi Emperor and interpreter during the negotiations with Russia for the Treaty of Nerchinsk; and Giuseppe Castiglione, painter at the court of the emperor Qianlong, who taught the secrets of perspective to the Chinese.[9] A wide spread of people and stories with great communicative effectiveness, they have succeeded in understanding and explaining the spirit of those who, abandoning their families and possessions with the perspective of leaving their country for good, and having to move to a place on the other side of the inhabited world, did so with enthusiasm, passion, a sense of duty and the spirit of sacrifice. This cannot but arouse our admiration.

The Jesuits held correspondence with the main European scientists and intellectuals in order to keep their technological and scientific

8 Bertuccioli, G. and Masini, F., *Italia e Cina, op. cit.*, pp. 90-140; Mungello, D. E, *Curious Land, op. cit.*, pp. 74-133.

9 A recent publication that summarises the life and the works of these missionaries is: Paternicò, L. M. (ed.), *The Generation of Giants. Jesuit Missionaries and Scientists in China on the Footsteps of Matteo Ricci*, Trento, Centro studi Martino Martini, 2011.

knowledge updated and to obtain the favour of the emperor. The results of this copious correspondence were some extremely important works for the knowledge of China in Europe and for the beginning of sinological studies: *China monumentis illustrata*, by Athanasius Kircher, published in 1667, the first general introduction to Chinese civilisation, containing information regarding its history, rituals, customs, usage, tradition and language, enriched by many images of strong communicative impact; *Description de la Chine*, by Jean-Baptiste du Halde, published in 1735, the first complete encyclopedia on all the aspects of Chinese life, including the State organisation, biographies of the emperors, agricultural techniques, the method for producing porcelain and much more; and last but not least, the *Novus Atlas Sinensis*, by Martino Martini, published in 1655, which is not merely a geographical description of the country with its maps but a an overview of each Chinese province based on original sources in Chinese and on direct observations.

The Jesuit presence in China coincided with the decline of the local Ming dynasty, which had ruled since 1368 after replacing the Mongolian Yuan dynasty. The Ming were defeated by the Manchu Dynasty of the Qing (1644), who reigned until the proclamation of the Republic (1912). After the conquest of Beijing, the Ming loyalists moved south and were finally defeated in 1661. The attitude of the new emperors towards the Christian religion varied considerably, according to the political situation and to personal inclinations. Periods of tolerance would be followed by persecutions. Even the attitude towards the missionaries residing at the court and towards the Chinese converts often changed. The encounter/conflict between the two civilisations could not but arouse fear and distrust. Both cultures were too proud to interact on an equal basis.

If the Jesuits were trying to present themselves as the champions of a civilisation, aiming at a peaceful exchange of scientific and technological knowledge, the Western merchants didn't hide their main intention of penetrating the tantalising Chinese market. Not only did they wish to directly reach the place of production of those goods that were most requested by the European upper classes, like porcelain, silk, lacquer, tea, etc., but they also hoped to sell some European products, which did not seem to be so appreciated by the Chinese. Their attitude caused misunderstanding and unfairness that, mixed with the corruption of the imperial bureaucracy, led to masking commerce under the shape of a tribute, saving the form but not the substance.

Their role of mediators continued even under the Qing rule. The Jesuits acted as interpreters during diplomatic negotiations, which resulted in the Treaty of Nerchinsk (1689), between China and Russia, the first treaty China had ever signed on an equal basis with a Western country. We also want to point out that since the appointment of Adam Schall, and for more than a century, all the Directors of the Astronomical Bureau – issuing the official annual calendar of the empire – were Jesuits. These elements, together with the Jesuit help in the field of war technology, persuaded the Kangxi Emperor, the second emperor of the Qing dynasty (r. 1661-1772) who was known for his mental openness and his support for intellectuals, to issue in 1692 the famous Tolerance Edict. The edict authorised the conversion to Christianity, annulled the previous laws against the missionaries and allowed them to build churches and preach the Gospel in public. The Tribunal of the Rites recognised the help of the missionaries in the long work of reforming the calendar. This task was started by Giacomo Rho and continued by Adam Schall. It was finally completed by the Flemish father Ferdinand Verbiest, to the great satisfaction of the Manchu court who saw the calendar grounded on a more firm basis than those first provided by ancient Chinese or Muslim astronomy.[10] The calendar was of vital importance because it would determine the best days to perform certain activities. The Christian faith was no longer considered a doctrine that might have caused uprisings among the common people, but was regarded as a support for public order. However, the imperial edict did not result in a mass conversion – there were still many obstacles to overcome.

This period also saw an exacerbation of the Rites Controversy, because of an edict issued by the Apostolic Vicar of Fujian, Charles Maigrot (1693), which dismantled the Jesuits entire approach to Chinese traditional culture.[11] The controversy concerned different aspects of Jesuit activities in China, the problem of which terms to use to indicate the Christian God and the worship of the ancestors of the Confucian tradition. The matter was whether to consider these customs as civil rituals or as expressions of another religion and thus incompatible with the Christian faith. The first decision in favour of the Jesuit approach, was made by Martino Martini, during his journey back to Europe (1656), when he had the chance to see most of his works through to publication. However, the rivalries among the religious orders and between the powers of Spain and Portugal – which supported them – did not diminish. This situation put all the accommodation efforts that the Jesuits had made so far, at risk. The problem was that neither the Dominicans nor the Franciscans, despite their good intentions, were able to really understand the Chinese culture and why such an ancient and

---

10 Golvers, N., *Ferdinand Verbiest, S.J. (1623-1688) and the Chinese Heaven,* Leuven, Leuven University Press, 2003, pp. 17-26.

11 Bertuccioli, G. and Masini, F, *Italia e Cina, op. cit*, pp. 148-159.

glorious civilisation could not have just accepted a foreign religion without any reworking and adaptation to national customs.

The visit of the Papal legate Carlo Tommaso Maillard de Tournon between 1705 and 1706, did not get the expected reaction from Kangxi. Instead, the emperor was actually annoyed by de Tournon's insolence and issued a decree forcing all missionaries to ask for a formal permit, called piao, stating one's religious affiliation and the will to remain in China forever. According to the Jesuits and many historians after them, this authorisation depended on acceptance of the "Chinese rites" that the Jesuits had always tolerated. Those missionaries who did not request the piao would have been expelled from the country. But the Church – following the Nanjing Decree issued by de Tournon in 1707 – threatened the excommunication of those missionaries who accepted the Chinese rites, considering them to be expressions of paganism and therefore incompatible with Catholic dogma. Most of the Jesuits requested the piao in order to be allowed to remain in China but also to show to the Europeans that they did not have any other choice. However, some non-Jesuit missionaries, despite possessing the piao, did not in fact accept the Chinese rites.

After Kangxi, the reigns of Yongzheng (r. 1723-1735) and Qianlong (r. 1736-1796) followed. They were characterised by less interest towards Christianity and Western missionaries, who often had to face persecutions. Qianlong enlarged remarkably the borders of the empire, to reach their maximum extension. He was very rigid towards the Europeans, as exemplified by his cold welcome to the British ambassador Lord McCartney in 1793 and by his constant persecutions of the Christians. China, after reaching the apex of its evolution during the Ming dynasty in the 16th century, seemed to have stopped its millenary evolution, being satisfied with its incomparable development. In the same period, Europe was going through an identity crisis, partly because of the Protestant Reformation. This would eventually lead to the Scientific Revolution of the 17th century and to the Industrial Revolution of the 18th century, until Europe reached an unprecedented level of socio-economical development.

The new emerging powers of Holland, France and England, above all, could not accept being treated like simple tributary countries. They wanted to play a key role in the East, taking advantage of the power of their fleets, of their merchants' initiative, of the productive efficiency of their newborn factories. Their growth corresponded with China's stagnation – it was so satisfied with its international prestige in Asia that it had not realised new threats were emerging. These threats were no longer from the nomads of the steppe – who had been definitively defeated by the field artillery – but instead were coming from those countries who had formerly helped China in making cannons.

Going back to the role of the Jesuits, after the Rites Controversy, the Society of Jesus was viewed with suspicion in Europe, since it had opposed the Holy See. The Catholic countries slowly began to change their attitude towards the Jesuits, who had been for centuries their best advisers and ministers. Now they were seen as champions of the most reactionary conservatism and obscurantism. Foreign missions were progressively abandoned, especially the China mission, which required a conspicuous financial support. The diffusion of the Enlightenment's ideas, stigmatising anything that could resemble religious superstition or doctrinaire intransigence, together with the loss of prestige of Catholic powers, made any missionary activities very difficult. Finally, in 1773, Pope Clemens XIV issued the bull *Dominus ac Redemptor*, suppressing the Society. The news arrived in China in 1775, marking the end of the Jesuit mission.[12] Other religious orders, like the Lazarist, took over from the Jesuits until the following century, when they had to leave the stage to merchants and official embassies, who were less interested in the health of the souls. After the Western triumph in the Opium Wars, the missionary presence in China was revitalised, thanks to the Protestant missionaries, who founded libraries, universities and research centres.

Most of the Christian missionaries shared a common attitude in China towards spread their religion with serenity: learning the local language and respecting the local political authorities. Like all the other missionaries, the Jesuits adopted a Chinese name, while the Chinese converts received a Christian name. Furthermore, the Jesuits also adapted to the local customs because, unlike any other mission in the world, the China mission was not attempting to convert a barbaric and primitive civilisation, but a learned, evolved and refined one, which was even superior to the West in some fields of knowledge. For this reason, from the very beginning, the Jesuits put into practice teachings coming from the Japan mission's experience – as Alessandro Valignano had wanted – with some difference on the linguistic strategy. Among the three Chinese religious beliefs (Buddhism, Confucianism and Taoism), Matteo Ricci highlighted how Confucianism was the closest to the principles of the Christian faith, at least in terms of individual and social ethics.[13]

---

12 For a complete overview of the Chinese Rites controversy see: Mungello, D. E. (ed.), *The Chinese Rites Controversy, its History and Meaning,* Monumenta Serica monograph Series XXXIII, Sankt Augustin, Institute Monumenta Serica, 1994.

13 Valignano, A., *Relación del Grande Reyno de la China*, manuscript preserved at Archivo de la Real Academia de la Historia, coll. Cortes, 562, ff. 519-542, 1584.

When Ricci arrived in China, he was dressed like a Buddhist bonze. However, he very soon (around 1594) decided to change into the Confucian scholars' robe, because the literati were more respected in Chinese society than the Buddhist monks. His new attire would help the conversions to avoid confusion. He understood that the social status of Buddhist monks in China was not as high as in Japan and that the Buddhist religion was strictly controlled by the imperial authorities (exactly like the other religions). Ricci also wanted to avoid any confusion with the Buddhist schools, since many Christian principles were not so different from Buddhist ones, and both religions came from foreign countries arousing distrust in China. The change of clothes took place when Ricci began the translation of the Confucian Classics into Latin. He thought that the role of the scholar would gain him the respect of the ruling class. Put simply, by wearing silk robes, growing a beard and using the palanquin, he could show a higher social status.[14]

The Jesuits aimed to introduce the Christian faith in China mainly through the conversion of the scholars and the Mandarins, rather than through that of common people. They believed that the conversion of the people would sooner or later follow that of the ruling class. All their efforts were therefore devoted to the upper classes, from the emperor himself to the literati. Their method would show results slowly, but it appeared safer that the constant and patient attempt at converting the common people on street corners. Furthermore, with the Manchu emperors, with their strong and authoritarian attitude, the missionaries had to start all over again, trying to obtain the favour of the new rulers. The Jesuit method was somehow opposite to that of the other orders, who were trying to convert the people directly. Despite obtaining some good results, they were often the targets of bans and their approach provoked a hostile reaction from the Chinese government. This difference of approach would also cause conflicts among the different missionary orders.

The Jesuit method was inspired by graduality: they wanted to obtain the respect of the literati first, and then they would attempt their conversion.

Despite the intense activity of the Jesuits, the Catholic religion they preached never obtained the expected results: the conversions were limited to a few tens of thousands and only in the bigger cities, because in the countryside the common people continued practicing their traditional rituals. Many Western scholars have analysed the China mission in terms of success or failure: Jacques Gernet ascribes its failure

---

[14] Bertuccioli, G. and Masini, F., *Italia e Cina*, *op. cit.*, pp. 92-108; Mungello, D. E., *Curious Land, op. cit.*, pp. 44-72.

to the cultural and linguistic difficulty in understanding the Christian doctrine. Paul Cohen ascribes its failure to the choice of acquiring the status of Confucians and thus challenging the local scholars.[15] Erik Zürcher, comparing the success of the spread of Buddhism and the failure of the spread of Christianity, explains the latter with the situation of the Late Imperial China: conservatism, xenophobia, sinocentrism, but also the difference between a guided conversion – that of the Christian missionaries, and a spontaneous diffusion – that of Buddhism.[16]

The best results the Jesuits achieved were in the scientific and technical fields. They were able to put into practice the formidable education they had received at the Roman College, one of the main educational institutions in Europe. The first map of China ever made in the West was that of the Portuguese father Luis Jorge de Barbuda and was published by the Flemish cartographer Abraham Ortelius in the edition of 1584 of his famous *Theatrum Orbis Terrarum*. We have already written about the works of Martini, Kircher and du Halde, which are just some of the 43 geographical and cartographical works compiled by the Jesuits during two centuries of activity in China. These works largely contributed to the European knowledge of China and its inhabitants, stimulating the sending of embassies and commercial missions to establish regular and lasting exchanges, but also inspiring the journeys of scholars, trying to imitate the best Chinese techniques of porcelain production – which at the beginning of the 18th century was finally reproduced in Dresden by a German alchemist.

The Jesuits' achievements in mathematical and astronomical fields were just as important and they started with the translation of Euclide's *Elements*, carried out by Matteo Ricci in 1607 in co-operation with the mathematician Paolo Xu Guangqi, *Colao* or Minister of the Ming Wanli emperor. One of their greatest achievements was undoubtedly the renovation of the imperial Astronomical Observatory and the production of a series of instruments by Ferdinand Verbiest, based on those of Tycho Brahe. These instruments, which are still preserved in the observatory, now a museum, represented an authentic innovation for the Chinese astronomers of that time, who were still using Mongol instruments.

Being able to use these new instruments (among which was the Galilean telescope), new astronomical tables, new calculation methods elaborated in Europe in the previous decades, the Jesuits appeared to be the bearers of a new and powerful science, which was more efficient in

15 Zürcher, E., *Bouddhisme, Christianisme et Société Chinoise*, Paris, Julliard, 1990.

16 Cohen, P., *China and Christianity: the Missionary Movement and the Growth of Chinese Antiforeignism 1860-1870*, Cambridge, Harvard University Press, 1963.

predicting astronomical phenomena and calculating the motion of the stars. This science was actually linked to schemes (like the Ptolemaic and the Tychonian systems, both replaced by the Copernican), which were about to be surpassed by the Scientific Revolution, started by Galileo, who was a friend and correspondent of the Jesuits. The information brought by the Jesuits eventually proved outdated when compared with the great progress made by the scientists of the Protestant countries, where the pernicious and obtrusive Inquisition did not exist and there was freedom of thought and research. These facts would demonstrate their importance only at the end of the 18th century, with the arrival of the first diplomatic expeditions of the English.

In the meantime, the level of education of the Jesuits was declining, as well as their moral rectitude and their respect for duties. As in nature, if a plant is not constantly and regularly watered, it will languish and die. However, the role of the Jesuits in creating a cultural dialogue between Europe and China cannot be denied because without their contribution, these two civilisations would have met later and with more difficulties in mutual understanding. The Jesuits somehow caused their own ruin because their numerous publications, which were meant to promote the success of the China mission, revealed the existence of a world, a culture, a tradition, that was just as valid as the Western one. Thus, there was no more reason to believe that the Christian religion was the best.

It so happened that the intellectuals of the Enlightenment, after sincerely admiring the results obtained by the Jesuits and exalting several aspects of the Chinese civilisation – like the examination system, the power of the scholars, the efficiency of bureaucracy, the strong control of the emperor compared to the apparent European anarchy – ended up considering China to be a kingdom of tyranny and obscurantism, which prevented the free development of the individual personality while trying to maintain the *status quo*, keeping the population in a state of brutal subjection.

The most important lesson taught by the Jesuits was that universal peace, harmony and concord are built through reciprocal knowledge and understanding. It is not possible to teach others what they should be, or think, but it is vital to accept their point of view without prejudice or bias, with the true will to proceed together on the path of progress.

Bibliography

Demarchi, F. and Scartezzini, R. (eds.), *Martino Martini. A Humanist and Scientist in Seventeenth Century China*, Trento, Università degli Studi di Trento, 1996.

Masini, F. and Paternicò, L. M. (eds.), *Martino Martini S.J.*, *Opera Omnia*, vol. IV, Trento, Università degli Studi di Trento, 2010.

Melis, G. (ed.), "Martino Martini: Geografo, Cartografo, Storico, Teologo," in Atti del Convegno Internazionale 1981, Trento, Università degli studi di Trento, 1983.

Mungello, D. E., *The Great Encounter of China and the West, 1500-1800*, USA, Rowman & Littlefield, 2005.

Ribadeneyra de, P., Alegambe, P., Southwell, N. B., *Bibliotheca scriptorum Societatis Iesu*, Roma, G.A. Lazzari Varese, 1676.

Ricci, M., Trigault, N., *De Christiana Expeditione apud Sinas*, Coloniae, Sumptibus Bernardi Gualteri, 1617.

Sommervogel, C., *Bibliothèque de la Compagnie de Jésus*, Bruxelles-Paris, Héverlé, 1890-1909.

Standaert, N., *Handbook of Christianity of China*, Leiden-Boston-Köln, Brill, 2001.

PART III

PERSPECTIVES OF A VALUE ORIENTED EUROPE IN THE WORLD

A Value-Driven Orientation: Introduction

Léonce BEKEMANS

Part III contains a variety of contributions which deal with the perspectives of a value oriented Europe in the world. They focus on basic applied dimensions such as the social market economy, the institutional context, the common good or the education perspective. Part III is further developed in papers which concern specific European/international issues related to the Islam tradition and the Eastern European area.

In his contribution "*The European Social Market Economy in the Economic and Monetary Union*," Dario Velo, Professor and chairman of the Jean Monnet Centre of Excellence of the University of Pavia, refers to the crisis of 1968 to describe the current process of the Economic Union. Velo argues for a European government of a European economy to manage the transition towards a new economic and social order. The issues in question are the relationship between the economy and society, between society and the State, the division of roles between State and the market, welfare reform, sustainable development and the need to remodel manufacturing processes in an environmentally friendly way. He favours a European social market economy, being a new order that reconciles freedom, solidarity and new forms of democratic participation in a way that is consistent with the emerging forces of European society.

The contribution by Luc Van den Brande, current president of the CIVEX Commission of the Committee of the Regions, dealing with "*Institutional and International Issues of the Europe 2020 Strategy*," introduces some new ideas and concepts as to how the European Union could better interact with regions, cities and citizens in a context of growing globalisation and EU institutional building. The principle of multi-level governance is said to respond to the current EU deficits and be a necessary condition for the future destiny of Europe. The author argues that such a response could be best embodied in the future European Charter on Multi-level Governance and the future developments of regional policy.

The paper "*A Common Goods' Understanding of Europe and the World*," by Peter Xuereb, Jean Monnet Professor of European Law and European Integration at the University of Malta, argues that global institutions are needed for the determination and pursuit of the global common good. Recent events (such as the Arab Spring or the current financial and economic crisis) illustrate the growing awareness of the potential and limitations of regional, national and global institutions and structures for pursuing the own interests as well as the universal common good. Positive lessons can be drawn from the European integration process, especially the combination of state equality, supranationality, solidarity and mutual respect. The author concludes with proposing the application of key procedural and substantive principles in promoting active solidarity and concrete measures to achieve the common good.

The contribution "*The Multiple Crisis of Europe*," by Ferenc Miszlivetz, a Hungarian Jean Monnet Professor of Global and European Studies, presents a very critical analysis of the impact of the current global financial and economic crisis on the elite-driven European integration process. He tries to explain the contexted structure and causes of the current European crisis, and analyses its consequences and perspectives. He argues that the exhaustion of the Community method combined with the lack of understanding of the cultural dimension of social and economic change, are a major impediment for deepening social and political integration and might eventually lead the EU to the fringe of disintegration. Miszlivetz favours a New Social Contract, which assumes a clear articulation of concept, method and vision. In referring to Jacques Delors' self-reflection on the revival of Europe, the author pleads for a polity at transnational European level, i.e. the politicisation of the empty European public space as well as the self-articulation of a great variety of still subterranean networks and movements.

Léonce Bekemans, Professor and co-ordinator of the Jean Monnet Centre of Excellence at the University of Padua, introduces his paper "*A Value-Driven European future: an Education Perspective of the European Civitas*," by identifying the value premises of the European Civitas, defined as a community concerned with education and citizenship. The first part of the paper deals with the conceptual context and content of the European Civitas. The author offers some important guidelines and a few intercultural practices for building a sustainable and value-driven European future. The second part focuses on the education perspective. He analyses the role, responsibility and objective of education, with particular and applied attention to citizenship education in its European and cultural dimension.

The starting hypothesis of the paper "*Cultural Relativism, Human Rights and the Co-existence of Contrasting Religious Prescriptions in the Islamic Tradition*," by Johannes Thomas, Prof. Em. of the University of Paderborn, is that radical cultural relativism can defend universal human rights only by decision but not with value based arguments. The author argues that in a situation determined by the contrast between universal rights and its limitations or invalidations in Islamic states, interfaith and intercultural dialogue seems to be the only promising issue. Such a dialogue is exemplified by the Regensburg lecture of Pope Benedict XVI and the subsequent messages to the Vatican and to Christianity as a whole by Muslim scholars. However, the affirmation of tolerance as an Islamic principle by Muslim authors is often in contrast with the real situation and even with some Islamic texts. These ambiguities can only be debated in a climate of friendship.

The European Social Market Economy in the Economic and Monetary Union

Dario VELO

Chairman, Jean Monnet Centre of Excellence, University of Pavia

In 1968, the crisis in the international monetary system marked the end of a long period of stable growth, which had been supported by the economic and monetary policy of the United States. Three years later, that crisis ended the convertibility of the dollar, resulting in the end of the Bretton Woods monetary agreement. Europe suffered the effects of the crisis more than any other part of the world. As a direct consequence of the absence of a single currency, the crisis caused fluctuations in national currencies with dramatic effects on the unity of the internal European market.

Against this background, the process of monetary unification began: a process that led, in a sequence of steps, to the creation of the European Central Bank. Having regained monetary stability, Europe was now able to create a single market. Throughout this lengthy process, a national approach opposed the European one. In turn, two very different schools of thought emerged within the European approach itself: one radical federalist and the other inspired by the ideas of Jean Monnet. These three alternatives can be summarised as follows.

a) The national approach. In the absence of a European government responsible for currency and the economy, the weaker European states tried to offload the burden of the crisis on to their partners, by devaluing the currency; the result was a vicious circle of competitive depreciation, the inflationary effects of which were particularly intense. In contrast, the stronger European states sought to protect themselves against chaos by revaluing their own currencies and acting as "islands of stability" on the international market. It soon became clear that this type of "two-speed" Europe would not last long. The European approach gathered pace, thanks to initiatives by France and Germany, which marked a decisive change of direction.

b1) The radical federalist approach. As mentioned above, the European approach incorporated two basic alternatives. The first European school of thought can be described as "radical federalist." According to this view, the crisis presented the opportunity for a leap forward in the unification process, by forming a fully-fledged European Federation, entirely comparable to the United States model. The European currency would have constituted an integral part of this formative process, as had been the case in the United States with the creation of the Federal Reserve System by Alexander Hamilton, after the ratification of the American Constitution.

b2) The "Monnet approach." The second school of European thought can be placed in the context of the Monnet tradition. Having identified the issues for which a solution was not only essential but also feasible, this school of thought maintained that it was now necessary to take the most realistic and evolved decision possible, in order to obtain the required consent. Events dictated that this alternative would be the one to hold sway, and the crucial decision was represented by the rules that were to govern Monetary Union, more specifically, the drawing up of the Statute of the European Central Bank. A fundamental part of that statute relates to the regularisation of currency management in order to neutralise inflation and devaluation as tools of economic policy.

The 2007 crisis shares many similarities with that of 1968. Also in this case, the international crisis originated in the United States, before spreading across the world. Ultimately, the crisis stemmed from the increasing difficulties in reconciling the United States' own internal objectives with international ones – the first of those objectives being the role of the USA as a global power. The crisis highlighted the absence of necessary resources. In 2011, the crisis extended to include a debate on the default of the US Treasury: the second earthquake to shake the foundations of the order created by the Bretton Woods agreement.

Once again it is Europe, more than any other part of the world, which is feeling the effects of the crisis. The impact of this second crisis on Europe has been lessened by the role of the European Central Bank (ECB), and the input of Eurozone institutions, which have provided coherent guidance for measures implemented at national level. The lack of a European government for the continent's economy has also exposed the Union to the backlash from the US crisis. Once again, Europe could become the worst-affected victim of the international crisis.

This is the context in which the process of Economic Union is now taking shape, albeit confusedly. Once again, three schools of thought have begun to form: one national, and two European. If the crisis deepens, this overlapping can be expected to become radicalised. Food for thought should come from the points of contact between the international monetary system's experience of the crisis and monetary unification on the one hand, and on the other, between the current crisis and the plan for European Economic Union, which is looming on the horizon.

First of all, a national (in actual fact, nationalist) approach has once again begun to oppose the European one.

a) The national approach favours the specific interests of each nation. Weaker countries are hoping to shift their problems onto the shoulders of their partners, while strong nations tend to impose tough rebalancing measures. There is a distinct possibility that the Union may run the risk of Europe becoming divided into two broad, but very different, areas. In this context, the national approach seems to be supported by a mood of nostalgia, and above all by the desire for monetary policy tools that were lost with the Monetary Union. This nostalgia feeds on the illusion that it is possible to maintain the benefits of European integration while recovering full freedom of action at the national level, especially in terms of the freedom to resort to inflation and devaluation as a way of reducing the weight of public debt.

This vision can be termed nostalgic as it cannot be linked to any rational theory, to the extent that it considers solutions drawn from radically alternative scenarios to be compatible. Nostalgia, by its very essence, implies a rejection of historical evolution. It is a desire to halt the march of time and progress, in order to return to a past whose negative aspects are forgotten and whose positive aspects are elevated to mythical status.

The full disregard for historical authenticity inherent in this nostalgia for the "old European order," can be illustrated by the emergence over time of the new continental powers which have, to quote Luigi Einaudi, rendered the smaller states of Europe "dust without substance." Nostalgia can – at most – only lead to Europe closing in on itself, consuming the capital accumulated in the past in order to finance a slow decline, shoring up consumption and shunning investment and innovation.

b1) The radical federalist approach. Once again, two basic alternatives are taking shape within the European approach. The first school of European thought is the radical federalist one, which draws on the analysis performed at the time of the Monetary Union and updates the results of that analysis to correspond more closely to the phase of Economic Union. According to this school of thought, the current crisis has again highlighted the need for a leap towards a full federation. This approach identifies several measures which would be necessary in this regard: an increase in the European budget, the institution of a Ministry of Finance, the possibility of issuing European Treasury bonds, and the setting up of a centralised government of the European economy.

b2) The "Monnet approach." The radical federalist line, whose cultural roots can be traced back to the views of Alexander Hamilton, is once again opposed by a Monnet-style alternative. In the current climate, this alternative can be identified more clearly by referring to a Monnet-style method rather than to specific content, as it cannot yet lay claim to any clearly defined project. As already mentioned, a distinctive feature of the Monnet approach is the attempt to seek realistic solutions, which are as evolved as possible, once any pressing issues that can be solved have been understood and identified. Ultimately, the Monnet method is a type of strategy intended to move the integration process forward. An essential factor in understanding the Monnet approach is the concept of integration as a "process."

Those who identify with this view are now busy attempting to identify the plans and rules that will attract the necessary consent, and support a joint approach to constructing an Economic Union. The task is all but impracticable, as the problems that Economic Union is expected to answer are many and complex. It is about giving Europe's economy a government, and reaching consent on the objectives and instruments of that government. There may be a debate as to whether there is a "key" to finding a unifying plan among all these complexities. These observations will appear clearer if we consider just some of the issues that Economic Union is asked to address. We are referring to the relationship between the economy and society, and between society and the State, the division of roles between State and the market, welfare reform, the issue of sustainable development and the need to remodel manufacturing processes in an environmentally friendly way. This list is by no means complete: in itself, it reveals the scope that an Economic Union may cover, in order to better define and consolidate the European model.

The Monetary Union essentially opened the debate on the relationship between national institutions and their European counterparts. It offered society an immensely valuable tool, the Euro, which had an inherent ability to direct public authorities towards an objective of good governance.

Economic Union cannot merely be interpreted as a new relationship between national economic institutions and their European counterparts. It is a project that raises questions about the social order and relations between society, the market and the State. A European government of a European economy will be asked to manage the transition towards a new economic and social order, by responding to the increasingly pressing concerns of society.

The plan, which is now taking shape in Europe as a part of Economic Union, is the European social market economy, a new order that will reconcile freedom, solidarity and new forms of democratic participation (subsidiarity, in constitutional terms) in a way that is consistent with the forces of European society that are emerging during the 21st century. The European social market economy has its roots in the continent's thousand-year history and the post-war experience of Germany. The project has yet to be defined fully, with the involvement of all Europeans, and recognition of the different experiences of each member state. It is this project that could give rise to consent for an Economic Union.

In order to move in this direction, some basic rules must be defined. The author is convinced that these rules are the neutralisation of monetary and financial policy, and the obligation for a balanced budget. Zero inflation, zero deficit, and zero public debt.

The plans for a European social market economy and the tools of government, referred to above, represent a historic turning-point. This began with Monetary Union, which introduced the neutralisation of monetary policy; what we have learned can be thrown open to questioning if the process of European integration fails to move towards Economic Union. The crisis will not then depend on Monetary Union, but the lack of an Economic Union. We can shed light on this by giving an extremely simplified summary of the relationship between the existing issues – monetary and real – facing Europe and the United States.

In the United States, a monetary and financial crisis goes hand-in-hand with an economic crisis. In Europe, the Euro is not experiencing a crisis, while certain member states are facing a financial and economic crisis. A case in point in Europe is that of Germany, which is not suffering from any particular crisis, either in monetary or financial terms, or at an economic level. It will only be possible to come out of this crisis with rigid financial discipline, by following the guidelines for monetary discipline of the ECB, and by favouring the implementation of economic measures.

This leads to the strategic importance of adopting the social market economy as part of the European Economic Union, by establishing fiscal federalism as a cornerstone of economic policy. This change will require a lengthy transition period. The strategic option, as indicated by Jean Monnet, is to begin the process after having made long-term decisions intended to give direction to the process itself.

It should be mentioned that the European Union has begun to incorporate a new dimension, compared with the past. The epic change now facing Europe is also taking place in the United States. Europe and the United States will be able to move forward more quickly and efficiently with the construction of a new order if they work in tandem, joining forces on a shared project and respecting each other's differences.

Europe is a laboratory for the world, and is now forging a new concept of statehood and a new social order. A convergence between the two Atlantic federations – the European Union and the United States – could point the international community in the same direction, which would render the objective of a new global federal order for the 21st century more realistic.

Bibliography

AA.VV., *L'Unione Economica e il problema della moneta europea*, Angeli, Milano, 1978.

Beck, U., *La società cosmopolitica*, ed. it. Il Mulino, Bologna, 2003.

Einaudi, L., *Problemi economici per la federazione europea*, Capolago, 1944.

Habermas, J., *L'occidente diviso*, ed.it. Laterza, Bari, 2005.

Maillet, P., "Un modéle de governance européen favorable à l'apparition d'une politique diversifiée et coordonnée," in *The European Union Review*, 1-2/01.

Monnet, J., *Mémoires*, Fayard, Paris, 1976.

Pernice, I., "Multilevel Constitutionalism and the Treaty of Amsterdam: European Constitution Making Revisited," in *Common Market Law Review*, 36/99.

Quadrio Curzio, A. (a cura di), *Profili della costituzione economica europea*, Il Mulino, Bologna, 2001.

Triffin, R., *Gold and the dollar crisis*, Yale University Press, New Haven, 1960.

Velo, F., "Fiscal Federalism: from the Gramm-Rudman-Hollings Act to the Atlantic Maastricht Treaty," in *The European Union Review*, 1-2/10.

Institutional and international issues of the Europe 2020 Strategy[1]

Luc VAN DEN BRANDE

President, CIVEX Commission, Committee of the Regions

Globalisation and inclusiveness in the EU are themes of crucial importance for understanding the path and destiny of the future European integration process. This paper introduces some new ideas and concepts in answer to the question: "How can the European Union better interact with regions, cities and ultimately its citizen?"

I. Context

The EU is facing extremely challenging times. Unemployment is at its highest point for two decades and we are officially in a recession. Young people are particularly feeling the effects, as many have enjoyed a sound education, but unfortunately do not yet have the necessary skills and work experience required to find decent and stable work. Many European leaders are cutting public expenditure, with the result being that in some member states, education, innovation and policies targeted towards investment in "human capital," are now suffering serious financing problems. In short, not only is Europe's social model under stress; so is its competitive position in the world.

First, the problem is not that at the EU level we do not know what to do. The challenges are clear and the Europe 2020 Strategy – a strategy for achieving sustainable, inclusive and smart growth – has been adopted. Equally, the Lisbon Treaty now provides the necessary institutional architecture to deal with the current crisis. However, our European Monetary Union was incomplete. Hence, a European Economic Governance system needed to be put in place for more fiscal discipline and a minimal form of reciprocal financial solidarity. This was done over the last two and a half years under the skilful leadership of Herman Van Rompuy and his fellow members of the European Council.

---

1 Adapted version Public Lectures, University of Padua, 19 March 2012.

Now we have to deliver on our Europe 2020 Strategy and come to an increased co-ordination of our economic and social policies.

Second, the Single Market needs to be deepened. In his former capacity as Special Adviser to Commission President José-Manuel Barroso, the current Italian Prime Minister Mario Monti has provided an excellent roadmap to make this happen. Commissioner Barnier has indeed built on his ideas and by the end of this year EU leaders have agreed to complete the adoption of the 12 legislative proposals of the so-called Single Market Act.

Third, the EU needs a modern and forward-looking budget. At the moment more than 70% of the EU budget is oriented towards agriculture and regional policies. We must also invest in policies of the future, such as R&D, innovation and the development of an EU industrial and entrepreneurship policy. Equally important, we must come to a Union in which the adage "*No taxation without representation*," is respected. Indeed, the time has come to have EU taxes, such as a genuine VAT at EU level and a European Financial Transaction Tax.

The key problem however, is that there is virtually no money left to finance the modernisation required throughout Europe. True, we must put in place Europroject bonds and other innovative financial engineering mechanisms, but this is not going to provide political leaders the necessary funds to make the change happen.

I believe that one way of helping to deliver on the Europe 2020 Strategy is to strengthen the pooling of financial resources of various entities, both public and private, at various levels of governance. In order to make this pooling happen, we must develop an intelligent system of making sure that all relevant partners can connect, dialogue and co-operate together to tackle share challenges on the ground. The good news is that such a system already exists. I am, of course referring to the emergence of a system of multi-level governance in Europe. The emergence of such a new culture of co-operation in Europe will require both time and persistence, but I am convinced it is feasible.

As a Belgian politician, I have worked in a complex and challenging institutional environment. Notwithstanding, I also had the privilege to gain policy experience at all levels of governance crucial for the future development of my city, region, country and indeed our European Union. It is by experiencing all the linkages between these various levels of power over the last 30 years, that I realised that fostering a culture of "multi-level governance" (MLG) is crucial for the future development of our continent. I often compare MLG to the image of the various layers of a delicious Italian "lasagne."

II. MLG Responses to the Triple Deficit of Democracy, Delivery and Destiny

It is my profound believe that in establishing an intelligent system based on the "principle" of multi-level governance, Europe will be able to overcome its "triple helix deficit." MLG will help Europe to overcome its three deficits: its "Democratic" deficit; its "Delivery" deficit and indeed its "Destiny deficit."

First, in providing for a governance system that is directly linked to member states and regions and cities, Europe provides citizens with more gateways to influence EU decision-making. Indeed, citizens will see their mayor, aldermen, provincial governor or regional president not only as a local politician, but also as a European politician. Hence, through their proximity with these politicians, citizens will feel more closely connected to Brussels. The EU democracy as such will ultimately be strengthened through MLG.

Second, various reports of the EU Committee of the Regions reveal that the EU does not deliver adequately on its policies because of the existence of a so-called "partnership gap." This is notably true for those EU policies with a territorial dimension, such as the Europe 2020 Strategy. Also, if we are to combat climate change and address energy or demographic challenges, we need to have regions and cities on board in order to meet the objectives set at the EU level. Again, MLG comes into play. The key words here are to achieve more solidarity through putting a greater emphasis on "responsabilisation." As pointed out by Prime Minister Professor Mario Monti, this time in his capacity as a member of the former Group of Wise Men on the future of Europe, there is a need for more direct "contractualisation" with regions and cities.

As the former president of the EU's Committee of the Regions and actual chair of its Committee on Citizenship, Governance, Institutional and External Affairs, we have indeed proposed the development of "Territorial Pacts." These contracts would put regions directly before their responsibility and indentify the milestones and policy objectives to be met in a given territory in order to deliver on the Europe 2020 Strategy on the ground. Yet another example of contractualisation is the "Covenant of Mayors." Today more than 2,000 mayors have signed and committed their city to respecting the EU's 20-20-20 climate change objectives.

Thirdly, I would like to reflect on the EU's future "destiny." Are we heading towards "less Europe," or, towards the "United States of Europe"? Will we see the development of various parallel forms of European integration that will co-exist?

III. Europe's Future Destiny

I would argue that setting up an intelligent system of multilevel governance is the *conditio sine qua non* for the future destiny of our continent. Why? Because, first I believe that the world will not wait for Europe. As observed by Professor Dominique Moisi (Special advisor to the Institut Français des Relations Internationales – IFRI), "[t]he key question is not to know whether there is less or more France, Italy or Germany in Europe. The question is rather whether there is more or less Europe in the world?"

That's precisely why I have congratulated the University of Padua as they have developed an academic programme on "globalisation" and "inclusiveness." Indeed, both concepts go hand in hand. The more we experience the consequences of globalisation, the more inclusiveness we will need in the end. As the emerging powers – or the so-called BRICS and Turkey – will only continue to grow and gain influence in world trade and politics, there is in my view no other way then going towards "more Europe"!

Both "inclusiveness" and "proximity" of the European project are thus crucial elements for constructing the strong Political Union we need. As I explained earlier, the development of multi-level governance is essential in the process of further integration. Hence, it may not sound as a surprise to you that the University of Padua was also the first European University to develop a Jean Monnet Centre of Excellence on "Intercultural Dialogue, Human Rights and Multi-level Governance."

The European Union faces extremely challenging times. Many of our democracies, both young and old ones, are under extreme pressure, including the European Union itself as a supranational identity. The difficulty is that the many multiple crises often require contradictory responses. Europe suffers at the same time from a sovereign debt crisis, a banking crisis, a social crisis, a competitiveness crisis, a political crisis, a confidence crises and indeed even an identity crisis.

The EU leaders are searching for adequate answers and much has been accomplished since the start of the crisis: (1) Greater budgetary surveillance through a new "Fiscal Compact Treaty," (2) higher liquid firepower to help Eurozone member states in financial difficulty through the new "European Stability Mechanism-Treaty," (3) the development of greater "European economic governance," through the new Eurozone Summit, the "Six-Pack" and the "Euro Plus Pact," (4) A new long term "Europe 2020 Strategy," with five headline targets for sustainable, smart and inclusive growth, (5) the adoption of the Single Market Act: a new strategy for completing our Single Market, (6) greater tax co-ordination and (7) the emergence of European Labour Law, as indeed enhanced monitoring and a peer review will be organised amongst member states evaluating each other's new "National Jobs Plan."

The crisis does unite Europeans. As President Herman Van Rompuy, has stated: "We are all in the same boat." However, greater budgetary surveillance and the EU's strong push for structural reforms also challenges its legitimacy and accountability. A punitive democracy will not deliver the appropriate change.

The crisis challenges member states too. Both Hungary and the Netherlands have been criticised for downgrading their fundamental rights and freedoms. Greece and Italy are now headed by a Technical Cabinet. New leaders have been elected too, but still many countries are under the strong monitoring of the European Commission, the European Central Bank and the International Monetary Fund. There's a growing tension between non-Eurozone and Eurozone member states. Politicians, eminent scholars and even chief EU officials are observing the emergence of a multi-speed Europe.

This process is only being accelerated by the extreme pressure put on the European "Social Rhineland Model." Finally, we can see a conflict emerging within certain member states; between the central level on the one hand, and the regional level on the other. This is not only the case for Belgium, but also in the United Kingdom, where Scotland, Wales and Northern Ireland are demanding PM Cameron take a different, more pro-European stand. Eventually, the emergence of a European Political Union will have to go hand in hand with a renewed discussion on the so-called "democratic deficit," in the EU. In my view, a new Convention should one day agree upon a renewed institutional architecture, enshrined in a Constitution for Europe.

In order to come to a "fiscal and social Union," one should indeed look into further strengthening EU democracy. *Inter alia* one could think of the possible direct election of the European Council President; the strengthening of both the European Parliament and the European Commission; the upgrading of the role of the Committee of the Regions and the European social partners; the emergence of fully-fledged European political parties and the election of a pool of MEPs within a newly elaborated pan-European constituency; or a reflection upon the development of additional tools for strengthening direct democracy, etc.

However, although all these ideas might be perfectly legitimate, this approach would probably take us another decade – years we simply cannot afford. So, the key question here is: "How can we generate a European Public Sphere without opening up an 'institutional Pandora's box'?"

The challenge is to provide for a system of innovative interest representation in which people feel represented on an equal basis in their various identities. The good news is that such a system exists. I am, of course, referring to the emergence of an intelligent Multilevel Governance system in the EU. Its full deployment would not require Treaty Change, as it could be done via secondary law. In the Committee of the Regions, we are convinced that both the restructuring of our economies and the creation of jobs and growth must happen "in partnership" between the institutions: with member states, regions, cities, socio-economic partners and civil society platforms. Policy co-ordination, budget synchronisation and a shared commitment towards the joint implementation of our future agenda for sustainable, smart and inclusive growth, are a top priority. We cannot fail.

This Reform Agenda can only be achieved if we work together. All policy-makers, socio-economic partners and civil society platforms should share the same policy agenda. This is precisely what MLG does. It ensures that all these actors work together – and not against each other. MLG does not question the state's authority, but on the contrary, it makes sure that those who have the expertise on the ground are also committed to implementing the grand strategies put in place by the state.

MLG strengthens openness, participation, co-ordination and commitment. It allows us to take account of the real territorial diversity in Europe. Due to globalisation and social informatisation, people identify with various groups and territorial levels. As has been observed in recent academic literature (see amongst others prof. Koen Lenaerts) "[t]he problem is that neither the classical 'trias politica' (Montesquieu) – neither the 'checks and balances system' were primarily thought of a system of territorial and functional interest representation in the 21st Century."

If we are to succeed, we need to strengthen our legal and political participatory instruments to come to a renewed governance architecture based on the "principle" of multilevel governance. I am convinced that the EU can demonstrate worldwide leadership in the development of sound multi-level and multi-actor procedures and policy tools. Therefore we should develop a "European Code on Participatory Administrative Procedures."

Of course, the new Citizen's Initiative would be a part of this EU Code as one of the participative instruments and methods allowing for greater involvement, dialogue, responsiveness and effective policy-making. Furthermore, the European Code must provide all the procedures necessary to operationalise all principles enshrined in the future "European Charter on Multilevel Governance." In my view, this European Charter would be open for signature to all public authorities in

Europe who wish to respect its key principles. The latter authorities would thus receive a MLG logo, recognised by the EU.

IV. Principles of the Future "Charter on Multi-level Governance"

The seven guiding principles that could constitute the main building blocks of the future "Charter on Multi-level Governance," could be the following: the respect of the subsidiarity and proportionality principles in both policy-making and implementation; the development of horizontal and vertical partnerships; a commitment towards enhanced inter-institutional co-operation; equal treatment amongst all institutional actors; respect for the principles of mutuality and loyalty; the encouragement of "active" citizenship; and a commitment towards multi-level fundamental rights protection.

In addition, public entities should subscribe to the five principles of Good Governance as identified by the Commission in its 2001 White Paper: Responsibility, Openness/transparency, Effectiveness, Participation and Policy coherence.

Finally, in my view, public entities that adhere to the Charter should also subscribe to the following six Good MLG Administrative Practices as identified in the 2011 CoR scoreboard on the monitoring of multi-level governance at the European Union level: provide timely information, dialogue and consultation practices; assure sound and timely stakeholder involvement; provide for a motivated response to stakeholders observations; cultivate territorial/integrated/place-based policy-making; respect the EU's Smart Regulation Agenda (impact assessment); and put forward innovative instruments for partnership.

V. Future of Regional Policy

Some first important developments have taken place, notably as regards the future of regional policy. As Special Adviser to Commissioner Hahn, I was extremely pleased that the Commission took up our advice to include a specific article on partnership and multi-level governance in the Regulations on the Structural Funds.

In its proposed regulation, laying down the common provisions on the structural funds and the cohesion fund, the Commission has proposed the following: 1) MLG is confirmed as one of the leading "general principles" of future cohesion policy; 2) Article 5 of the Regulation states that member states "shall" organise a partnership in accordance with the MLG approach. MLG is thus a legal principle to be scrutinised by the EU Court of Justice; 3) MLG is to be respected within the Partnership Contract and all Operational Programmes. The partners "shall" be involved in the full policy process, in the preparation, implementation, monitoring and evaluation of programmes; 4) The Commission will propose a European Code of conduct that lays down objectives and criteria to support the implementation of MLG and partnership; 5) Every Partnership Contract "shall" detail "the actions taken to involve the partners and their role in the preparation of the Partnership Contract and the progress report as defined in Article 46 of this Regulation."

These positive developments in regional policy are all very promising. In the future, I hope this renewed regional policy will inspire politicians to cultivate a partnership and multi-level governance approach in all EU policies with a territorial dimension. Hopefully, the member states will also agree with these proposals put forward by the European Commission.

VI. Conclusion

Regions and cities have a strategic place in building a Common European Identity based on shared values. Through their position, they are able to promote multi-dimensional partnerships and networks bringing together all relevant actors in an intercultural dialogue resulting in joint action on the ground. Multi-level Governance is the way forward to a more involved and accountable Political Union. The important issue is to discuss and mainstream European policies. In a world that has become interdependent and competitive, Governments – together with socio-economic and civil society actors – at all levels of governance have to seize opportunities together.

There is a window of opportunity to make the case for a strongly connected European Union, both horizontally and vertically, in order to make a Citizens-Europe a reality. This is my belief: a Political Union committed to work *together* with its citizens, through its regions and cities and its living European civil society. *Costruiamo insieme Europa.*

A Common Goods' Understanding of Europe and the World

Peter G. XUEREB

Professor of European and Comparative Law and Jean Monnet Professor of European Law and European Integration, University of Malta

I. Introduction: the Common Good Context(s)

This paper[1] raises as many questions as it attempts to answer. It does this from several perspectives, i.e. law, international relations and politics, and emphasises fundamental principles including human rights and moral principles.

The Common Good is a function of space, time and forum (or "level"). It will mean something different depending especially on the "level" – the polity – at which the decider is deciding what is required by "the" common good, whether at the level of the locality, nation state, grouping of states (and peoples, in the case of the European Union), or the globe. Each level will determine what is required for the common good of that level in accordance with the principle of subsidiarity. But no forum or level is an island.

Through the pursuit of their objectives and aims, the EU Treaties and its policies and laws claim to embody the "European" common good from the perspective of all member states both as a whole and singly. Initially the "context" and "scope" were defined in economic terms (mainly by reference to the scope of the European Economic Community Treaty and its stated aims), and specifically in terms of markets and the single market. However, certainly since the Treaty of Maastricht – and even more so after the Lisbon Treaty – the Common Good of the Union and its member states has been "defined" more

---

1 This paper is the substance of an address delivered by the author in the session titled "Perspectives of a Value Oriented Europe in the World" at a Workshop with the theme of "Cultural and Value Roots for Intercultural Dialogue in a European Context," organised by the Jean Monnet Centre of Excellence at the University of Padova on 25-26 October 2011.

widely, in terms of a wider range of core values such as democracy, the rule of law, solidarity, protection of human rights, protection of minorities and of the rights of the child, gender equality and sustainable economic, environmental and social development, but also by wider aims and objectives that include principled relations with the world beyond. The Treaties are clear about the Union's obligation to pursue the implementation of these values in and throughout all EU external relations. Further, the EU is to contribute to the development of International Law, in addition to being committed to its observance. In this very broad sense it is at least in part also an "international protection regime," as well as being an institution for the common good, as will be elaborated in this paper.

We have at least, and at last, come to realise that our core values cannot be taken for granted even with the achievement of higher levels of prosperity than ever imagined – and also, tellingly, even as we see them "erode" around us and work to stem the flow. Indeed, values appear to be taken for granted in times of relative prosperity, but come under real test in times of economic recession or any other crisis. It is also true that both unrest in Europe itself, and the current financial and economic crisis that has fuelled much of it, have shocked us into reality on this point.

We, healthily, have to "re-evaluate" and redefine our "values." Many assumed that these basic values, and the broader values we espouse (family values, consumer protection, social justice in general, fair dealing, freedom in general and freedom of speech, association and the press in particular, and so on) would forever continue to form the bedrock and the cause of social and economic stability and prosperity and the ability to maintain it (sustainable growth and progress). We now realise that our value system was not as strongly embedded or as perfect as many thought. In short, we need to rediscover and re-order our values in order to restore ourselves to health.

Moreover, we recognise that we have to do this with an overall focus on global peace and stability for all around the globe. And this has to be achieved in a sustainable long-term context that includes the welfare of future generations. We in Europe share responsibility (and are beginning to realise this) for the wider world with which we deal and interact, not only in trade terms but also for a "common project" of democracy and peace building for our world. We are finally shifting our world-view by absorbing the concept and implications of our global Common Destiny. For many of us, the starting point is that our values indicate the way to the common good, not only for ourselves but for the peoples of the world, i.e. the realisation of the global common good.

Such a project must be carried out with others. The means or the way to this end is what I like to call the Common Destiny "Project," emphasising that the adjective "common" refers to the word *project* as well as to the word *destiny*. By definition, a Common Destiny Project must be worked out "in common" with our neighbours and all others. Success can only be reached if multiple perceptions of the common good are melted into *a common perception of the universal common good and the means to attain it*. In practice, of course, the various global cultures will take different starting points and perhaps propose different routes, but if we believe that we are all one, then we must process the various approaches into a common approach. There must be "mediation" between different perceptions if we are to reach our ultimate goal – namely, a world order through which not only the survival, but the prosperity in justice of all humankind can be assured.

II. "Levels of the Common Good" (or Overlapping Circles of Different-level Perceptions of "the" Common Good)

In the daily practice of policy-making and decision-making, at the various "levels" at which a measure of sovereignty is exercised and decisions are made, these processes follow a perception of the common good. It is, however, the end of the matter if competence stops at that level. On the other hand, if that level is in some way subordinate to, or dependant upon, a wider level of decision-making (that is, co-operation with others, at what becomes a higher level) then that perception will need to be "represented" at that higher level and be tested against the perception of the "wider" common good as formulated at that higher level. A proper process of "mediation" based on accepted common principles will ensure that the wider – and out of necessity dominant – perception has taken due account of the "lower" level perception and somehow accommodated it.

The level matters, but equally important to the ultimate ideal of the attainment of the universal common good is *how each level acts* – that is, comes to its own determination of the common good in the first place. For a lower level perception can be "narrow" (more inwardly focused) or "broad" incorporating, with goodwill and commitment, a perception of the wider common good. For example, the national determination can be made to take fully into account the regional or the global common good.

The widest perception of the global common good can – and must – be made to encapsulate the perceptions produced at the "narrower" regional levels, which ideally will have already taken into account the various relevant national or local level perceptions. It is the constant mediation of these perceptions that will produce the greatest harmony.

Of course, each perception must first be produced. Then the process of mediation can start in earnest. This entire process will be more or less successful as each level produces its own perception – of "its own" common good – in full awareness of the other perceptions, both lower and higher. So that the distinct single level processes must not be entirely separate but must develop in tandem. Arguably, this is what happens within the European Union, and we can draw lessons for the wider global blueprint from the European experience.

However, in practice, no matter how culturally or psychologically open to considering the wider common good a lower level may endeavour to be, it remains likely that – by dint of political realities, democratic demands made at its own level and usually a "level-based" degree of expertise – the lower the level of decision-making the narrower the definition and ambit of the Common Good as perceived at that level will be. For example, a national government, formulating national policy, will tend to formulate its perception of the national common good, albeit hopefully also by reference to its international obligations, with national goals, priorities and parameters (the "national interest") uppermost in mind.

However, national perceptions of the national common good as perceived by the national authorities of each member state at their level, when brought to the "higher" level, say to the EU institutions, will need to be "mediated" among themselves and also with the independently proposed perception of the higher level common good, as proposed (usually) by the European Commission. This institution exists indeed in order to propose a European-level common good. The theory is that the European Common Good as determined at that higher level is also for the good and in the interest of each member state and people.

The reality can be very different, since one or more member states can singly, or in tandem, block moves to achieve even the *Union's* common good, as perceived by the independent European Commission, the majority of the member states and the European Parliament, and thereby also prevent the Union from adopting a Union common good position and from interacting with yet higher levels, pursuing, at least in theory again, an even wider and "higher" common good – *the global common good.* This means that the national or the regional levels can, in certain cases, block the higher level common good even within the European Union.

Therefore, if maximum harmony and efficiency are to prevail, decision-making at all levels must be structured so as to bridge the potential gaps between common good perceptions. The best chance of this at the global level would lie in a world order – supported by the consent of all players – that sees all lower level determinations (subject to the application of the principle of subsidiarity) as being preliminary or contingent only, that is to say, being open to further mediation at the wider/higher level.

III. The Problem – Some Examples

A. The Proposal for a Directive on the Common Consolidated Corporate Tax Base (CCCTB)[2]

The Commission recently proposed a Directive to bring in a common consolidated corporate tax base in Europe. In the view of several member states, the measure, if adopted, would have the effect of hitting their service economies hard while benefiting the manufacturing and consumer economies of other member states, and at the same time doing no good to the European economy as a whole. They do not see any "common" good in it for them, or rather they do not see their reality reflected by the Commission's perception of the Common Good; they see it as contrary to their own "common good" perception at their level (but argue also that it would not advance the Union's common good either). Other member states see it as consonant with their individually conceived version of their national "common good" and argue that it is also a necessary measure for the Union's common good.

From these various views it seems clear that mediation is required in order to produce a common perception of the common good of each and of all. Each "side" will make legal, economic, social and political arguments, including competence arguments, in order to seek to ensure that their view prevails. The question is: what lessons can be learned from the way in which the member states of the Union resolve competing common good perceptions in the context of the wider common good?

This example illustrates one particular type of scenario, and not the typical one in the Union. In the taxation context, the Treaty builds on a mechanism that permits one single member state to trump the majority-perceived common good, not through any process of mediation leading to some middle way – but by exercising a right of veto. In some contexts the resort to enhanced co-operation, where permitted by the Treaties, is a possible response to this kind of blockage, but only if applicable and capable of effectiveness in the particular circumstances. If not, what are the principles involved?

In the case of the CCCTB proposal, the measure requires unanimity in the Council for adoption. In this instance, the Treaty excludes action by majority, because the member states reserved their own taxation

---

2 See at http://ec.europa.eu (accessed 23 January 2012).

powers. So it cannot be forced upon the minority of States, or even upon a single state. It appears as if the system allows the minority to obstruct the achievement of the higher level common good (assuming that the Union common good as rooted in Treaty objectives requires such a measure).

Arguably, by excluding majority voting as the decision-making procedure, the member states in essence declare that there is no room or call for any considerations of the higher, wider and longer term common good, at the wider Union level. The decision to maintain the unanimity requirement in specific cases may or may not be objectively founded on a studied position based on a strong application of the principle of subsidiarity, namely that the matter as to whether or not there is to be a common approach or co-operation can ultimately be safely (and without consequence to the wider common good) left entirely to the individual level. Yet such an assumption, namely that there are certain "no go" areas for a wider common good approach, needs to be tested, for it could *ex ante* exclude the pursuit in common of a wider/higher common good where one state made a (non-reviewable) objection. Does this mean that our notion of sovereignty requires yet further adaptation in the interest of fully allowing the pursuit of a majority-determined (with safeguards) "wider/higher level" Common Good?

Surely an absolute condition for the step towards greater supranational majoritarianism would be the guarantee that, in the case of conflicting perceptions, a wider common good decision that trumped a narrower one was properly functionally produced by agreed institutions to which a higher but reviewable power of decision-making had been entrusted and subjected, in its exercise, to appropriate provisions for minority interests, with proper safeguards and controls.

Assuming that such provisions, including mechanisms, safeguards and controls, could be put in place, who or what could then justify the obstruction of the pursuit of the wider-level Common Good? Is a system that continues to allow such to happen one that is to be tolerated in the future? Could it also be that we as EU member states sometimes act in this way and obstruct the wider global common good in international fora by using, maintaining and defending rules of decision-making that permit this? Is any kind of veto, in any kind of forum, acceptable in principle anymore?

For as long as we fail to put in place better designed mechanisms, safeguards and controls, which assure that the lower (national) level will not suffer grave prejudice from a system of majority voting, the veto will remain. Only full solidarity mechanisms can unblock this. By the same token, what do we say of the now general situation in the EU, where in fact and in law, in most areas of policy, the majority's perception of the Common Good (as articulated at that level) can trump that of the minority?

Clearly "mediation" between perceptions/levels of the common good is necessary and already occurs successfully within the EU. However *externally* we may doubt whether we as the European Union have the will to subject our vision to wider mediation – even as the European Union endeavours to propose its vision of what is for the common good at even higher levels. So, the complexity of the dilemma is of course magnified when the *Global* Common Good is at stake.

The basic provisional conclusion is clear: if the global common good is to be identified independently and then pursued with hope of success, we need (1) common "global institutions for the common good," (2) which are capable of seeking and identifying the common good properly perceived at that level, and (3) which are capable of actuating that common good by securing agreement to its implementation at all levels, through (4) the practice of active solidarity. This calls for a global organisation with institutions, that in full solidarity, mutual loyalty and trust will take full account of all common good perceptions (including national interests) arrived at, at the lower levels. Its primary task would be to mediate such perceptions with the perceived Universal Common Good, as identified at that widest level by some supranational objective mechanism.

Such an institutional device would permit action to be decided at those higher levels but implemented through action at the lower levels of region and nation state, provided the outcome has taken full account of legitimate positions at the lower level. If this system were put in place, it is a difficult question as to whether and on what conditions any kind of veto could be justified. With certain exceptions, the EU has shown the way in moving away from decision-making by unanimity to majority determination, by establishing the essential conditions for making the latter work.

B. Migration

In a post-Stockholm scenario,[3] the EU has been planning and putting in place a series of new measures, as part of a Common European Asylum Policy and a Common Migration Policy. The latter will favour the skilled worker from outside the EU over the unskilled. Yet it is hoped and expected that the EU will also champion the cause of all who flee oppression, discrimination and persecution and fully commit to the

[3] The so-called Stockholm Programme. See at http://eur-lex.europa.eu (accessed 22 January 2012).

global challenge of saving those who hunger or face death from disease and climate change, or are otherwise rendered less than fully human.

It is lamentable in view of Europe's Christian heritage that there are those in the EU who would question whether there be any obligation upon the EU to show the fullest solidarity with the oppressed and the suffering across the globe, or to do so even when it "hurts" financially or in other perceived ways. Are the parameters and limits, of our concern to be drawn at the good or the perceived (sometimes xenophobic) interests of the member states and their peoples? Is some conception of "limits" to our individual and collective responsibility in fact being pursued? For example, are we prepared to help, but only as long as it does not hurt us too much? Or even worse, do we only help as long as it benefits us, or "protects" us? How will others judge our "perception" of our own and of the wider common good? Will they conclude that the EU has no mechanism for aiming for the universal common good at all?

This particular example, of EU Migration and Asylum Policy, raises directly and in a "difficult" context the question of whether the "European level" understanding of the common good includes the individual's good, and the "non-EU individuals'" good in particular? The real question is whether we Europeans really think and act on the basis that for us to fail by all means, internally and externally, to address the plight of others, diminishes us. At the very least, do we truly realise that practising solidarity with others not only furthers the good of others but also our own good (including spiritual and moral good)? Do we recognise that the human rights of others are our responsibility also, and that failing to support those rights diminishes our own freedom, and our own respect for our own rights, leading to erosion and degeneration within our own society?[4]

We need to listen harder to NGOs such as Amnesty International and Statewatch UK. In the European Parliament itself (perhaps rightly viewed as the conscience of the Union), certain groups have expressed their opinion about the recent internal agreement on Frontex:[5]

> We don't need Frontex but a humanised refugee policy to deal with situations in Africa where people are living in dire conditions, an asylum

---

4 Commissioner Malmstroem certainly does. See Malmstroem, C., *How Europe Failed*, Times of Malta, 19 January 2012 at http://www.timesofmalta.com (accessed 19 January 2012).

5 The excerpts that follow were taken from the website of Statewatch UK: www.statewatch.org (accessed 24 September 2011).

system based on solidarity and a new neighbourhood policy more in tune with our values.[6]

Speaking after the vote, Marie-Christine Vergiat said:

We do not want this Europe, this fortress Europe that gives lessons in human rights and democracy and is unable to reach out and help thousands of refugees. The Parliamentary Assembly of the Council of Europe is currently investigating the deaths in the Mediterranean and the EU will have to account for its own failures.

And the Green/EFA Group declared that:

The European Parliament today adopted a final compromise revising EU legislation on FRONTEX, the EU's agency for external border operations. While recognising that the final compromise will bring some improvements, the Greens regret that the revision will fall short of providing necessary guarantees on human rights protection.[7]

These statements deserve to be taken seriously. On the same lines of thought, the AEDH[8] published the following reaction to the recently proposed Directives on foreign workers:

Within the framework of regulating foreign workers in the European Union, the European Parliament will vote this autumn on two directives concerning seasonal workers and intra-corporate transferees. After a comparative analysis of the texts in the legislative package on foreign workers, which includes these two directives, the AEDH is concerned about shortcomings in the texts and the possible infringement on the right to equal treatment. The AEDH maintains that all workers must enjoy the same rights on European territory, regardless of their country of origin or skill level. The AEDH believes that it was imperative to draft a European text with a view to ending the exploitation of seasonal workers and guarantee them a minimum of rights. However, the Commission's proposal is insufficient and will not allow these objectives to be obtained. The rigidity of the seasonal worker status, the weakness of the assurances provided, and the non-transferability of social rights to the country of origin are all reasons that will encourage workers to work illegally, in turn greatly exposing them to exploitation. In addition, the AEDH criticises the fragmentation of the labour market by the Commission, which creates different working conditions and therefore variable rights according to worker category. A separate framework will be created for third-country national seasonal workers, thereby creating a

6 *Ibidem*, EU-FRONTEX: European Parliament: GUE/NGL group: *New Frontex mandate a "wolf in sheep's clothing."*

7 *Ibidem, FRONTEX/EU border control: Half-hearted improvements on human rights protection fall short* (Press release).

8 AEDH, European Association for the Defence of Human Rights 33, rue de la Caserne B-1000 Brussels Tel: +32(0)25112100, Fax: +32(0)25113200, Email: aedh@aedh.eu, http://www.aedh.eu (accessed 17 October 2011).

> discriminatory policy of unequal rights due only to the worker's nationality. Seasonal workers from other Member States remain subject to Council Regulation (EC) No. 1408/71 (1). As an example, the duration of seasonal work is fixed at a maximum of six months for foreign workers while Europeans are allowed eight months. Although very positive provisions have been created for intra-corporate transferees, this leads to differences in treatment according to worker skill level, which the AEDH considers to be contrary to the principle of equal treatment. In particular, the right to family reunification will be accorded to manager level staff and not seasonal workers. The respect of private and family life should never be dependent on a worker's skill level or remuneration. The AEDH criticises the utilitarian vision of the EU's legal immigration policy and finds it inadmissible that foreign workers be considered as economic tools for European growth and thereby subject to different rights than European workers. This type of approach endangers the principle of equal treatment and thereby social cohesion in Europe.[9]

We fully agree with this criticism voiced by the AEDH. I would even add that such a mere economically driven approach to migration by the EU erodes our very souls. These are serious charges! They beg the question of whether the EU sees its mandate from its Members and Citizens in purely utilitarian terms or whether the EU can regard itself as "an institution for the Common Good" in the terms in which some international relations thinking has proposed.

IV. The Freedom to Pursue the Common Good

This leads me to the question: How free are decision-makers to pursue the common good? How free do we, their electorates, leave them? Is it we, the citizens, who compel them to follow our prejudices, fears and short-term demands? Are they as much victims or prisoners of "the system," constrained collaborators, rather than the solely responsible perpetrators? No one would deny the essential democratic value of our constitutional espousal of the concept of "*alternance*" of five (or so) yearly national elections. Yet, the political short-termism that this creates is just as erosive of values and soul as the short-term pressures placed by demanding investors on the captains of industry.

What must be the answer at the wider/higher level – assuming that the wider common good demands a different approach – is for the higher level to "pull" all lower level polities in the right direction. This it can do if it is so structured as to fully take account of and provide for – that is, to show full Solidarity with – those States which will otherwise be "forced" to be guided by self-protective concerns.

9 AEDH, *Foreign workers in the EU: moving towards multiple standards, founded on unequal treatments?*, Press release, 17 October 2011.

In a very real sense, in the internal EU context, a form of solidarity is what the relatively stronger member states have been asked to show in support of the weaker member states throughout the current euro-zone crisis. The question of the nature of this explicit form of solidarity has been raised elsewhere.[10] However a convincing and all-embracing answer is difficult to give today, even for the Union. As recent events in the Union have shown, state sovereignty needs to be constantly re-evaluated. Otherwise national interest will be pursued not through co-operation, but through the power of the veto, and even when this obstructs the pursuit of the wider common good. This makes it a constitutional issue for all member states and the Union as a whole.

The above examples indicate that a move to ever wider/higher political, economic and indeed moral levels of thought and action, and a further supranationalisation of the EU and beyond, requires guarantees that the Good pursued at the higher levels is objectively for the good of all, and is in fact pursued without unreasonable (disproportionate) and uncompensated detriment to any group or "individual" lower-level entity. This is the pre-condition for the required Consent to a system that allows the wider common good to be independently identified, proposed and pursued. This is an ambitious task to be undertaken, especially at the global level. However, many lessons from the European integration process, including the most recent developments, should give us reason for hoping that such a blueprint is possible, in all groupings of States and at the global level itself.

V. The External Dimension and Mediating the "Wider" Common Good

The second example well illustrated the importance of the external EU dimension for a blueprint for global policy-making. Globalisation does not imply the disappearance of the nation state but it will surely result in the solidifying of great regional blocks (or "groupings of states"). The greater and more powerful the grouping of states, the greater the impact of its decisions on the Non-Members and citizens of the latter.

What principle(s) might constrain such a group(s) of states to act primarily in the wider common good of all, Members and Non-members? The Members of the Union are expected to work towards the common good of all member states and to show mutual loyalty. I argue

[10] See Editorial, *European Constitutional Law Review*, no. 7, 2011, pp. 169-172. In the view of the editors, solidarity in this explicit form not of one-sided transfers from the well-off to the needy but in the form of mutual responsibility – and responsibility that is explicit, articulate and creative – is at the heart of the "social contract."

that what goes for the individual member state within the context of the Grouping of States must also go for the Group itself in the wider context, at the global level. Such a Group should fully take into account the interests of its neighbours and others. It should also formulate a perception of its own Common Good, which encapsulates the wider common good, and makes consensus at the global level more possible and likely.

Such a Grouping of States, working with an international society mind-set, would make a real contribution to the evolution of global governance and a beneficial new world order. It would be capable of acting with moral force in the world, as we would expect from the EU. It ought always, therefore, to be prepared to subject its own perception of the common good, including its own interests and any perception of the wider common good that it might have formed, to still further mediation of that vision by participation with others in a wider forum. Anything less is, if not actually the case, easily perceived as attempted hegemonic pursuit of selfish interests.

In democratic and pragmatic terms, for the taking and actualisation of enlightened decisions *affecting the globe*, the entire globe would need to be "represented and participate" in the identification of the *universal* common good from the global perspective. Decisions that *concern the globe*, should be taken *by the globe*, through structured solidarity at the world level through carefully designed global institutions. A democratically legitimate global body would be needed for the purpose. How participation in such a global body would be structured is a matter of crucial importance for the sake of workability, but Universal consent to such structured decision-making with solidarity is the underlying fundamental condition. This is now an urgent task.

It is true, of course, that even without such a global body, some systems and principles (such as the United Nations Charter) currently seek to ensure that, however powerful a single state or group of states may be, that state or group of states may not with impunity override individual human rights, the self determination of peoples, and other universal precepts. This is a glorious human achievement, incomplete and defective as it may still be.

In support of human rights and self-determination, the world community has felt entitled and obliged to intervene in what would have been considered in the past to be "domestic" or "internal" affairs (as in the case of Libya, for example). The co-ordination of this global response to date can hardly be called "structured." Yet, taking the case of Libya, the "common good" as identified by the rest of the world, and defined as rooted in the rights and interests of the Libyan people, as individuals and as a community, as well as the concern of the world community for democracy in Libya and stability in the world, appears to have been the moral, political, and legal justification for measured international action in support of the universally acknowledged rights of the Libyan people.

The Arab Spring has caused us to eschew easy *clichés* and prejudices. We have come to realise that, behind the veneer of acquiescence to authoritarian rule, "people" do share in their hearts and minds the same values of liberty, democracy, and respect for human rights. The Arab Spring has demonstrated this in a most powerful manner. This lends credence to the concept of universal values, on which a Common Good Framework may be constructed.

VI. Principles

Yet, as the first example showed, there are cases even within a group of like-minded and more or less homogenous States, where "the majority" may not act – where they are expressly precluded by their own international agreement from acting – for what at least some argue was for the common good. This is so, largely, it seems, on the tenet that some areas are "no go" areas for common action in the absence of specific universal consent (the veto issue). At the same time, there are many cases where the majority may act in such a way as to bind the minority, there having been some form of *ex ante* consent to this by all members (as with the acceptance by all member States of the Union's ordinary legislative procedure in so many areas of policy).

It seems clear that a fundamental criterion for the permission (authority) for a "higher" level to determine and pursue the wider Common Good in such a manner as to "trump" any lower level determination of the common good, is the principle of Consent. This concept would be at the root of the legitimate pursuit in law and practice of the higher or wider common good. Without that, we would have to continue to hope and pray that smaller-than-global might, (in the form of action taken by a super-power or by a strong group of states) is in fact guided by "right."

Without Universal Consent to the global structure and decision-making process, however obvious to some or even to the majority the route to the common good may be, there can be no fully legitimate majority decision-making, obligation-imposition and enforcement from a wider/higher level. This is what the EU Treaties teach us. But we have also learned, through the current economic and other crises, that we would each individually be wise to take the path of sovereignty-pooling and mutual co-operation if we wish to "regulate" the manner of "other-level" influence, de facto as well as de jure, on our individual state futures. If it is such wisdom that explains the decisions of states to join in larger structured groups of states as well as their consent to wider-level decision-making in such a structure, it would also explain the general consent to, and legitimation of, global level decision-making for the universal common good. Global institutions and mechanisms – most likely based on the participation of groups or blocks of states – are crucial, and must be developed at the global level on the basis of these principles.

A next step in the argument can be taken. While a political and legal basis for the authority and obligation to pursue the "wider" common good can be set out for all members of a grouping of states and for the institutions that they may set up for the pursuit of the common objectives, it nevertheless remains for them, through these institutions, to decide what is or is not to be regarded as being for the common good in any concrete case. Democracy and legitimacy require full participation in this process. Commonality requires solidarity. Solidarity requires procedural fairness in the first place, but also "just content" in the second. "Just content" can only be achieved if the principles of equality, mutual loyalty and respect for the identities, circumstances and needs of each member are fully taken into account and incorporated into the final measures to be taken in pursuit of the common good.

In other words, the decision-making process and principles must be demonstrably appropriate for attaining the truly *common* good. Everyone must benefit or stand to benefit, and be assisted to benefit. All action must be directed to benefit and calculated to benefit all involved. It will demonstrably not be so if only some stand to benefit while others stand to suffer detriment, or if it involves disproportionate sacrifice or costs for some members without adequate compensation or compensating advantages that will place the latter in a better position than they previously stood. This is practical commonality and solidarity.[11]

What follow are some conclusions. First, it is clear that structures/organisations/institutions to serve the common good must be built with the participation and consent of all. Second, it follows that all must be given equal (fair) treatment. Third, it is clear that the Common Good must be enshrined as an objective value, to be arrived at by impartial judgment that takes interests into account but is not ruled by any majority or minority interest. Fourth, it must be somehow assured that what is pursued is in itself Good, that is to say that the structures/institutions must be created and empowered for, be capable

[11] See Xuereb, P. G., "The Future of Europe: Solidarity and Constitutionalism: Towards a Solidarity Model," in *European Law Review*, issue no. 6, vol. 27, 2002, pp. 643-662.

of, and have their competences limited by, the "Good"; hence core values are crucial and must be agreed on and secured. Fifth, it must be for an independent – but accountable – authority to ascertain and propose a concrete vision of the common good and propose measures to attain it. Sixth, all states and groupings must commit to pursuing the widest common good, singly and collectively, and owe such obligation to all others, albeit being represented within the global body in principle via the principal grouping to which they belong. Seventh, the ultimate determination of the universal common good must itself be objectively reviewable; this implies that all and especially the minority must be "protected" by the system or order, so that they do not need to resort to self-protective measures that serve as an obstacle to the achievement of the common good; the rule of law, including of the "higher law"[12] would then prevail, by consent.

Imperfect and incomplete as the European Union itself may be, there are many lessons to be learned from the European institutional and "rule of law" experience, even as lessons continue daily to be learned by the member states.[13]

VII. Institutions

The need for global institutions is clear. Singly, each "unit" (State/Group) must remain free to establish a position as to what is for its "own good," at its own level. This can be identified through the exercise of 'sovereign' competence at that level in accordance with the principle of subsidiarity.

---

12 Itself a contested concept, but a crucial one.

13 Generally, by the author: Xuereb, P. G., "Infusing the Euro-Mediterranean Partnership with the Supranational Dynamic. A Euro-Mediterranean Community and a Step towards Global governance?," in E. Lannon (ed.), *The EU Neighbourhood Policy's Challenges*, Brussels, P.I.E. Peter Lang, 2012, pp. 159-187 – a shorter and modified version is to appear as one of the conference papers in a Conference publication by the European Commission titled: "Evolutions in the Southern Mediterranean – Implications for the European Union," due out in 2012; Xuereb, P. G., "Values, Intercultural Dialogue and Making it Pay to be Good: More than a Research Agenda but also a Policy Approach for the European Union to Promote in the World," in *Pace Diritti Umani/Peace Human Rights*, vol. 2, 2010, pp. 69-95; *id.*, "Making it Pay to be Good – Intercultural Dialogue, Virtue in the Public Sphere, The Common Good, Global Governance, and the European Experience," published in the proceedings of the Jean Monnet Conference of 8th September 2009, *20 Years of Support for European Integration Studies* (European Commission 2010). For a study of the international relations (economic) dimension of some of the ideas expressed in the above, see Petersmann, E.-U., "International Economic Law and Public Reason: Why do Governments Fail to Protect International Public Goods More Effectively?," *EUI Working Papers*, Law 2010/17, http://hdl.handle.net (accessed 9 February 2012).

Yet in a world where "own decisions," even about one's "own good," are increasingly contingent on the co-operation of others, wise decision-making at that level will already take account of the wider perspective – the "wider" good. In other words, it must be accepted that the capacity of national decision-making to rule the outcome even within one's own polity is increasingly limited. In this sense, all national "planning" is contingent. It is the same at the level of the grouping of states. Henceforth, there is an urgent need for effective global institutions that will ensure global solidarity, not least in order to turn our own contingent plans – whether formulated at single state or grouping level, and albeit in modified form – into reality.

To summarise, the determination of the common good at the wider/higher level requires the application of three essential conditions: (1) a full interplay, dialogue, exchange and compromise from preliminary "own level" perceptions of the common good (i.e. mediation across levels of common good perceptions); (2) institutions designed for the purpose and structured in such a way as to bring forth legitimate proposals based on independently and impartially identified wider Common Good requirements (in the EU, it has been the role of the Commission to prepare preliminary "wider common good perception" for the EU); (3) some form of majority decision-making and the enforceability of the resulting decisions must be agreed, "concretising" the wider common good into real measures, subject to those decisions having been taken legitimately and lawfully. This begs the question as to what makes such decisions legitimate, and therefore acceptable and applicable.

Proposals and decisions should be made to pass through the "filters of legitimacy."

They will be passed through the filters of subsidiarity and proportionality, to leave each lower level free to pursue their "own" common good, freely, if no higher level action is warranted.

They will be tested against the principle of real or actual Solidarity, both procedural and substantive, so that any higher level common good will not be pursued at the unjust expense of any "lower" level common good determination, i.e. in a manner that harms a particular state or group without a counterweighing benefit.

They will be forged in democratic exchange and in full dialogue,[14] with full respect to cultures and common values. This is perhaps the

---

[14] See Köchler, H., *The Philosophy and Politics of Dialogue*, keynote lecture delivered at the Global Dailogue Conference 2009, University of Aarhus, Denmark, 6 November 2009, http://en.wikipedia.org/wiki/Hans_K%C3%B6chler (accessed 18 February 2012).

most challenging part of the process, for in the absence of a universal culture, and in the light of the imperative of respecting individual cultures; a new "intercultural understanding" must be forged around universal core values. This will be the main challenge in the common good(s) mediation process.[15]

I argue that it is crucially important to understand that the concept of the Common Good – whether for a state, a group of states or the world community of states – is to be rooted in and reducible to one fundamental objective, namely the recognition, respect and promotion of the rights of the human person. This happens to be a main tenet of our Christian heritage, but can be regarded as the subject of universal acknowledgment. The human person is equal everywhere. No one may be made to suffer in order that another may benefit. In positive terms, it implies that authority everywhere is subservient to the aim of the promotion of the well-being of each and every person, and responsibility for that well-being is shared by all in authority at whatever "level." The exercise of that authority is only well directed when it is calculated to lead to the benefit of each person.

This is the proper conception, in my view, of the Common Good. It is certainly not rooted in the concept of individualism. Because we have not always practised what has been preached, and may have strayed from this path, it requires an evolution in our thinking about authority, sovereignty, constitutionalism, and law – whether domestic or global/transnational. "Events" and the correlative "people" response to these on a global scale, are pointing the way forward for society, law, economics, politics and institutions. Those in power must surely respond to this challenge. They must now allow for the evolution of the political, economic and social developments of this age – illustrated so vividly by the broad response to the economic and financial crisis and its causes, or by the Arab Spring – that have already acquired a solid impetus. World society is in formation.[16]

---

15 Stephanie Lawson has written that "the objectification of culture as a thing is based on a conservative and static notion of culture that largely ignores – or at least glosses over – its contingent nature as well a its social, political and moral dynamism." See Lawson, S., "Global governance, human rights and the 'problem' of culture," in R. Wilkinson and S. Hughes (eds.), *Global Governance – Critical Perspectives*, London, Routledge, 2002, p. 87.

16 Generally on this theme see Buzan, B., *From International Society to World Society? English School Theory and the Social Structure of Globalisation*, Cambridge, Cambridge University Press, 2004.

VIII. Organisation and Institutions for the "highest," "widest" or "universal" Common Good

Without pretending to have all the answers, or being comprehensive in my analysis of the "international relations" debate, it is useful to pursue some recent "international relations thinking" about "institutions for the common good." As one example of some thinking on the subject of "institutions for the Common Good," and specifically drawing on thinking about so-called "International Protection Regimes," I cite Bruce Cronin. He writes as follows:[17]

> International politics is as much about defining the structures and rules of interaction as it is about achieving specific material benefits or gaining strategic advantage [...].
>
> [...] international protection regimes are part of a class of institutions that are designed to promote the 'common good' for a collectivity of states. Unlike functional institutions that seek to provide consumable benefits to their participants, 'institutions for the common good' are concerned with the preservation and general welfare of the international order itself [...].
>
> [...] While these institutions may not provide direct benefits to participating states, they help to advance the broader goals of an international order by helping to maintain a preferred social or political framework through which states can co-operate and compete on the international stage.

The key idea which I wish to draw out in the context of this paper, relates to the recognition that such organisations have a function that goes beyond pursuing the sum or distillation of the "national" interests of the members as put forward by their governments, whether these interests cover the long term as well as the short term.

I would argue that this kind of thinking is directly relevant to the post-Lisbon EU itself. Clearly, the Union, as its predecessors, was founded to advance the interests of its members. But, membership has always been open and national interests have always been broadly defined in terms of values as well as interests. The European Union surely is, and wishes to be seen also as an international protection regime. One major aim of the EU is the promotion of its own values (which it hopes are shared not only by the member states but also by the rest of the world), within the context of (beneficial) development and observance of international law and therefore the universal common good. This does not exclude its vocation of advancing the interests of its Members or the interests of the Union. However, one presumes (1) that

---

[17] Cronin, B., *Institutions for the Common Good, International Protection Regimes in International Society*, Cambridge, Cambridge Studies in International Relations, Cambridge University Press, 2003, p. 4.

the EU is always prepared to subordinate interests (in purely utilitarian terms) to values, (2) that it is prepared to engage in constructive dialogue about values, and (3) that it will always give "priority" to the rule of just international law and a just world order built upon the development of such.

In orientation, one part of the EU identity of the Union is that of an international protection regime as well as an institution (organisation) for the common good and a contributor to the ascertainment of, and the common pursuit of, the wider global common good. The EU has a vested interest, as do its member states, in operating within a just international (global) climate and international (global) order. It has, on the whole, shown itself to be able and prepared to make its own contribution to the evolution of such an order.

The obligation imposed on the EU by the Treaty on European Union itself is a larger one than that of the protection or advancement of its own "interests." The Treaty clearly acknowledges that others co-habit the global space and exhorts the Union to take up its responsibilities in this regard.[18] It also recognises the global level as yet another level (the "highest/widest" level) for "common good determination and action," for the sake of which, national and even "EU" common good determinations, will need to be "mediated" with common good determinations made in other fora. The EU accepts its responsibility to play its part in furthering the universal common good – with a major responsibility to do so ever more in a globalised world where the concepts and the conditions of world order, global justice and universal morality need to be articulated as a matter of international relations, politics, economics and law.

Thinking along these lines is alien in many respects to many people. The new world that such ideas presage is still beyond the ken of most of us. The structures that we have put in place at the global level were premised on the old Law of Nations. New world concepts and structures have been slowly taking shape. Global regulation has emerged in many new spheres. The failures of the past are pushing us to new solutions, new structures, new economics, new politics and new laws.

---

[18] Articles 3 (5) and 21 of the Treaty on the European Union, Official Journal of the European Union C 083, 2010. For a recent contribution on the trend of "dynamic constitutionalism" and the EU constitutional dimension of some of the themes in this paper, see Lark, J., "Shaping the International Order as a Union Objective and the Dynamic Internationalisation of Constitutional Law," in *Cleer Working Papers*, 2011/5. For a view of the European Union as a polity of States and Citizens, a transnational democracy – a concept that I would seek to transpose to the global level – see Hoeksma, J., "The EU as a Democratic Polity in International Law," in *Cleer Working Papers*, 2011/2.

The good news is that this new world appears to acknowledge such values as democracy, human rights, the rule of law, international obligation, individual freedom, societal values, or systems such as parliamentary democracy or even capitalism (properly re-directed), and is itself premised upon the pursuit of them, as witnessed by the Arab Spring. What we see is a continuum – evolution (or what I would call re-evolution)[19] not revolution – in terms of declared universal values. We seem to have rediscovered that the human spirit is one and that, wherever on the planet it may reside, it craves the same fulfilment and is prepared to suffer for the opportunity of such. Most importantly, it is a spirit that is open to Dialogue.

But the conditions of dialogue must be created. The parameters of "power" must be clearly set out. Loyalty must have a basis in Trust but also in remedy. *Solidarity in values and action must be the cardinal principle that may never be transgressed or compromised.*

While preserving all the major gains in terms of European and international orders that have been made over the last two hundred years, the European Union (and its Members) must be prepared, as one player among several strong players, to see past its own – especially its short-term – interests,[20] and to propose better global organisations/ institutions and a better (more Good) international order. We can go beyond the historical European and international order constructs in order to construct a just and effective global framework. We should recognise how past constructs may at the same time have imprisoned us; we should therefore act increasingly actively in accordance with the Values that we proclaim.

Otherwise, how can the Union be a credible player on the global scene? We cannot expect the "better" conduct of others unless we engage in it ourselves. Indeed, the EU will lose credibility in so far as it puts (crude) interest before Values. Rather, a new moral playing field must be created under an order that "makes it pay to be good" – for States and Groups of States as for Enterprises. We should hope for the same commitment from all our partners in return, but we can take the

---

19 See, for an example of such thinking, Kobrin, S. J., "Back to the Future – Neomedievalism and the Postmodern Digital World Economy," in A. Prakash and J.A. Hart, *Globalization and Governance*, London and N.Y, Routledge, 1999, pp. 165-187.

20 The recent announcement of the Commission's plans to decouple economic growth from natural resource consumption (suggesting that the member states sign up to a myriad of short and long-term environmental targets by the end of 2013) shows an ability and a determination to prioritise accordingly and to put long term over short term considerations. We should study such initiatives for the ingredients of good governance in global terms. *Euractiv Newsletter*, 21 September 2011.

initiative in opening up a real dialogue in any event. On certain conditions, the Union can be a true player, a leading player, in the shaping of the new global order for which the citizenry of the world is crying out.

IX. Conclusion

The universal common good needs to be pursued by appositely designed global institutions, but these do not yet exist. This means that the development of a new system for the pursuit of the universal common good must with urgency be pursued by the existing global organisations, but also by regional organisations such as the EU, and also – though with less direct effect – by each State. Where a Grouping of States exists, it can, acting as an international protection regime and, further, as an institution for the common good, act as a vital intermediate stage in the process of identification and pursuit of the new global system for achieving the universal common good.

As to the ultimate result, what we certainly do not want, in my view, is a world order in which the global good is perceived and determined by any superpower, oligarchy of states or even by some crudely-operating majority of states – and certainly not one in which it is pursued in crude opposition to group or national interests, i.e. without the various level-defined perceptions of the "common good" ever meeting in structured dialogue such as to lead to legitimate global decision-making.

We can accept that the idea of a "common good" is not a rejection of individual interest, as Cronin has put it.[21] Equally, the mediation of common good determinations made at "lower" levels with a global-level-produced determination, undertaken in order that such mediation might produce the concrete universal common good in action, is not – indeed is the opposite of – a denial of those lower level determinations, for it should render those determinations more achievable.

We need organisations, institutions and mechanisms that are capable of ensuring the meeting, through dialogue, of "individual" interests while filtering out "individualism." At the same time, the pursuit of the global common good must take place within a context of full cognisance of the democratic self-determination of the individual and of the local, national or regional common good. In short, the world order must be designed in such a way that the global level will always practice full

---

[21] Cronin, B., *Institutions for the Common Good, International Protection Regimes in International Society*, Cambridge, Cambridge Studies in International Relations, Cambridge University Press, 2003, p. 13.

Solidarity with the lower levels, for all "levels" are intimately bound up. A "constitutional" framework is indispensable for this purpose.

The sole purpose, legitimation and effectiveness of any global authority must reside in, and be bound by, its orientation towards creating a global environment in which all levels can, and do, carry out their responsibilities and pursue their goals with the universal good – which they participate in identifying – in mind, and in greater freedom and security. The United Nations may be the obvious main candidate for a large part of the global institutional role advocated here, if appropriately reformed, but other organisations such as the World Trade Organisation and some others must be brought into the equation in what must be the greatest global institutional reform programme since the middle of the last century.

I would argue that unless we and all our global partners make this mental, philosophical and cultural leap at both the national and regional level, and develop appropriately the international (global) policy/ decision-making level, we will find justice, peace and prosperity increasingly elusive within our own regional groups, and within our own states.

To conclude, the challenge for the EU and the member states post-Lisbon is to make the European Union work at the global level as envisaged by the Lisbon Treaty. The Union will do so not least by offering its vast (and chequered) experience of combining intercultural dialogue with supranational decision-making, as a partner in creating global institutions and governance for the Universal Common Good. A global Jean Monnet conference on this specific subject would be an important step forward in the process.

The Multiple Crisis of Europe[1]

Ferenc MISZLIVETZ

Jean Monnet Professor, West Hungarian University;
Director of the Institute for Global and European Studies,
Corvinus University, Koszeg, Budapest

I. Why Europe is not Leading the 21st Century?

Europe is in a deep crisis today, a fact that is recognised by an increasing number of analysts, experts and observers. The crisis of the Euro-zone has been on the front page of leading newspapers for a long time. A lot has been said and written during the past year or two about the impact of the global economic and financial crisis on the EU. But frustratingly, the recognition that the crisis is actually far more complex and also a deepening political and social crisis for the European Union as such, grasped the attention of analysts only recently.

Although there were enough reasons after the 2004 Big Bang Eastern enlargement and the 2005 double "no" votes to the constitution to think about emerging crisis symptoms, lingering questions were swept under the carpet. Against promises, European integration remained an elite-driven and non-democratic process, and Eurocrats, experts and national politicians remained uninterested in identifying or understanding the deeper structural causes of its failures and negative tendencies. The lack of a proper diagnosis left no chance for effective therapy. Self-congratulatory official EU and national propaganda about successful accessions has possibly led to self-deceit: "Unity in Diversity" remained a main slogan while increased diversity further undermined transnational solidarity and silently turned core European societies against further enlargement.

Before and around Eastern enlargement the proclaimed self-image of the EU was elevated to great heights. Books were published under the title "*The European Dream*" (Jeremy Rifkin) and indeed for a while many believed that the fading away of the American dream would open

[1] A first version of this paper was published in *Délkelet Európa – South-East Europe International Relations Quarterly*, vol. 3, no.1, (Spring 2012/1), pp. 1-7.

up new horizons, not only for new visions of Europe but also for the realisation of those visions. It seemed that the European construction had gained new momentum and that Europe would gain greater political significance on the global level and become a model for further regional integrations and as such, a shaper of a new post Cold War world order.

Marc Leonard wrote in 2005: "[…] far from being the problem, the EU is the remedy: giving countries control over policies that had become global."[2]

He continues:

> By giving national governments a voice in the world, the EU has saved national democracy from becoming a mere talking shop that comments on global events while the real decisions are taken elsewhere […] The EU is the only way that small countries can have a measure of control over global markets.[3]

The buoyantly optimistic title of the book "*Why Europe is Going to Lead the 21st Century*," speaks for itself.

However, this overwhelmingly self-congratulating optimism did not last too long. Opinion polls clearly showed that old core Europe had lost its enthusiasm about Eastern enlargement (if it had any) rightly seen and interpreted as an elite decision made above the heads of European citizens. The accession of former Soviet bloc countries had unforeseen and rather frightening consequences and European citizens understood that in the lack of democratic decision-making on the transnational level, decision-makers would remain unaccountable. The double "no" votes in 2005 were an expression of dissent about the previously successful and celebrated European construction method and procedure.

European politicians, Eurocrats as well as their expert groups and think tanks, had a bubble around their head – a self-image determined by an idealised and desired image of Europe. Instead of facing the harsh reality after 2004/2005, postponement and avoidance was accomplished through declaring time for "years of reflection" and projects like Plan D: Democracy, Dialogue, Debate. The Commission recognised the democracy deficit but couldn't find the method to cure it. Plan D did not produce sufficient dialogue and deliberation on any European, transnational or regional level and failed to strengthen citizens' identification with the EU, bringing them closer to the European project. As opinion polls and Euro barometer data suggest, trust in EU institutions has further declined and in 2009 the turnout in EP elections

2 Leonard, M., *Why Europe Will Run the 21st Century?*, London and New York, Fourth Estate, 2005, p. 90.

3 *Ibidem*, p. 92.

reached a negative record. Margot Wallström, the commissioner with a human face, created sympathy during her meetings with European NGO leaders, but the campaign did not galvanise and couldn't even empower the so-called "European civil society" which largely remained a metaphor from above – an invention of European think tanks and the White Paper on European Governance. This time the genie remained in the bottle – societies remained passive, apathetic and increasingly sceptical.

The "period of reflection" concluded with an open letter of 27 recommendations at the end of 2007. The European demos remained an abstraction; the European polity remained a non-democracy with diminishing chances for becoming a political authority with global aspirations. The eruption of the global crisis found a Europe weakened by the diminishing trust of its citizens in its non-transparent institutions, by its over ambitious and less and less convincing social policy contradicting its de facto neo-liberal economic policy, and by its political philosophy. Europe was left without real leadership and the capacity for comprehensive crisis management to deal with growing discrepancies between its different regions of North and South, East and West.

Instead of expanding, de facto solidarity has been rapidly diminishing and bilateralism based on national interests has taken momentum. For the first time during the entire post World War II history of integration, the German population became Eurosceptic, and those who did not believe that European integration was a good thing, started to outnumber its supporters. In the absence of strong institutions, accountable leaders and an empowered parliament, Europeans once more became increasingly inward looking. An emphasis on national interests in economic and energy policies was followed by the articulation of the pre-eminence of national vernacular, culture and belonging: the social need for an exclusive type of democracy has been strengthening, followed by the growth of rightwing populism and extremism. Germany and Britain have announced the end of multiculturalism as a new political doctrine. This has begun a new period in the history of European integration.

In 2011, after the NATO intervention in Libya led by the French Air Force, the French president Nicholas Sarkozy, supported by other Western European countries, raised the question of suspending the Schengen treaty and reintroducing national border control, in order to be able to legally turn away refugees from MENA countries. During a long half decade, the celebrated European dream has turned into a European nightmare.

II. The Deep Structure and Causes of European Crisis

Up until 1989/2004, those who saw, interpreted and preached post World War II European construction as a success story were not far from reality. The foundation of functioning trans or supra-national institutions by discovering and applying a new methodology of integration was not only unprecedented and unique since it had been happening among former rivals and ardent enemies, but thanks to its success it became an emerging model for regional integration and development co-operation throughout the world. What was less – or not at all – understood, was that the conditions for the obvious achievements of European integration were guaranteed by the bipolar logic and military stalemate of the Cold War. Western Europe's integration with itself was a nested and well-protected integration – Marshal Aid, the Berlin Wall, NATO and the Soviet (Warsaw Pact) Army guaranteed the peaceful, step by step and undisturbed process of building new institutions, introducing legal guarantees and creating the largest single market of the world. Liberal democracies nurtured upon that base became attractive models for many countries, especially in East Central Europe: it seemed – especially from the outside – that welfare and democracy were inseparable.

1989 – as unexpected and undesired as it was for the beneficiaries of this *status quo* – created completely new conditions: the Berlin Wall collapsed, the Soviet Union dissolved, the logic of bipolarity disappeared. The entire Eastern border of the European Communities became open; both in the physical and political sense. Helmut Kohl, an apt politician, jumped on the bandwagon. German reunification, interpreted as the first step towards Eastern Enlargement, started building immediately upon the debris of the Berlin Wall. What belonged together started to grow together but nobody seemed to care too much about what did not belong together and therefore could not integrate. It was neither politically nor morally possible to deny the right of post-Solidarnosc Poland, post-Charta 77 Czechoslovakia and post-Kadarist Hungary, to "belong to Europe" or in a more profane way, to access the integration process. After the collapse of the Soviet Union the same was true in the case of the Baltic Republics. It was possible to postpone the date of enlargement but it was not possible to avoid it. Maybe due to the lack of sufficient time, but most likely thanks to the lack of enough interest, political will and wisdom, potential challenges caused by an immense increase in diversity, were not discussed or understood and were rather swept under carpet by both Eurocrats and their experts, gurus and advisors in the Brussels labyrinth and by old-new political elites of transition and accession countries of East and Central Europe.

The inapplicability of the old community method under completely new circumstances, was overlooked by the masters of Eastern enlargement. By formally accepting the *Acquis Communautaire* as well as the economic conditions dictated by the EU, the accession countries contributed significantly to the enlargement of the European Single Market, without contributing to the creation of a European demos and a clear-cut European polity.

The number of European market-citizens grew significantly while their identification with the European project stagnated with rapidly fading illusions about material progress. Democracy and welfare was decoupled, causing disillusionment, apathy and anger first mostly in "New Europe," and then with the escalation of global crisis, everywhere.

Economic calculations behind the political ornament proved to be wrong: poor and exposed countries as proper peripheries might contribute to economic stability of the centres in the short term, but increasingly complex diversity has destabilising effects on social and political integration processes in the medium term. The boomerang effects of the one-sided and not well thought out enlargement were felt immediately after the Big Bang and were exacerbated together with many other symptoms of the global crisis.

III. Consequences and Perspectives

The exhaustion of the Community method combined with the lack of understanding of the importance of deep cultural determinants of social and economic change ("ligatures" in Ralf Dahrendorf's terminology) became a major impediment for deepening social and political integration. National democracies, emptied out by international guardian institutions including the unaccountable institutions of the EU, became "no-choice democracies" with increasingly frustrated citizens who felt disempowered and paralysed at the national level and, at the same time, never empowered as European citizens at the transnational level. As a consequence, Europe has to face a double democracy deficit, a primary source of its escalating and deepening political crisis.

Instead of offering an alternative model of regional integration to the unregulated system of the global economy and its discredited ideology of market fundamentalism, Europe remained exposed to and entrapped by financial market players and neo-liberal economic policies. As a result, it de facto turned against its own aspiration to implement the European Social Model and equal out regional disparities. The East-West divide as well as the North-South divide is stronger – or at least more obvious – today than before 2004/2005. The process of neo-peripherialisation, conducted by German-led ordo-liberalism, has provoked national resistance and led to a further and sharp decline of public trust in both national and European institutions.

The political landscape of Europe is equally intriguing and troublesome. Propagating an obscurant and misleading ideology called the "third way," the left became captivated by neo-liberalism and had less and less to offer to its voters. Facing the devastating social consequences of the crisis, it does not have an agenda. Differences between centre left and centre right are continuously diminishing, while inward-lookingness, xenophobia, racism and exclusivist tendencies are strengthening in both visible and invisible ways. As a consequence, rightwing populism as well as extremism has been on the rise during the past half decade almost everywhere in Europe, including in model democracies such as France, Holland, Denmark, Sweden and Finland. *De facto* solidarity is shrinking instead of expanding, as if the spirit of Marie Le Pen is about to replace the spirit of Jean Monnet.

Instead of deepening integration, the famous Franco-German engine now represented by the Merkozy-Sarkel tandem brought the EU to the fringe of disintegration. Where does the road lead from here? Will Europe blow up, as some of its rivals and adversaries hope and suggest, or are there options and alternatives for reinventing itself?

In a recently published paper about the possible scenarios of Europe's self-invention, Marc Leonard heralds the "near collapse of the EU's political system."[4] Not referring to his earlier prediction about Europe's leading global role in the 21st century, Leonard puts forward four alternative scenarios: what he calls "asymmetric integration," the creation of a "smaller, more integrated eurozone," a "political union through treaty change" and finally a "deal among the vanguard" (a Schengen-type treaty).

These scenarios are based upon the tacit assumption that the elite driven integration can be continued with the same methods and in the same spirit. In my understanding this is not the case, since the lack of democratic legitimacy and therefore the lack of trust in transnational decision-making, procedures and institutions, are among the deep causes of the present failure of the European construction. Instead of being based upon the economic, financial and power interests of an elite which has proven to be incapable of transnational leadership, a real alternative should be based upon a new concept and vision of democracy which combines the deep human aspirations for wellbeing and dignity; in other words, a combination of economic, social and legal/institutional aspects

4 Leonard, M., *Four Scenarios for the Reinvention of Europe*, European Council on Foreign Relations, November, 2011, available at http://www.ecfr.eu/ (last visited 28 May 2012).

of democracy. The new method for further construction needs to be based upon social and cultural constructivism, a permanent feedback and consideration of the different and at the same time changing values of stakeholder societies. Europeans can escape the iron cage of their nation states only if they are able to find their belonging in a larger, transnational social space. The "cold projects" of the market and of open society (to borrow Dahrendorf's words again) combined with and guaranteed by European institutions, are unable to offer this feeling of belonging and thus do not contribute to a stronger European identity.

The process of an emerging European demos and clear-cut polity might not be fast or easy and certainly is not possible without conflict. In fact the democratisation of the European project presupposes the politicisation of the rather empty European public space. Transnational – European political movements, networks, coalitions of civil organisations, etc, need to move into this vacuum to compete for the support of an increasingly transnational post-national public and by doing so must define and redefine the European public good.

Europe's political and social turbulence, amplified by the global financial and economic crisis as well as by the crisis of democracy, has paved the way for a new public discourse and deliberation. Strongly institutionalised neo-liberalism, rapidly growing national populism and escalating far right parties and movements need to be challenged and counterbalanced by newly emerging or reinvigorated democratic movements capable of representing the interests and aspirations of local, national and regional societies.

IV. No Alternatives Without Self-reflection

In 2000 I had the honour to participate in the Reflection Group on Eastern Enlargement, led by Jacques Delors. After a short introduction during our personal conversation over dinner, Delors showed great interest about East and Central European countries preparing for accession and the next morning he asked me about my view of Central Europe and my major concerns about Eastern enlargement during the group's working session. I briefly summarised the dangers of the historically-based cultural differences and the developmental gap between Western and East-Central Europe and suggested a cautious, well-negotiated, step-by-step enlargement which would better guarantee proper social, economic and political integration. Otherwise, I said, the EU might lose face and Eastern enlargement could lead to failure. "Wishful thinking" – was the short comment of the former (and probably last) legendary head of the Commission. The debate was over.

It took me a while after this episode to understand that the major questions of enlargement, i.e., its size and timing, had been already decided: Big Bang (10 countries) in one step instead of the original three-to four and a step-by step formula. The details about the process and major stakeholders of the decision-making, however, remained unknown. Our discussions in the Reflection Group, whose meetings lasted for a year and a half, were summarised in a publication with the interesting title: "The Political Dimensions of Eastern Enlargement," but the Group's impact on the course of events was most likely less then minimal.

After a long period of silence, in April 2012, Delors, the father of the Euro and Economic and Monetary Union (EMU), published a self-reflective article in *Tribune*: "For a Revival of Europe."[5] In the article he acknowledges the "decline of Europe" *vis-à-vis* the world as a whole and that the euro and the EMU are in a "difficult stranglehold situation." Delors tries to learn the lessons of the past and understand what went wrong and who was responsible for the present state of affairs. He notes that the uncontrolled single market with a single currency gave rise to increasing and in the end unmanageable diversification, out of which basically one country, the economically mightiest and most efficient, benefited – Germany.

The EU is supposed to celebrate the 20th anniversary of the Single Market this year, which, in Delors' design, was based on three notions: competition (which stimulates), co-operation (which strengthens), and solidarity (which unites). The roots of the present European crisis lie in the malfunctioning of this theoretical mode: out of the three assumptions only competition has been realised. The EMU in Delors' view functioned well until 2007, but could not resist the global crisis since it did not have an economic pillar. Since the co-ordination of economic policies did not work, nothing has counterbalanced the power of the European Central Bank (ECB), which, according to German interests, only pursued price stability. Besides making the ECB as well as heads of national banks responsible for the lack of co-ordination and the neglect of amounting public debt as well as lack of financial stability, Delors points to his own responsibility as well. He thinks it was naïve to believe in "co-operation" in the absence of supranational federalist governmental guarantees. Indeed, neither co-operation, nor solidarity came out of this elite-driven model, dominated and controlled by multinational companies and global financial players besides the European Central Bank.

5 Delors, J., "For a Revival of Europe," in *Tribune, Notre Europe,* 11 April 2012, based on the speech delivered at the meeting of the S&D group of the European Parliament on 28 March 2012, available at www.notre-europe.eu (last visited 6 June 2012).

Delors believes that he learnt the lesson: "Economic and social union should have been reinforced at the initiative of EMU," and besides, the common currency is not possible without a minimum of federation – as he was warned by American economists before the introduction of the Euro. But to suggest that the implementation of the federalist scenario would have failed at the time when Delors was the president of the Commission – at least he was convinced that it would have been rejected by the nation states – is a hypothesis that cannot be proved or falsified retrospectively. It seems that a profound and multifaceted crisis had to arrive to throw light on the weaknesses and exhaustion of the old methods of pursuing elite driven, non-democratic integration. The time has arrived. It seems that all of a sudden everyone seems to be surprised although almost everyone knew it was unavoidable.

This new era is the time of politics at the transnational European level: the politicisation of the vacuous or rather empty European public space. Since early 2012 there have been a lot of suggestions and claims for the reinvigoration of a rather paralysed left, which is sandwiched between a neo-liberal ideology and the old labour paradigm. Many authors (Francis Fukuyama, George Schopflin, John Palmer, etc.), independently from their political belonging, suggest that the left does not have an agenda and therefore cannot offer relevant answers to the formidable challenges caused by the manifold crisis. They also conclude – and one cannot but agree with this – that this is the moment for the reformulation of a new agenda, on all possible levels of political activity, but most prominently on the European level. In this crisis situation Delors himself turns to politics, suggesting that Europe is at the beginning "of an offensive of social democracy in the broadest sense […]."

As a result of less obvious, more undercurrent social and cultural processes of Europeanisation, everyday co-operation among civil society activists, student movements, professional circles, artists, journalists and public intellectuals has become routine. The open question of the European social and political crisis is whether the emerging European society will provide enough of a basis and framework for a new public discourse and the politicisation of the empty European public space, or whether Europeans will choose to submerge themselves in their national and sub-national interests.

Against all odds the European construction can be continued if Europe finds a new method and is able to step out from the double trap of neo-liberal economic policies and rightwing populism. Debating, deliberating and identifying the new European public good might conclude in a new politics of de facto solidarity. But this has to be seen clearly: the social contract upon which democratic decision-making is built, has been broken or seriously damaged in most of the member states of the EU. At the same time, it does not exist on the EU level. To recover Europe from the present social, political and economic turmoil, new social contracts are needed on all levels of governance. For this to happen, a broad consensus is needed within and among European societies about the European project. Amidst the present apathy, scepticism, frustration and inward-looking tendencies, the chances for such a broad social and political agreement are slim. But for exactly the same reasons, the politicisation of the European public space is inevitable. In the vortex of the downward spiral, alternatives are popping up. Europe has arrived at its political moment. It can no longer be disguised that alongside national democracies the left has emptied out as well. Its main stream being entrapped in neo-liberalism, it lacks a credible agenda. If it falls back to the old state-socialist, distributive paradigm, its revival won't last very long. If it opens up towards other progressive groups and new initiatives – including those social movements or subterranean networks who deliberately chose to stay outside the "system" – it will enhance the chances for renewal and getting rid of old hierarchical and vertical power structures as well as obsolete dogmas and attitudes toward society and social change. In a sense, the global crisis and especially the crisis of Europe, is crying out for new visions and is thus offering a great chance for progressive forces to come out of their trenches and deadlocks.

This alternative is not a given, it won't occur as a natural side effect of the crisis. It needs political will, courage and imagination, which presupposes self-reflection. New coalition building would have a significant impact on public discourse and political culture. It could prove the willingness of different old and new, post-modern, post national etc. players to take responsibility in a social sense and on a social scale both on national and supranational levels. New European alternatives and new coalition building might not occur within the imagined "left." In the spirit of the founding fathers like Spinelli and Spaak, a broader coalition of democratic post-nationalist political forces is inevitable, as is evident from recent calls and memorandums of the European Movement and other pro-European organisations. The lingering questions of this New European Political Movement is if, when and how these different fragments, isolated parties, marginalised, self-entrenched, subterranean networks can emerge and create a political platform in the sense of a European People's Assembly.

There are no clear answers to these questions. There are no guarantees that this will happen and if it happens, that it will be successful. Grasping a political moment also means taking risks; creating long lasting and effective new coalitions requires self-limitation and getting rid of the narcissism and self-justification of political fragments and social movements. Democracy itself needs renewal or rather rebirth. As an outcome of the present global and European turmoil, the processes of fundamental social, political and economic transformations will accelerate. At the end of this robust transformation we might have more, but possibly also less democracy. A European renewal would certainly push the pendulum of global democratisation.

V. Conclusion

Building efficient and long lasting institutions marked by high levels of public trust needs special methods which correspond to the logic of a given historic period's techno-economic paradigm and legal-political regulations and needs to be adjustable both to the conditions of the international system and that of the expectations of stakeholder participants. Looking at the no longer short history of the European integration, one can observe that its first period ended with 1989, the collapse of the bipolar logic of the political and military world system, out of which a transformation process began that concluded in 2004/2005 with Big Bang eastern enlargement and that, symbolically enough, was immediately followed by the collapse of the process of European constitutionalisation by the double "no" votes in Holland and France. During the third – rather short – period, the process of integration, or rather construction, has reached a critical point where its previously and partly hidden contradictions and weaknesses, first of all the exhaustion of the community method, have become clear.

The crisis of the EU developed from a fiscal debt crisis to the crisis of the Euro zone and soon thereafter into a complex social and political crisis whose end and consequences are not yet foreseeable. The global financial and economic crisis hit the EU in a moment of rapidly increasing diversification, disorientation and regional disparities when its polarising single market was not counterbalanced and coupled with common or co-ordinated economic policies. Neither was it extended by de facto solidarity from its centre towards its periphery. Lacking legitimate and accountable supranational governance, good leadership and crisis management capabilities, the EU has embarked on a self-destructive phase.

Any further attempt and co-ordinated aspiration to continue the European construction will depend on the capability of European democracies and social, economic and political actors to reach a new consensus about the European public good, redefining the scope, the speed and the method of integration. The European construction has arrived at a turning point. Europe is a complex system that requires the identification of new ways and methods, complex thinking, understanding and analysis. Oversimplified, one-sided and superficial "solutions," such as further austerity measures, treaty amendments or introducing new fiscal policies, will not be able to serve as real therapies but might instead further exacerbate and speed up the already dangerously fast downward spiral.

There is nothing 'natural' about the European construction; neither markets, nor will individual nation states be able to provide automatic solutions. Quite the opposite, so-called 'solutions' reflect particular vested interests against the neglected and vanishing European public good. They are rather the causes of problems than viable remedies. The new paradigm – or "development model," in Delors' words, requires the understanding of increased interdependence and the acceptance of the growing uncertainties of our age. Alternatives can be worked out and legitimated by the major players and stakeholders of the European project only in open social debates and deliberations.

Bibliography

Bauman, Z., *Europe, an Unfinished Adventure*, Polity, 2004.

Barber, B., *Fear's Empire; War, Terrorism and Democracy*, W.W Norton, New York, 2003.

Collignion, S., *Democracy and Europe's crisis of legitimacy*, www.stefancollignon.de, 2006.

Grant, C., *A time of Austerity and German Leadership*, Centre for European Reform, 2012.

Habermas, J., "Europe's Post-democratic Era," in *The Guardian*, November 10, 2011.

Hughes, K., "EU Democracy in Crisis," in *Open Democracy*, January 16, 2011.

Jones, E., "No Four Leaves Cover for Europe," in *ALDE Europe*, December 2011.

Krastev, I., "Europe's Democracy Paradox," in *Democracy Digest*, February 28, 2012.

Laqueuer, W., *After the Fall. The End of the European Dream and the Decline of a Continent*, Macmillan, 2012.

Menon, A., "Europe's coming political crisis, E'Sharp," in *ALDE Europe*, December 2011.

Overholt, W., "The Price for German Leadership," in *International Economy*, Winter 2012.

Palmer, J., "EU voters may finally be given some real choices," in *Open Democracy*, March 22, 2012.

Rifkin, J., *The European Dream*, Jenny P. Tarcher/Penguin New York, 2004.

Rogoff, K., "The End of Europe," in *Time*, August 2011.

Schmidt, V., *Democracy in Europe*, Oxford University Press, 2006.

Schmitter, P. C., *How to Democratize the EU and why Bother?* London, New York, Rowmen and Littlefield, 2000.

A Value-Driven European Future: an Education Perspective of the European Civitas

Léonce BEKEMANS

Jean Monnet Chair "Globalisation, Intercultural Dialogue and Inclusiveness in the EU," Academic co-ordinator of the Jean Monnet Centre of Excellence "Intercultural Dialogue, Human Rights and Multi-level Governance," University of Padua

In UNESCO's Constitution, the key concept of equal human dignity is one of the basic pillars of the "democratic principles" of justice, equality and solidarity – "intellectual and moral solidarity" in order to be able to ensure that educated human beings are "free and responsible" (UNESCO 1945: Article I). The Universal Declaration of Human Rights, adopted by the General Assembly of the United Nations on 10th December 1948, provides directions on how to behave in order to respect human dignity and equality. It is indispensable therefore to better share not only material goods, but knowledge and experience and most of all – wisdom. In a humanity committed to its common destiny, dialogue means to fully express our views and to listen to those of others. Dialogue is to respect and to show respect for views completely opposite to our own ideas, to interact with all partners in a setting of mutual learning. A value-driven and education perspective of the European future is therefore of crucial importance.[1]

Education at various formal, informal and non-formal levels of learning, should foster a culture of peace, understanding and dialogue. This might finally lead to an active and responsible citizenship-building, which favours the integral human development perspective of education. It is important to recall the major characteristics of the socio-cultural transformations that are challenging education in the global and European context:

1 See Reflection Group on the Future of the EU 2030, *Project Europe 2030, Challenges and Opportunities*, May 2010.

– (neo) liberalism: a society based exclusively on markets and laws leads to a commodification, marketisation and monitarisation of societies and human relations;

– democratic practices and the challenge of multi-level governance are confronted with a plural vision of the world and human beings;

– existence of multi-cultural societies: the recognition of this multi-culturality implies the need for an interdisciplinary language, for new concepts, approaches and mechanism and for pedagogy to learn to dialogue and to manage diversity towards interculturality;

– the growing complexity of our societies leads to growing uncertainties and human (economic, social, political, etc.) insecurity. This existential situation of instability produces a crisis of the sense of belonging at a social level (i.e. growing individualism, the principle of the predominance of "I," individual and collective egoism) as much as at the cultural level (i.e. cultural relativism, attitudes of indifference, neglect and intolerance);

– the Globalisation vs. Europeanisation debate shapes the nature of internal and external relations within and beyond Europe with consequences for leaning competences and "good" citizenship-building at the European and global level.

In short, the ongoing interaction between these societal characteristics leads to increasing pluralism, to the need for reading the signs of our time and of quickly changing societies, and for responding to the challenges of our fragmented, post-modern culture with a new culture of education and citizenship. Moreover, the role and responsibility of education in multi-cultural and complex societies rooted in a community of shared values should reinforce the overall substance of the challenges: the search for adequate and concrete responses in the learning agenda dealing with education and active citizenship.

Premises: Value Premises of a European Civitas

Europe is a multi-faceted and multi-dimensional society exhibiting multiple characteristics. Therefore it is important to identify the general principles of the European Civitas as a community in dealing with education and citizenship. We are aware that these principles have to be understood and translated within the globalisation context that often produces changing and paradoxical realities. They have an impact on current European identity, citizenship and solidarity building.

1) European Civitas as a Community of Destiny: the process of European civilisation has led to an increasing interdependence and complexity of interactions and relations, which shape our common

destiny in a globalising world. The maintenance of peace, the conservation of the environment, and the means to enable people to live their lives with dignity, all demand common policies. Unifying Europe in diversity is the response to past suffering and the challenge of history. All Europeans are called upon to work responsibly together to build a peaceful European order. The concrete realities of every day however, illustrate a growing tension and differentiation amongst member and non-member States as to the role, responsibility and finality of Europe within the global context.

2) European Civitas as a Community of Values: the aim of European integration and inclusion is to carry out, test, develop and safeguard the community of shared values. These are rooted in common legal principles, acknowledging the freedom of individual and social responsibility. Fundamental European values are based on tolerance, humanity and fraternity. Building on its historical roots in classical antiquity and Christianity, Europe further developed these values during the course of history, which finally led to the development of democracy, the recognition of fundamental and human rights and the rule of law, now enshrined in binding legal frameworks.

The great currents of culture and art, the scientific discoveries and their application for the common good, as well as the critical analysis of accepted views and perceptions have created an area of freedom, justice and democracy. These principles for international relations have opened the way to a free and peaceful future. However, Europe has repeatedly called these values into question, causing conflicts and wars. Therefore, in the name of the preservation of the collective memory, intellectual, cultural and artistic built and non-built heritage needs to be cherished and protected in treaties, programmes and projects. Potential conflicts can then be overcome through the European dialogues framework, peace-building and non-conflict initiatives, reciprocal understanding and mutual learning processes, thereby stimulating a sense of common purpose and an awareness of a shared European identity.

European identity requires the free exchange of persons and ideas, and finds its expression in the common protection of our values. The 1950 Convention for Human Rights and Fundamental Freedoms, the EC Charter of Fundamental Social Rights of 1989, the creation of European Union citizenship by the Treaty of Maastricht and the European Charter of Human Rights, constitute important steps towards consolidating a European community of shared values. The promotion of European citizenship however, should be conceived as part of global citizenship.

A truly good European citizen, assimilating multiple identities, is therefore a good global citizen within cosmopolitan thought.[2]

3) European Civitas as a Community of Life: in order for the European Union to become a citizens' Europe it must develop into a tangible, living community. To that end, citizens must be given the opportunity to participate more fully in the process of European integration. A unified Europe implies further developing European citizenship to the point at which all citizens in all member states have the same rights and duties. The democratic and federal structures must therefore be strengthened and individual decision-making procedures and policies made more transparent. All citizens must be informed of important proposals for reforms at an early stage, and be involved in the public debate.

Therefore, a cultural and education policy fostering European identity is necessary for the Union and its member states. While drawing attention to common roots and values, as well as to Europe's diversity, the aim must be to develop a spirit of tolerance, dialogue and mutual learning towards other people and cultures, to convince all citizens of the European idea, and to enable them to play their part in the process of European integration. This should be favoured at formal, informal and non-formal levels of learning.

4) European Civitas as an Economic and Social Community: the first steps were taken when six countries founded the European Coal and Steel Community in which basic industries important for the conduct of war were placed under a common authority. This neo-functional approach resulted in the European Economic Community, and eventually the European Union, in a process that led to peace between the member states and a higher standard of living.

The driving force behind European integration was economic, though it has become clear that achievement in this field alone is insufficient for the development of a European identity. It implies that the social objectives of the economy must be identifiable. Therefore, a social community is an essential aspect of European identity and would lead – for reasons of internal and external solidarity – to sustainably cohesive societies. European governance on economic, fiscal and environmental issues has become central to Europe's responsibilities in these present confusing times.

5) European Civitas as a Community of Purpose and Responsibility: in today's globalising and individualising world, the European Union carries a particular responsibility. The European continent has close

[2] Beck, U., *Cosmopolitan Vision*, Cambridge, Polity Press, 2006; Beck, U. and Grande, E., *Cosmopolitan Europe*, Cambridge, Polity Press, 2007.

economic, political and cultural ties with many regions of the world, set in various co-operation agreements. Conflicts and crises – whether within or beyond our continent – threaten both European states and citizens alike. Only through co-operation, solidarity and unity, can Europe effectively help to solve world problems. Discord in European policies would be irresponsible and can only lead to chaos.

Global responsibility has various dimensions. It means responsible co-operation in conflict prevention and mediation within the scope of the common foreign and security policy, neighbourhood and development policy. However, this also includes conducting trade and ecological negotiations with other regions of the world in a fair and helpful manner. In accordance with its values and its policy of peaceful integration, the European Union should set an example, in particular in relation to upholding human rights and the protection of minorities. By this means, Europe can remain true to its own heritage.

6) European Civitas as a Community and Meeting Place of Multiple Identities: freedom, peace, dignity of mankind, equality and social justice are Europe's greatest common goods. To protect and further develop these aims, Europe needs a morally acceptable political structure and policies which strengthen the sense of common purpose while establishing the credibility of the European Union and making its citizens proud to be Europeans through the building of meeting places and the recognition of the wealth of its multiple identities. When that point has been reached, then a stronger, an added, European identity will also exist. In this perspective, the city dimension becomes more and more a space of recognition and true citizenship-building. Reality shows how individuals are bound to territorial places to define and contextualise their identity, within the combined global-local aspects of globalisation. Cities have become laboratories of conviviality and living together with all the problems and opportunities multicultural societies offer.[3]

7) Europe as a Community of Multicultural Learning: in order to build up a common European identity as an added value, a common background and future is needed, one which takes into account the specific multilayered and diversified institutional and cultural European context. This however implies enough sharing to create a multicultural learning space that supports integration and human integral development. Although a legal framework exists in which education/learning is set in the European context, there still exists a

---

3 Bekemans, L., "Urban Environment of Intercultural Dialogue: Why Cities Matter in Building a Democratic 'Urban Civitas'," in Bekemans, L. *et al.* (eds.), *Intercultural Dialogue and Citizenship. Translating Values into Actions. A Common Project for Europeans and their Partners*, Venice, Marsilio, March 2007, pp. 113-134.

problem of "*closer information*" about the principles and practices of Europe, as well as a problem of a too limited European dimension of education, referring to basic knowledge of the European space and environment. These problems seem paradoxical when the living reality of daily experience refers to an unaware europeanness, which could increase the awareness of a European citizenship and the multi-faceted identity of Europe.

This paper is divided in two main parts. The first part deals with the conceptual context and content of the European Civitas. We present major guidelines and a few intercultural practices for building a sustainable value-driven European future that might shape the European Civitas. The second part focuses more on the education perspective of the European Civitas. It analyses the role, responsibility and objectives of education paying particular attention to citizenship education in its European and cultural dimension.

I. The European Civitas

A. The Conceptual Context

The concept of the "European Civitas" refers to the combined and overlapping themes of inclusion, integration and diversity. It is said that integration cannot be achieved without inclusion and that a society that exhibits respect for diversity and dialogue needs both integration and inclusion. The concept links the "demos" with the "polis," embodies these three interlinked phenomena in a given community and applies it to the city level.

Inclusion is defined as people's capability to participate fully in economic, social and political life. The growing interest in the inclusion of wider social, cultural and environmental concerns into all areas and levels of policy-making has led to the adoption of the now fashionable term of mainstreaming. As a consequence, policies have moved from a narrow basic human needs approach to a wider view of an inclusive and cohesive society.

The essence of integration is the acceptance and tolerance of and respect for people possessing different values and beliefs who behave differently; while at the same time being committed to a common future in which all will have a fair share. Living with differences in societies requires the management of differences. In order to live together in a cohesive community with different cultures, synchronisation in public spaces is necessary to prevent open conflict and promote co-operation and a sense of belonging to the community. We perceive integration therefore not as a flattening process of assimilation but as a two-way process, based on a framework of basic values, in which equal opportunity, cultural diversity and mutual tolerance are respected.

Furthermore, the European context implies that integration is understood from within its existing multicultural environment. Multiculturalism advocates that society allows and includes distinct cultural groups with equal status but differing cultural identities. A useful reminder in this perspective is the distinction Amartya Sen makes in his book "*Identity and Violence*" between the idea of cultural liberty, which focuses on the freedom either to preserve or to change priorities, and that of valuing cultural conservation.[4] In reality, multicultural practices sometimes lead to an entrenchment of cultural identity, a "ghettoisation" of particular groups or a policy of separate development of ethnic minorities.

Diversity is a much more nebulous concept than inclusion or integration. Within the context of this paper diversity is defined as recognising, appreciating, valuing and utilising the unique talents and contributions of all individuals regardless of their differences in values, beliefs and lifestyles, culture, language, religion, etc. Diversity means more than just acknowledging and/or tolerating differences. The Human Development Report 2004 of the UNDP refers to a set of conscious practices that involve:

> a) understanding and appreciating interdependence of humanity, cultures, and the natural environment; b) practising mutual respect for qualities and experiences that are different from our own; c) understanding that diversity includes not only ways of being but also ways of knowing; d) recognising that personal, cultural and institutionalised discrimination creates and sustains privileges for some while creating and sustaining disadvantages for others; and e) building alliances across differences so that we can work together to eradicate all forms of discrimination.[5]

The Report concludes that an enriching effect of the recognition of diversity for democracy and progress can be obtained through building multicultural democracies and various forms of advanced democracy.[6]

B. Conceptual Guiding Lines

We believe that the future of the European Civitas should be characterised by a number of shaping trends that will determine Europe's future.

---

4 Sen, A., *Identity and Violence. The Illusion of Destiny*, New York, W.W. Norton, 2006.

5 UNDP, *Human Development Report 2004*: *Cultural Liberty in Today's Diverse World,* New York, Oxford University Press, 2005, Ch.1.

6 *Ibidem*, Ch. 3.

1. Moving from Multiculturalism to Interculturalism

In accepting "European Civitas" as the underlying vision for linking intercultural dialogue with citizenship, we propose an anthropological definition of culture as one's capital, creativity and way of life.[7] Three main functions of culture can be distinguished: i) The conservation of culture, culture as an asset, tangible or intangible and a carrier of local identity. Its protection against territorial and market trends shapes the urban context; ii) The production of culture: culture as a commodity which needs to be re-produced not only to reconstitute the cultural capital but also as a source of economic development insofar as it is embedded in production processes; and iii) The valorisation of culture: culture as a set of norms and capacities which enrich the local communities and may be used as bridge builders and carriers of good relations for social and economic exchange. A dynamic and interactive process between these three functions of culture implies not only the peaceful co-existence of different cultures within society but also a mutually influencing and open dialogue between cultures.[8] Such a conceptual change from multicultural co-existence to intercultural dialogue may avoid the trap of cultural relativism and provide the base of an interreligious dialogue.

2. Recognising Multi-faceted Identities and Cosmopolitan Citizenship[9]

The debate concerning identity and citizenship is crucial for understanding the role of intercultural dialogue in developing advanced forms of democracy. Identity-building is not a constant and invariable process, but changes over time according to criteria such as birth, family, language, religion, territory, etc. This process has become even more complex and disturbed by growing individualisation, intolerant and distrustful behaviour, as well as by the vagueness of the moral norms within society. In short, identity is becoming more and more a relation identity with no exclusive characteristics in modern societies.

The inclusion of a European dimension as an added (enriched) value to our relation identity reinforces our conceptual point of departure.

---

7 Stavenhagen, R., "Cultural Rights: a Social Science Perspective," in *Culture Rights and Wrongs*, Paris, UNESCO, 1998.

8 Parekh, B., *Rethinking Multiculturalism. Cultural Diversity and Political Theory*, London, Macmillan, 2000.

9 Stevenson, N., *Cultural Citizenship: Cosmopolitan Questions,* Maidenhead, Open University Press, 2003; Bekemans, L., "A Cosmopolitan Perspective of Multi-level Govenance," in Bekemans, L. (ed.), *Intercultural Dialogue and Multi-level Governance in Europe. A Human Rights Based Approach*, Brussels, PI.E. Peter Lang, 2012, pp. 163-186.

Multiplicity is therefore the basis of European identity, shaped by a community of shared values (such as solidarity, the rule of law, respect for diversity, attention to the person and the human dignity). This enriching effect is certainly true for the cultural identity, which binds and unifies countries, regions and groups of persons by shared memories and expectations. The political meaning of the recognition of multi-faceted identities lies in mutual respect for the uniqueness of the person. It constitutes the basis for more and certainly better dialogue and solidarity within and outside Europe, rooted in the universal human rights paradigm.[10]

3. *Humanising Globalisation*[11]

A process of humanising globalisation, defined as a multi-faceted phenomenon and process, provides another guideline for the "European Civitas." The mainly economically dominated globalisation process has led to a commodification and depersonalisation of economic and social relations, a radical decrease of the power of states in managing socio-economic activities and an increasing control of democratic societies by transnational networks. Europe is however not an exclusive economic space, but in the first place a community of shared values, which is forced to re-visit its premises in a newly emerging geo-political and economic setting.[12]

Dealing responsively with the various consequences of globalisation is based on a common pattern of values and mutual respect of differences. A more "compassionate globalisation"[13] (or a cosmopolite humanism) is required against any cultural relativism. Structures are needed that create both zones of common interests and shared values, for civilised confrontation and disagreement. At the same time, different cultures need to re-examine their own realities in the context of globalisation in order to re-locate themselves in this new reality. This implies the emergence of a global consciousness and the acceptance of

10 Papisca, A., "Droits de la Personne et Démocratie – Les Cultures à la Source de l'Universel," in European Commission DG EAC, *Intercultural Dialogue*, Luxembourg, Office for Official Publications of the European Commission, March 2002, pp. 132-140.

11 Baudot, J., *Building a World Community: Globalisation and the Common Good*, Copenhagen, Royal Danish Ministry of Foreign Affairs, June 2000, p. 272.

12 Bekemans, L., "The Idea and Practice of Europe in a Globalising World: Reality and Responsibility," in *Pace Diritti Umani/Peace Human Rights*, vol. 1, April 2004, pp. 121-133.

13 Falk, R., "Realizing the Copenhagen Vision: The Political Imperative," in J. Baudot, *Building a World Community: Globalisation and the Common Good*, *op. cit.*, pp. 156-166.

multi-faceted identities and multiple modernities.[14] The role of education is herein fundamental through the introduction of learning processes that replace a culture of competition, distrust and fear with a culture of co-operation, peace and mutual respect.

4. Revalorising the Role of Cultures in Europe

In accepting an anthropological definition of culture we identify European culture(s) as a dynamic interaction of the historic, spiritual, religious, intellectual, material and artistic characteristics and attitudes. These characteristics illustrate the multiplicity and wealth of European cultures, cultural expressions and traditions. These diversified but shared cultural expressions finally make up Europe's social, cultural and human capital. This cultural multiplicity is also a source of inner strength and outer pride. No culture can be missed in the European cultural landscape.

Although Europe is pre-eminently a space of cultural diversity, respect for cultural diversity should not lead to ethnic reflexes and exclusive attitudes. The binding role of an internal and external open culture approach is to be a guarantee for further European integration and a renewed co-operation with other cultures. As a consequence, we conceive culture in the first place as a source of inspiration for social integration, socio-economic development and societal inclusion. It certainly may give an impulse to greater commitment and participation of the citizen to the European project.

5. Stimulating Intercultural Dialogue[15]

The term intercultural dialogue is strongly normative and is seen as a pathway towards the goal of attaining ways of living together in diversity. Ray Isar's definition[16] of intercultural dialogue as an inherently normative and voluntaristic practice of "learning to live together,"[17] very well suits the purpose of this paper. Intercultural dialogue can be instrumental in softening and avoiding the (negative)

---

14 Eisenstadt, S., "The Dialogue Between Cultures or Between Cultural Interpretations of Modernity – Multiple Modernities on The Contemporary Scene," in European Commission DG EAC, *Intercultural Dialogue*, *op. cit.*, pp. 59-68.

15 World Commission on Culture and Development, *Our Creative Diversity*, Paris, UNESCO Publishing, 1996; European Commission DG EAC, *Intercultural Dialogue*, *op. cit.*; UNDP, *Human Development Report 2004, op. cit.*; Council of Europe, *White Paper on Intercultural Dialogue "Living Together As Equals in Dignity*," Strasbourg, 7 May 2008.

16 Isar, Y. R., "The Intercultural Challenge: an Imperative of Solidarity," in European Commission DG EAC, *Intercultural Dialogue*, *op. cit.*, pp. 169-183.

17 This concept was used by the Delors International Commission on Education for the 21st Century, in *Learning: The Treasure within*, Paris, UNESCO, 1998.

consequences of the globalisation process (i.e. the issue of minorities, migration, poverty, etc.). A dialogue between peoples and cultures can also be constructive if it is based on common and moral values. In the current tension between (economic) globalisation, need for internal and external solidarity, and respect for different cultures and religions, such a dialogue can be a vehicle for conviviality in which cultures influence each other without destroying each other or clashing with each other.

As to the specific European dimension of intercultural dialogue, it is clear that Europe as a global actor has an important responsibility in enabling and facilitating intercultural dialogue.[18] Europe should be a communicative bridge builder and a boundaries-breaker in such a dialogue. The specificity of the underlying characteristics of the European model is much related to mutual understanding and learning in open dialogue. Within this context initiatives have been taken and policies developed to reinforce the dialogue between peoples, cultures and civilisations.[19] As such, intercultural dialogue is an integrative force of (re-) creating the European Civitas and providing urban spaces for interreligious dialogue.

6. Promoting Creative Urban Realities

Cities can be seen in today's Europe as major vehicles for creating a European Civitas, representing local communities of diversified values and practices at the citizen level. They are changing places, where tradition is continuously confronted with modernity. Today they may offer inclusive environments for practising democratic citizenship and dialogue. Urban realities are increasingly playing a role in stimulating creativity for economic, social, political and cultural development. Cities are breeding grounds for inclusion, integration and diversity and are a major shaping actor in the promotion of intercultural dialogue and finally in building a European Civitas.

The specificity of the urban context is determined by the various governance levels that move from hierarchical to networking relations. Conditions of urban policies that respond to this renewed role of cities as reference frames in economy, polity, society and culture, are

---

18 Bekemans, L., "Culture vs. Globalisation in Europe: Actual Tension or Possible Dialogue?," in L. Anckaert, D. Cassimon and H. Opdebeeck (eds.), *Building Towers. Perspectives on Globalisation,* Leuven, Peeters, Oct. 2002, pp. 191-211; *id.*, "Globalisation and Solidarity: Europe's Duty in Intercultural Dialogue," in *Intercultural Dialogue*, *op. cit*., pp. 152-168.

19 High-Level Advisory Group, European Commission, *Dialogue Between Peoples and Cultures in the Euro-Mediterranean Region*, 2003; Bekemans, L. *et al.* (eds.), *Intercultural Dialogue and Citizenship*, *op. cit.*; European Institute for Comparative Cultural Research, *Sharing Diversity, National Approaches to Intercultural Dialogue in Europe*, Study for the European Commission, March 2008.

manifold. They may vary from the need to develop global strategies, to master spatial cohesion, to propose qualitative density in space and environment, to stimulate innovating and creative power, to create urban diversity and flexibility within multi-faceted identities and to guarantee urban solidarity, social justice and cultural diversity. The creation of such a favourable environment presupposes an active investment in strong development coalitions between public, private and civil society stakeholders at territorial and issue levels. If positive answers are given to these urban challenges, cities can be the main actors for creating a European Civitas, in particular for providing the environment for intercultural and interreligious dialogue, and finally for citizenship building.

a. Cities are Sources for European Identity, Imagination and Integration

Throughout history, cities have always been the driving forces of culture, civilisation and development in Europe.[20] They express the richness of Europe, its cultural and spiritual memory and its creative will to make history. Cities are the meeting places on the road to intercultural dialogue.[21] The spirituality of the place can be a driving force for city planners and local decision-makers in rediscovering the European identity.[22] Cities are the stories they tell about themselves. Pride, confidence and identity come from the collective imagination of people across the city. The opportunity is there to reconcile the past and to realistically link it to different possible futures through encouraging public participation.

This is why policy at regional, national and European levels needs to have a citizenship dimension: to exchange experiences and best practices, to help overcome social and cultural ruptures and finally to bring forward new investment in social capital development. An imaginative human-centric approach may help to design principles that allow for creativity and experimentation and favour citizens' participation from the grass roots level.

---

20 An excellent overview of the role of cities in history is given by Hall, P., *Cities in Civilisation. Culture, Innovation and Urban Order*, Phoenix, Weidenfeld & Nicolson, 1998. Also relevant are Amin, A., Massey, D. and Thrift, N., *Cities for the Many, not the Few,* Bristol, Policy Press, 2000; Bekemans, L. and Mira, E. (eds.), *Civitas Europa, Cities, Urban Systems and Cultural Regions Between Diversity and Convergence*, Brussels, P.I.E. Peter Lang, 2000.

21 The programmes of cultural routes by UNESCO, the Council of Europe and the European Union relate to itineraries that connect people. They very much focus on practising dialogue of cultures and civilisations as a factor in the creation of a culture of peace.

22 Flanaghan, B., *The Spirit of the City, Voices from Dublin's Liberties*, Dublin, Veritas, 1999.

b. Cities are Engines for Sustainable Growth, Social Cohesion and Urban Quality

Cities have also often been engines of economic and social development, creating growth, innovation and employment. Economic and social sustainability is in this perspective a key concept in urban policies.[23] Economic, social and urban policies are mutually reinforcing: economic growth is sustainable when it goes hand in hand with efforts to reduce poverty, fight social exclusion and tackle urban problems. However, significant disparities in economic, social and urban opportunities as well as contradictory developments between Northern and Southern European cities exist. They often necessitate diversified urban policies and different types of urban action.[24]

Despite the crisis, cities may provide today a political platform for realising the objectives of sustainable growth and social cohesion within an increasing urban quality context. People want to live and work in cities with clean air, green and secure spaces, attractive architecture and high quality services, including cultural and recreational amenities. When cities have the structures and means to create urban quality they provide the conditions of an inclusive and democratic urban civitas for the multicultural composition of their inhabitants.

c. Cities are Facilitators For Innovation and Entrepreneurship in the Knowledge Society

Cities often provide a stimulating environment for creativity,[25] innovation and businesses. In the emerging European creative urban reality, cities may stimulate the creation and development of SMEs, micro-enterprises and social economy enterprises, set up business incubators and provide access to finance and other business services. In addition, experiences and practices illustrate that cities can simplify administrative demands, improve education and training opportunities, facilitate networking between education and enterprises and stimulate the co-operation between companies, research institutes and universities. Being laboratories of innovative democratic initiatives, they fully contribute to the development of sustainable knowledge societies and citizenship building. In short, a new equilibrium between change and tradition in a stimulating urban environment with citizens' involvement can be searched for.

---

23 See Giradet, S., *Creating Sustainable Cities (Schumacher Briefings)*, London, Green Books, 1999.

24 Hall, P., *Cities of Tomorrow, An Intellectual History of Urban Planning and Design in the 20th Century*, Oxford, Blackwell Publishing, 2002.

25 Landry, C., Bianchini, F., *The Creative City, A Toolkit for Urban Innovators*, London, Demos Publishers, 2000; Florida, R., *The Rise of the Creative Class*, New York, Basic Books, 2002.

d. Cities are Promoters of Social Inclusion, Equal Opportunities and Security for Citizens

The urban reality often reflects disparities between neighbourhoods, a problem that confronts Europe's large and medium-sized cities. According to the data of the Urban Audit,[26] most cities experience deprived neighbourhoods (where high unemployment is linked to poor housing, poor environment, poor health, poor education, few job opportunities and high crime rates) as well as certain disadvantaged groups. Cities should therefore pay special attention to integrating immigrants, and preventing the social exclusion of young people. In short, they can favour social inclusion through measures of security and facilitate the professional, social and cultural integration of fragile communities.

Social exclusion is at odds with the European social model, which guarantees opportunities for every citizen. It has consequences on the local business, the living environment, and the inhabitants and on the growth potential of the city. Tackling social exclusion is therefore crucial to sustainable urban policies. Connected to the promotion of social inclusion is also the need to guarantee citizens' security. Cities are at the foreground for creating favourable urban environments for social inclusion and security, and consequently, for genuine intercultural dialogue and democratic citizenship building.

In summary, cities are important sustainable and living sources for building and experiencing the multi-faceted identity of the citizens of multicultural Europe. Throughout history they have been shaping actors for promoting and facilitating creativity, imagination and integration. They have always been places on the road to dialogue and learning. Today they are laboratories and breeding places for innovative democratic processes in which dialogue can be an important vehicle. They provide learning places, built and non-built environments and meeting spaces for the daily experiencing of intercultural and interreligious encounters and the practising of democratic citizenship. If some conditions are met, a liveable urban context provides a favourable, attractive and creative environment for citizens' participation in (formal and informal) democratic processes of active citizenship. Roads of dialogue interconnect cities through the creation of occasions and areas of interchange and encounters. Interconnecting cities can, as history has proven, create the environment for intercultural practice between people and the meeting point for interreligious encounters.

---

26 For valuable data on city developments see http://www.urbanaudit.org/.

C. Intercultural Practices

In the following section I briefly present two relevant illustrations of intercultural practices, which respond to the underlying characteristics of the European Civitas in dealing with managing diversity and promoting intercultural integration

1. Intercultural Cities: Towards a Model for Intercultural Integration[27]

"Intercultural Cities" is a joint EU-Council of Europe project that was launched in 2008. It questions the role of cities in fostering dialogue between people from different cultures in their daily lives – at school or at work – and in managing diversity within a space of conviviality. The project aims at stimulating an inclusive debate and policy making in pilot cities, taking an intercultural approach to migration, integration and social cohesion, encouraging pilot cities to develop comprehensive intercultural strategies to manage urban diversity and acting as inspiration for other cities in Europe. It proposes practical policies and methods to help cities review their policies through an "intercultural lens," including tools like expert reviews, study visits, city-to-city mentoring, thematic workshops and public events.

We believe that an intercultural city presents a vision for the future that accepts diversity as the norm and perceives it as a source of dynamism, innovation, creativity and growth.[28] Public spaces, schools, homes, workplaces and cultural forums are designed to enable people from different cultural backgrounds to mix, exchange and interact productively and creatively. Public consultation, debate and decision-making reflect the community's cultural mix – cultural conflict is accepted and dealt with – often at the grassroots level. Politicians and the media encourage citizens' participation in creating a shared identity. However, to make this vision a reality, cities should develop an inclusive strategy which transforms their policies, public spaces, institutions and relationships between communities, expressing respect for diversity and dialogical conviviality in the European Civitas.[29]

---

27 Wood, P. (ed.), *Intercultural Cities: Towards a Model for Intercultural Integration,* Joint action of the Council of Europe and the European Commission, October 2009, pp. 17-46; Bonniel Chalier, P., *Interculturalism in the Cultural Policies of European Cities*, October 2009 available at: http://www.coe.int/t/dg4/cultureheritage/culture/Cities/Publication/.

28 Bloomfield, J. and Bianchini, F., *Planning for the Intercultural City,* Stroud, Comedia, 2004.

29 Westendorff, D., *From Unsustainable to Inclusive Cities*, Geneva, UNRID, 2004.

2. Cultural Routes: Spiritual Spaces and Routes

As was said above, today's Europe is experiencing a transformation in the perceptions of the role that places can play in developing sustainable communities of common interest and shared values. The "genius loci," i.e. the spirituality in the space of the city in the 21st century, is realised both by secular and sacral objects. As described by many cultural researchers, spiritual spaces and routes are built around the existential problems common to all people. They deal with the problems of life, love, suffering and death. Problems are common but emotions and the ways of expressing them vary between cultures, creeds and communities. Urban spaces can then be understood as the lived spaces that shape collective imaginaries. These are created by history, architecture, people's perception and their culture. In particular, cities are increasingly seen in a wider societal context, linking places, territories and scale with governance, inclusion and identity-building. Cities are hubs for diversity, integration and intercultural encounters and are of vital importance to mobilising citizens. They are perceived as economic, political and social assets in the changing European societies. Within this emerging new environment, culture and intercultural dialogue are mobilising sources in building a democratic "European Civitas" and, consequently, giving a renewed spirit to the European future.

Within this space-specific perspective, "Cultural Routes" represent interactive, dynamic and continually evolving processes of human intercultural links that reflect the rich diversity of the contributions of different peoples to cultural heritage. Though cultural routes have resulted historically from both peaceful and hostile encounters, they present a number of shared dimensions, which transcend their original functions, offering an exceptional setting for a culture of peace. This culture is based on ties of shared history as well as on the tolerance, respect and appreciation for cultural diversity that characterise the communities involved. Cultural routes reveal the heritage content of a specific phenomenon of human mobility and exchange that developed via communication routes. In other words, cultural routes are not simple ways of communication and transport, which may include cultural properties and connect different people, but are special historic phenomena that create added (cultural) value (such as monuments, archaeological remains, historic towns, architecture, intangible heritage, cultural and natural landscapes, etc.). The Route projects launched by UNESCO[30] are very illustrative for the promotion of mutual knowledge

[30] See http://www.unesco.org/en/dialogue/routes-of-dialogue/.

between civilisations and cultures while renewing a dialogue between civilisations, cultures, religions and spiritual traditions.

Cultural itineraries facilitate an effective merging of cultures through the discovery of a common heritage and multiple identities. This is the case in particular with the Roads of Al-Andalus,[31] which are part of the UNESCO Programme of Interreligious Dialogue. The purpose is to bring out the dynamic nature of the reciprocal cultural, artistic and textual interactions and influences between religions and spiritual traditions, which resulted from the movement of persons, ideas and goods along the roads taken by pilgrims, migrants and tradesman. It has resulted in encounters along the roads of Faith. The sacred monuments, sites and texts, illustrate a common heritage with shared ethical and spiritual values. These spiritual sites have become meeting places for spiritual leaders to work together for peace, intercultural and interreligious dialogue.[32] Cultural routes are therefore an instrument for reading the European values that emerge from the complexity of the cultures and societies constituting Europe.

Spiritual rebirth, linked with the renaissance of pilgrimaging – which we observe today – is carried out by the authenticity, identity and genius loci, of particular places and routes of the pilgrimage. There is still a danger that pilgrimage destinations are becoming a mere component of the tourist industry and losing their soul. Today's challenge is to keep or find an expression and a context for contemporary spirituality in the places for pilgrimages, which remains loyal to a value-driven European Civitas.

II. The Education Perspective of a European Civitas

Part II focuses on the crucial role of education in developing a European Civitas within the globalising context. The learning processes for intercultural dialogue, respect for religious diversity and civic education, should be based on shared social responsibility and integral human development. Places for educational and cultural encounters are crucial for practicing Europe's unity in diversity. Objectives, competences and aspects of education need to be revisited and strengthened in view of developing proper answers to current society challenges.

---

31 The "Routes of al-Andalus: spiritual convergence and intercultural dialogue" project by Unesco seeks to highlight the heritage of dialogue that gradually developed in medieval Spain and study and promote the creation of areas of dialogue between cultures and civilisations.

32 A good example is the annual Assisi interfaith gatherings for peace between religious leaders.

A. Point of Departure: Shared Social Responsibility for Human Integral Development

Education plays a central role in the development of both human beings and modern societies as it enhances social, cultural and economic development, active citizenship and ethical values. Education is to build peace, foster dialogue and enhance understanding in order "to build peace in the minds of men," as enshrined in UNESCO's Constitution (UNESCO 1945) and further developed in its various recommendations, declarations, resolutions and initiatives.[33] To be educated is to learn and to be able to feel free of any kind of dependence, submission or fear. It is to be able to create, to think, to imagine, to dream – all distinctive and decisive capacities of the human condition. According to the Delors Commission, there are four pillars in the education process: learn to know; learn to do; learn to be; learn to live together.[34] Learning to live appropriately with others is as important in everyday life as in the wider society. It requires awareness of and respect for human rights and the responsibilities of local, national and global citizenship. Moreover, learning to live together as responsible citizens can help reduce tensions due to ethnic or other divisions and social disparities.[35]

The current crisis of socialisation and value transmission has made the task of education difficult but vital for society building.[36] The crucial role of education needs therefore to be reset within the dramatic

---

33 It is useful to recall the major general UN contributions to Education since 1990: Education for All (1990); Agenda 21 for the Environment (1993); World Plan of Action for Education on Human Rights and Democracy (1993); Vienna Conference on Human Rights (1993); The Contribution by Religions to the Culture of Peace (1994); Declaration of Principles on Tolerance (1995); Copenhagen Declaration on Social Development (1995); Fourth World Conference on Women, Beijing Declaration (1995); International Decade for a Culture of Peace and Non-violence for the Children of the World (1998); Declaration and Programme of Action on a Culture of Peace (1999); UN Millennium Declaration (2000); The Earth Charter of Amsterdam (2000); Universal Declaration on Cultural Diversity (UNESCO, 2001); Declaration on Dialogue among Civilizations (2003); Culture of Peace (UN Recommendations A/Res/63/113, 26 February 2005); The Hague Agenda on City Diplomacy (2008); Charter for a World without Violence (2009); etc.

34 Delors Report, *Education for 21st Century "Learning: the Treasure Within,"* Report to UNESCO of the International Commission on Education for the Twenty-first Century, Unesco Publishing, 1996. The Report focuses on the relationship between education and the six subject areas of development, science, citizenship, culture, social cohesion, and work.

35 Cernilogar, K. and Coertjens, M., "Towards a Europe of Shared Social Responsibilities: Challenges and Strategies," in *Trends in Social Cohesion*, no. 23 (Provisional Version), Council of Europe Publishing, Spring 2011, pp. 229-235.

36 See *Education Together in Catholic Schools*, published by the Congregation of Catholic Education, Rome, September 2007.

acceleration in the speed of social change brought about by the process of globalisation. I am referring to the works of sociologists such as Zygmunt Baumann, Ulrich Beck and Anthony Giddens, talking about education in a liquid society, risk society or reflexive modernity.[37] In such a changing context of the processes of transformation at the global level, there is an urge to rethink the meaning of education as well as the use and practices of teaching and learning, the opportunities of communicating interaction offered by new technologies and the dangers of the commodification of human relations caused by the new relation between culture and economy.

B. Objectives and Competences

Education is a dynamic process of learning that creates added value and forms the person to integral development. It is to transmit possibilities and opportunities with conviction, intuition and motivation. It is always a meeting with the other, henceforth the role of teachers as key agents for change and the need to accompany and respect their role in the educational landscape. Henceforth, Europe and the international context are an integral part of the general educational project as well as of each individual learning path. This implies transmitting in an open and critical way, the ideals and principles that valorise the person at the centre of education systems and national curricula recognising the European and international context.

The first task of education is to form (young) people to become responsible citizens, providing them with information, knowledge, competences, skills and an open behaviour, in line with fundamental values such as peace and tolerance of diversity, etc. Key competences refer to knowledge, skills and attitudes that serve personal fulfilment, social inclusion and active citizenship. These include the traditional competences but also the more transversal ones such as learning to learn, social and civic competences, cultural awareness and expressions.[38] In this context the reference to Edgar Morin, the French sociologist, is compulsory. He proposes four objectives in the transmission of knowledge and the activities of teaching:[39] to form a

37 Bauman, Z., *Liquid Modernity,* Cambridge, Polity, 2000; *id., Europe: an Unfinished Adventure,* Cambridge, Polity, 1994; *id., Liquid Times: Living in an Age of Uncertainty*, Cambridge, Polity, 2006; Giddens, A., *Europe in the Global Age*, London, Polity Press, 2007; Habermas, J., *Europe. The Faltering Project,* Cambridge, Polity, 2009.

38 The European dimension of such an education is very well captured by Zani, A. V., *Formare l'Uomo Europeo: Sfide Educativie e Politiche Culturali*, Roma, Città Nuova, 2005.

39 Morin, E., "Réforme de la Pensée et Éducation au XXI Siècle," in J. Bindé (ed.), *Les Clés du XXI Siècle*, UNESCO/Seuil, Paris 2000, pp. 271-275.

well developed mind (better than a too full mind), to teach the human condition, to educate to live (learning does not mean only the acquisition of knowledge, techniques and productive modes, but also an interest in relations with the other and with oneself); and to learn the dignity of the citizen.

C. Citizenship Education: Education for Responsible Citizenship in a Plural Europe

Education has the priority task of transmitting knowledge and competences that give scope and responsibility to the development of each person.[40] A number of fundamental questions need to be addressed: education to and for all, education of humanity – this concerns crosscutting the dichotomy between a culture of education and a professional education; education to change – this deals with the meaning of creativity and the use of a critical mind, to master a variety of "languages"; finally, continuity in the search of values – this implies surpassing the so-called contradiction between tradition and innovation.

In the education processes and transmission of knowledge it is not sufficient to affirm the principle of the centrality of the person. The educator and the teacher have to act within the socio-cultural context responding to the challenges of globality and complexity, cultural disintegration and the dispersion and fragmentation of knowledge. This requires integration of a diverse range of learning sources and levels.[41]

As was said above, Europe is part of such a learning process. The question however remains open as to what extent a common vision, founded on common goods, can survive in a context of economic globalisation and cultural relativism. The problems of social inequality and poverty, values of solidarity, responsibility and respect for differences, as well as the non-accessibility of the benefits of globalisation, have to be tackled by various forms of learning. In short, the current situation requires an inspiring vision and a strategy that embodies such a vision. Europe cannot be taught as a technical project, but requires scope and engagement. Education has the task of being an agent of change and has the responsibility to revitalise its original project and consequently, mobilise its citizens, in particular the youth. This can only be done through the (formal, informal and non-formal) education of active citizenship, which stimulates the commitment of (young) people to the European project, the plural Europe, the Europe of

[40] Commission of the European Communities, *Schools for the 21st Century*, Staff Working Paper, Brussels, 11/07/07.

[41] Cernilogar, K. and Coertjens, M., "Towards a Europe of Shared Social Responsibilities," *op. cit.*, pp. 229-235.

dialogue and the intercultural Europe. Various aspects of the education agenda of a European Civitas can be distinguished.

1. A Modern and Dynamic Concept

The notion of 'responsible citizenship' concerns an awareness and knowledge of rights and duties. It is closely related to civic values such as democracy and human rights, equality, participation, partnership, social cohesion and social justice as well as the knowledge and exercise of rights and responsibilities, beyond the legal status and judicial relationship between the citizen and the State. A citizen may be regarded as a person co-existing in a society. In recent decades, societies have changed along with the theoretical conceptions and practical implementation of citizenship. The concept is steadily broadening and changing, as lifestyles and patterns in our relations with others become more diversified. Far from being limited to the national context, the notion of harmonious co-existence among citizens relates to the concept of a community embracing all contexts – local, regional, national and international – in which individuals live. The Council of Europe has done much work on this.[42]

The link between citizenship and education is very close. Today's challenge is to strengthen the need for citizenship in societies and develop learning modes which respond to the need for information, knowledge, capacity and quality that citizens should be equipped with to deal with the societal developments of today's world. This is the core of the pedagogical approach to citizenship. However, the teaching of citizenship is not sufficient; it is the learning of citizenship that is essential. This consists of the development of intercultural skills in context by acquiring operating, social and communicative competences through practice, experience and dialogue in formal and non-formal instruction. As a consequence, the concept of citizenship could (and should) be integrated into the educational process in a very integrated way with a horizontal focus from different perspectives.[43]

Moreover, active citizenship is a lifelong process. Learning citizenship is interactive and deeply embedded in specific formal, non-

---

42 We refer to: Final Declaration Second Summit of Heads of State and Government of the Council of Europe (Strasbourg. 10-11 October 1997); Committee of Ministers' Declaration and Programme on Education for Democratic Citizenship, Based on the Rights and the Responsibilities of the Citizens (Strasbourg, 1999); Recommendation on Education for Democratic Citizenship (Strasbourg 2002); Recommendation on the Charter on Education for Democratic Citizenship and Human Rights Education (CM/Rec (2010)7), etc.

43 Gollob, R., and Krapf, P. (eds.), *Teaching Democracy, a Collection of Models for Democratic Citizenship and Human Rights Education*, Strasbourg, Council of Europe Publishing, December 2008.

formal and informal contexts. Support should therefore also be given to citizenship learning within the civil society as well as within the informal setting of the family. Also, churches can play a role in the field of education for democratic citizenship.[44] Teaching to learn to become active citizens implies giving people access to these capacities and skills, of which they are in need, to efficiently participate in economic, political and social life. This also means the knowledge of languages. In fact, the educational dimension of European citizenship has as much to do with rights as with responsibilities and duties. Accordingly, the "European citizenship" cannot be merely reduced to forms of individual participation to political life or to bilateral economic relations, but it should take into account the acquisition of skills that have been previously acquired during the formal and non-formal process of education. This process should be favoured from below by concrete projects at local and regional citizens' level with exchanges between schools, students and teachers. Extra-curricular opportunities for citizenship learning should therefore also be encouraged through international exchanges.[45]

Accordingly, the concept of citizenship education relates to educating young people to become "responsible citizens" who are capable of contributing to the development and wellbeing of the society in which they live.[46] Education traditions and approaches to citizenship vary across Europe. The basic idea of democratic citizenship in a modern society is the active participation and engagement of each. Although the sense of citizenship is embedded in each individual's life history and its relationships with others, no standard model for developing citizenship can be applied.[47] Till recently, the concept of citizenship was conceived in mainly state and institutional terms.[48] In today's Europe the concept of citizenship has become more fluid,

---

[44] Conference of European Churches, Church and Society Commission, Church and Society Commission, Education for Democratic Citizenship: *A Role for the Churches?*, Strasbourg, 5-7 October 2011.

[45] See EU Citizens' programme.

[46] See the definitions given in: O'Shea, K., *Developing a Shared Understanding. A Glossary of Terms for Education for Democratic Citizenship*, Council of Europe, Strasbourg, 2003.

[47] Holford, J. and van der Veen, R. (eds.), *Lifelong Learning, Governance and Active Citizenship in Europe*, ETGACE project, European Commission, EU Research on Social Sciences and Humanities, Luxembourg, Office for Official Publications of the European Communities, 2006.

[48] Steele, T. and Richard, T., "Citizenship and Global Chaos – Education, Culture and Revolution," in D. Wildemeersch, V. Stroobans and M. Bron (eds.), *Active Citizenship and Multiple Identities in Europe, a Learning Outlook*, Frankfurt, Peter Lang, 2005, pp. 88-97.

dynamic and contextual, linking it to the multiple identity of Europe.[49] This means that learning to live together positively with differences and diversity is becoming the central dimension of practising citizenship in Europe. Therefore, citizenship education is a modern and dynamic concept with a European dimension.

2. Objectives

While its aims and content may be highly diversified, key objectives of responsible citizenship education in today's complex world should relate to (1) political and (multi) cultural literacy, (2) critical thinking and the development of certain attitudes and values and (3) active participation.

1) The development of political and cultural literacy may involve: learning about social, political and civic institutions, as well as human rights; the study of the conditions under which people may live harmoniously together, social issues and ongoing social problems; teaching young people about national constitutions so that they are better prepared to exercise their rights and responsibilities; promoting recognition of the cultural and historical heritage; promoting recognition of the cultural and linguistic diversity of society. In this perspective, increased literacy should favour active communication and participation in democratic societies; in short, responsible citizenship-building. In other words, political and cultural literacy requires a lifelong and a lifewide education. However, the impact of globalisation on our lives necessitates a growing awareness of the existence of different cultures, religions and political systems, in order to develop respect for the otherness. In other words, increasing the diversity of peoples in European societies requires a reconceptualisation of literacy towards a political, multicultural literacy, which might be a vehicle for mutual understanding and learning in European multicultural societies and beyond.

2) The development of critical thinking and the adoption of certain attitudes and values may entail: acquiring the skills needed to participate actively in public life; developing recognition of and respect for oneself and others with a view to achieving greater mutual understanding; acquiring social and moral responsibility, including self-confidence, and learning to behave responsibly towards others; strengthening a spirit of solidarity; the construction of values, with due regard for differing social perspectives and points of view; learning to listen and resolve conflicts peacefully; learning to contribute to a safe environment; developing more effective strategies for fighting racism and xenophobia.

---

[49] Wildemeersch, D., Stroobans, V. and Bron, M. (eds.), *Active Citizenship and Multiple Identities*, *op. cit.*

3) Finally, the active participation of youngsters may be promoted by: enabling them to become more involved in the community at large (at international, national, local and school levels); offering them practical experience of democracy at school; developing their capacity to engage with each other; encouraging pupils to develop project initiatives in conjunction with other organisations (such as community associations, public bodies and international organisations), as well as projects involving other communities.

In short, it should be clear that citizenship education is not just concerned with imparting theoretical knowledge to enhance political and (multicultural) literacy in issues such as democracy, human rights, the functioning of political institutions, the cultural and historical heritage, etc. It is crucial for integral human development that positive civic attitudes and values should also be developed and that active participation should be promoted by pupils – be it at the school level or in society at large.

3. *European Dimension of Citizenship Education*[50]

Citizenship always has a territorial-based connotation, whatever its scale and limits, although education processes should take account of

---

[50] The European Commission has published various White Papers and studies on European citizenship education such as: White Paper on "*Teaching and Learning: towards the Learning Society*" (1995):
http://ec.europa.eu/languages/documents/doc409_en.pdf
Memorandum on Lifelong Learning (2000):
http://www.bologna-berlin2003.de/pdf/MemorandumEng.pdf
Resolution on Lifelong Learning (2002):
http://eurlex.europa.eu/LexUriServ/LexUriServ.do?uri=OJ:C:2002:163:0001:0003:EN:PDF)
European Commission: *Open Learning Environment, Active Citizenship and Social Inclusion. Implementation of Education and Training 2010 Work Programme: Progress Report,* Brussels, November 2003; European Commission: *The Future of Education and Citizenship Policies: The Commission Adopts Guidelines for Future Programmes after 2006,* Brussels, 2004; *Learning for Active Citizenship. A Significant Challenge in Building a Europe of Knowledge: Education and Active Citizenship in the European Union (*2006):
http://ec.europa.eu/education/archive/citizen/citiz_en.html
Programme in the field of lifelong learning 2007-2013:
http://ec.europa.eu/education/lifelong-learning-programme/doc78_en.htm
Interesting policy-oriented studies were made by GHK, *Study on Active Citizenship Education*, commissioned by DG Education and Culture, Feb. 2007:
http://ec.europa.eu/education/pdf/doc248_en.pdf
And Eurydice, *Citizenship Education at School in Europe*, May 2005:
http://www.moec.gov.cy/programs/eurydice/publication.pdf
The most recent Report concerns *Citizenship Education in Europe*, Education, Audiovisual and Culture Executive Agency (EACEA P9 Eurydice), May 2012: http://eacea.ec.europa.eu/education/eurydice

the fact that citizens identify with different entities and dimensions, whether local, regional, national, European, international or global. Four aspects should be considered in developing the European dimension of education: curriculum building, teacher education, and support for teachers and teaching materials and extra-curricular activities involving mobility and exchanges.

1) Curriculum building: the European/international dimension of citizenship should be part of the overarching general aims of various levels and phases of education to stimulate a sense of belonging to Europe and of involvement. Aspects which could be addressed in education/learning paths are the rights and obligations of EU citizens; the contemporary history of European nations and the EU integration process; the functioning of European/international institutions main economic/ political/social issues in European/international co-operation; the knowledge and promotion of socio-cultural diversity; learning about European culture/literature/values guidelines, etc. From the curricular standpoint, citizenship education can be offered as a separate stand-alone compulsory or optional subject, or integrated into one or more other subjects (such as history, social studies, geography or philosophy), or as a cross-curricular educational theme, so that the principles of citizenship education might be present in all subjects of the curriculum. These different approaches are not mutually exclusive.

2) Teacher Education: the European dimension of citizenship education should be taken into account in the initial teacher education, as well as in the provision of in-service teacher training.

3) Support for Teachers and Teaching Materials: teacher support measures relevant to the European dimension of citizenship education may exist in a wide variety of forms and bodies. They may be devised by the education authorities of a particular country, public research institutes, institutions for teacher education, associations and NGOs as well as by a variety of European institutions, such as the European Commission or the Council of Europe. They may involve materials or facilities intended directly for teachers, or information materials on the European Union for the general public.

4) Activities in the wider school context: learning about the European dimension of citizenship means acquiring formal knowledge and developing awareness about a set of societal and political issues. However, this learning process also requires above all that students should be able to gain experience of a practical nature, as in simulation games or various exchange programmes. Many European, national and regional education programmes and schemes exist for promoting the European dimension and awareness.

If Europe wants to carry out its destiny, a drastic increase in the engagement of citizens and (young) people to the European project is necessary. Strengthening a holistic and integral approach to the concept and practice of citizenship enriches the possibility of promoting active citizenship together with the European dimension. From the Tindemans Report "Europe of Citizens and Peoples" (1976) onwards, many community action programmes have been launched to contribute to the building of active citizenship, mainly in the fields of education, training and youth (e.g. Socrates, Leonardo, Culture 2000, the Lifelong learning programme, "Youth on the Move").

In short, the European dimension of active citizenship goes beyond the economic, political, social and cultural boundaries. Such integration can lead to the recognition and acceptance of a European citizenship covering multiple identities and nationalities. This is not the exclusive responsibility of governments, but also the responsibility of citizens and their organisations. Consequently, diversified forms of civil society participation emerge and develop in Europe, to concretise active citizenship at the local and regional level. However, a certain level of common identity is needed to strengthen European citizenship. This identity exists in different complimentary forms, creating a multilayered identity. It is a process that should be enhanced, as long as it goes along with the recognition of diversity. Intercultural learning could be the key to this strengthening.

4. *The Cultural Dimension of Citizenship Education: Intercultural Education*

The specificity of intercultural education refers to learning processes that lead to a knowledge of other cultures and install behaviour patterns of availability, openness and dialogue. It concerns a rather complex type of knowledge. The primary objective of intercultural education is the promotion of the capacity of constructive conviviality in a multi-form cultural and social context, valorising the cultural dimension of active citizenship. It consists not only of the acceptance and respect of diversity, but also the recognition of the place of the proper cultural identity in a perspective of mutual learning. The challenge of such education to comprehension can be expressed at two levels: the cognitive level of knowledge and information of the world and the others, and the affective level of attention to the relation, interaction and the story.

The unifying perspective of intercultural education lies in the reconciliation between unity and diversity in various situations of multicultural and plural Europe.[51] Out of tolerance and respect, dialogue and mutual enrichment can be developed to manage cultural diversity and strengthen citizenship. The notion of solidarity may then open up to the concept of hospitality; the principle of equality may integrate with the recognition of diversity and finally lead to mutual responsibility. In short, education will need to play a key role in developing the ability to conduct authentic intercultural dialogue, being an integral part of developing democratic culture.[52] Intercultural education accepts the paradigm of human rights as the universal point of departure, implying the importance of human rights education and consequently of education to democratic citizenship. Therefore, we plead for a multi-dimensional approach to intercultural education. Such an education responds to the learning objectives of reciprocity, complexity, interpersonal communication, conflict prevention, conviviality of differences and value-driven peace building.

Conclusion

The knowledge society requires an in-depth development of lifelong learning, benefitting from a variety of interconnecting learning resources for citizenship building. However, today's policy towards a learning society implies a more innovative capacity to (re)design (new) institutions of political, economic, social and educational governance, which can respond properly to the challenges of the multi-faceted process of globalisation. The learning society manifests fundamental structural trends towards the individualisation of risk and the threat of social exclusion, while promoting social inclusion, personal fulfillment, and lifelong learning for employability and adaptability. Learning new skills should therefore be envisaged for citizenship as much as for employability. This includes learning for personal, civic and social as well as for employment-related purposes. It implies raising investment in people and knowledge and broadening opportunities for innovative, more flexible forms of learning, respecting multiple identities within the European meeting place.

The policy consequence of such a thesis is that education institutions should accept lifelong learning as their collective responsibility, that governments should invest in training teachers and trainers for all stages

---

51 Illustrative are the Conclusions of the International Conference *Intercultural Education and Religious Pluralism* (Rome, 27-28 March 2008) organised by the Congregation of Catholic Education (CEC), the Catholic Association of Institutions of Educational Sciences (ACISE) and the World Federation of Catholic Universities (FIUC), in *Atti e Documenti 31*, Libreria Editrice Vaticana, 2009.

52 Sjur, B. and van't Land, H. (eds.), *Speaking Across Borders: the Role of Higher Education in Furthering Intercultural Dialogue*, Council of Europe, December 2010.

of informal, non-formal as well as formal education and that Europe should strengthen its lifelong learning agenda on active citizenship. New inclusive education policies on citizenship, which should respond to the very requirements of an education for a risk society, need to consider the following three elements: a differentiated discourse, curriculum content and a social and cultural relevance.

– Discourse refers to people's internalised values and the way they behave. A deeper understanding of how people build up a self-image will help educators provide effective and adequate learning programmes for those most excluded from the mainstream. Educational inclusion for a responsible citizenship also means that different and alternative ways of knowing and doing within our mainstream learning programmes should be recognised.

– The development of a curriculum content in a European context needs i) to contextualise the curriculum building in critical, reflexive learning experiences, with the goal that understanding the role of the self is critical to learning how to contribute actively to a changing world and ii) to introduce the idea of an alternative curriculum, alongside the conventional mode of disciplinarity, as a new mode of knowledge that is context specific, transdisciplinary and created and transmitted largely outside of universities.

– Social and cultural relevance: the most common method proposed for democratising the selection and control of knowledge is through discussion and dialogue. There is need for a critical dialogic approach to learning that recognises community experience as a contribution to knowledge and as a means of understanding their cultural relevance to the curriculum. This also implies recognising values outside the dominant perspective of the education system, in particular an education of intercultural dialogue, human rights and democratic citizenship.

Consequently, the promotion of an education of responsible citizenship and multiple identities needs to be understood and realised in a wider societal context of the knowledge triangle. A more comprehensive, international and multi-perspective analysis of the interconnection between education and society is proposed for both economic and societal reasons, to make societies more cohesive and responsible citizenship an instrument and a goal. In order to respond to these contextual and societal developments, the educational and cultural dimension of the European Civitas should be prioritised with the following broad guidelines:

– A value orientation and a community of shared values, i.e. a vision based on universal values which support and guide concrete action to build a European public space.

– A request for integral human development and the acceptance of education as a common good: this implies an educational approach that places the individual as a person at the centre of the pedagogy to learn to think, reflect and act.

– An identification of learning objectives and competences which make intercultural dialogue worthwhile and intercultural communication possible in times of ongoing change.

– An equality of respect and opportunities of democratic principles in citizenship building.

– The recognition of (cultural) identity building to be understood in its social context.

– Launching innovative pedagogical projects of citizenship in the European context.

– Sharing best learning practices of responsible citizenship in a positive and pro-active manner.

– A dialectics of thinking and acting together with a view to learning to fully participate in society building.

Cultural Relativism, Human Rights and the Co-existence of Contrasting Religious Prescriptions in the Islamic Tradition

Johannes THOMAS

Professor Emeritus, University of Paderborn

I. Preliminary Remarks

For John Rawls, the modern democratic state is an "association consisting of equal citizens." The state has no competence in religious, philosophical or moral matters, and it "has neither the right nor the duty to do what it or a majority […] wants to do in questions of morals and religion." It should be "neutral" towards different beliefs and values and only guarantee "the conditions of equal moral and religious liberty." The pursuit of the interests of the population is limited only by the state's duty to preserve "public order and security."[1]

Under these liberal conditions the threat posed by moral or religious convictions cannot be contested on the basis of other beliefs but only empirically. There must be "some considerable risks for the own legitimate interests," for preservation of equal liberty, public order and security. When there is no danger for liberty and security, "there is no reason to deny freedom to the intolerant."[2]

That means that the state does not have values and a worldview of its own besides the principle of equal liberty. Consequently, it is not the state but the society and the individuals who have to bear the burden of tolerance. The different groups within a given society and the individuals must tolerate beliefs and behaviours with which they disagree, even intolerant attitudes and propaganda for intolerance. Because of this disharmony, the state is constrained to continuously supervise the society in order to guarantee that no group imposes its

1 Rawls, J., *A Theory of Justice*, Cambridge MA, Harvard University Press, 1971, pp. 212-213. For criticism of Rawls see Casey, M. A., "The Puzzle of Intolerant Tolerance," in A. Rauscher (ed.), *Toleranz und Menschenwürde – Tolerance and Human Dignity*, Berlin, Duncker & Humblot, 2011, pp. 151-157.

2 Rawls, J., *A Theory of Justice, op. cit.*, pp. 218-220.

beliefs on others. When there is a conflict between different groups and beliefs they must acknowledge that "the principles of justice override beliefs."[3] Every group has to accept that its rights must be limited to protect the rights of others.

But the forced acceptance of limitations of its own rights which is believed by the group to be derived directly from what is held to be the truth, is inevitably felt as an acceptance of an act of intolerance. In order to avoid conflicts because of the belief in different truths, truth has to be eliminated:

> In the light of the copious plurality of human existence, the abundance of conflicting views, values and desires, and the adamant insistence on our supremacy, truth appears to be not only implausible but tyrannical […]. Its categories of truth and evil and true and false, exclude and rise to division and intolerance. For those who follow this reasoning, relativism seems to be the only option to ensure respect […] for freedom and human rights […] relativism has become the only form of moral philosophy safe for democracy.[4]

Relativism in its general and radical form, however, is not what people normally are willing to accept for themselves. The belief in what is just and what is good, especially beliefs in fundamental and universal human rights, continues to be held by most people, even if they do not know exactly what the fundaments of their beliefs are. They do not need to know something about them or, more exactly, they cannot know anything about them because, according to the relativists, there are no fundaments at all. That is why governments simply have to decide for example in favour of the general validity of human rights and introduce them into the law of their states without caring about their possible or impossible value-fundaments; they just make a decision, one which normally follows the opinion of the majority. Thanks to such a decisionism, relativists like John Rawls or Richard Rorty[5] hope to escape from the dilemma that is posed by the affirmation of radical relativism on the one hand and the affirmation of the binding character of the universal human rights in the form given to them by the UN, on the other hand.

This presumed way out of the dilemma, however, is illusionary. Once a government has fully accepted the validity of the UN Declaration of Human Rights (UDHR, 1948),[6] it cannot avoid affirming

---

3 *Ibidem*, pp. 220-221.

4 Casey, M. A., "The Puzzle of Intolerant Tolerance," *op. cit.*, p. 155.

5 Rorty, R., *Contingency, Irony and Solidarity*, Cambridge, Cambridge University Press, 1989.

6 http://www.un.org/en/documents/udhr.

at the same time, at least implicitly, the validity of the value foundations of these rights – in the first place the absolute value of the human person, independently of its socio-cultural and religious context. This basis, which relativists do not want to elucidate and to define, is clear enough insofar as it allows us to differentiate it from other, non-universalist conceptions of human rights.

II. Human Rights in Islamic Societies and States: the Cairo Declaration on Human Rights in Islam (CDHRI, 1990)[7]

The declaration concludes in articles 24 and 25 that "all the rights and freedoms stipulated in this Declaration are subject to Islamic Shar'iah," which "is the only source of reference for the explanation or clarification of any of the articles of this Declaration." The Declaration is therefore patently in contradiction with the universalist pretensions of the UDHR.

Whereas the UDHR had affirmed the "faith in fundamental human rights, in the dignity and worth of the human person and in the equal rights of men and woman" (Preamble), the CDHRI in its preamble affirms "his (man's) freedom and right to a dignified life," only insofar as it is "in accordance with the Islamic Shar'iah." It states that "fundamental rights and freedoms" are binding insofar as they are "binding divine commands." The rights of the individual resulting from his being a human person are not mentioned and could not have been mentioned, given the belief that they exist and have to be safeguarded only as an expression of God's will and of his commands "contained in the Revealed Books of Allah."

The right to life is limited by the prescriptions of Islamic law that can "prescribe(d)" to "take away life" (art. 2, a). The same is valid for the protection against corporal injuries:

> Safety from bodily harm is a guaranteed right […] it is prohibited to breach it without a Shari'ah-prescribed reason. (art. 2, d)

The right to marriage for men and women cannot be easily restricted, but among the restrictions excluded one misses the mention of the religion. That means that because of religious prescriptions this right can be abolished (art. 5).

Women are accorded a lot of rights and duties, they are "equal to man in human dignity," but do not enjoy equal rights in general. The preeminent role of the husband is not put into doubt:

> The husband is responsible for the maintenance and welfare of the family. (art. 6)

---

7 http://www1.umn.edu/humanrts/instree/cairodeclaration.html.

The education of children is equally bound in Islamic law:

> Parents [...] have the right to choose the type of education they desire for their children, provided they take into consideration the interest and future of the children in accordance with ethical values and the principles of the Shar'iah. (art. 7)

Proselytism aiming at converting a Muslim to another religion or to atheism is strictly forbidden, not only if one has recourse to "any form of pressure" or tries to "exploit the poverty" of the Muslim; it is even forbidden to take profit of his "ignorance." And a Muslim must be ignorant if he converts to another religion, because otherwise he would know that "Islam is the religion of true unspoiled nature," as is explained in the same article (art. 10). The question of apostasy and the death penalty foreseen by several Islamic States for this crime are neither mentioned nor discussed in the Declaration.

"Free movement" and free selection of the "place of residence" is allowed only within the "framework of the Shar'ia" (art. 12).

And "there shall be no crime or punishment except as provided for in the Shar'iah" (art. 19, d) which means that the corporal punishments prescribed by the Qur'an (from cutting off the hand of a thief to the stoning of an adulterer, a prescription which, by the way, is only presumed to have figured in the earliest Qur'an) are generally accepted.

Very strict limitations are applied to the freedom of expression. Every information or opinion that seem to be contrary to the principles of Islamic law or which could "harm the society or weaken its faith" is absolutely forbidden. Only those opinions and judgements are allowed that move within the boundaries of Islamic law:

> Everyone shall have the right to express his opinion freely in such manner as would not be contrary to the principles of Shar'iah. Everyone shall have the right to advocate what is right, and propagate what is good, and warn against what is wrong and evil according to the norms of Islamic Shar'iah. Information is a vital necessity to society. It may not be exploited or misused in such a way as may violate sanctities and the dignity of Prophets, undermine moral and ethical Values or disintegrate, corrupt or harm society or weaken its faith. (art. 22)[8]

I would like to make one remark: it is not at all clear what Shar'iah really means because, as I will demonstrate later on, Shar'iah is an

[8] The menacing consequences of the CDHRI were clearly pointed out for example in a joint statement to the UN Commission on Human Rights by Adama Dieng, its Muslim secretary-general, a prominent Senegalese jurist. See Littman, D., "Universal Human Rights and Human Rights in Islam," in *Midstream*, New York, February/March 1999: http://www.dhimmitude.org/archive/universal_islam.html.

ambiguous concept. This does not exclude, however, that there is in any case a conflict between those who defend universal rights and freedoms and those who limit them to rules prescribed by religious laws. The only peaceful issue and the only alternative to aggravated cultural conflicts seem to be the interfaith and intercultural dialogue. One of the most prominent examples of such a dialogue is that between Pope Benedict XVI and several representatives of the Islamic world.

III. First Steps Towards a Catholic-Islamic Dialogue: The Regensburg Lecture

Pope Benedict delivered a lecture at the University of Regensburg on 12 September 2006, that was entitled: "Faith, Reason and the University."[9] It seems worth quoting at least one of its key passages:

> In the seventh conversation (between Manuel II Palaeologus and an educated Persian) edited by Professor Khoury, the emperor touches on the theme of the holy war. The emperor must have known that sura 2, 256 reads: 'There is no compulsion in religion.' According to the experts, this is one of the suras of the early period, when Mohammed was still powerless and under threat. But naturally, the emperor also knew the instructions, developed later and recorded in the Qur'an, concerning holy war (jihad: in the original German version, not in the official English translation, J. Th.). Without descending to details, such as the difference in treatment accorded to those who have the 'Book' und the 'infidels,' he addresses his interlocutor with a startling brusqueness on the central question about the relationship between religion and violence in general, saying: 'Show me just what Mohammed brought that was new, and there you will find things only evil ('bad' would be more correct, J. Th.) and inhuman, such as his command to spread by the sword the faith he preached.'

The reflections and statements of the Pope evidently fall into the category of opinions strictly forbidden by CDHRI, art. 22. The violent and sharp reactions of the masses in the streets, the killing of Christians, the burning down of Christian churches and the aggressive protests formulated by political representatives of Islamic countries like Recep Tayyip Erdogan, prime minister of Turkey, should insofar have been expected. None of these political representatives, by the way, condemned the violent actions of the Muslims perpetrated against Christians.

A few days later, the Vatican released a declaration saying that the Holy Father "sincerely regrets that certain passages of his address could have sounded offensive to the sensitivities of the Muslim faithful" but

9 http://www.vatican.va.

he insisted again on his "clear and radical rejection of the religious motivation for violence, from whatever side it may come.."[10]

The Pope here is in full accordance with the UDHR, which stipulates:

> Everyone is entitled to all the rights and freedoms set forth in the Declaration, without distinction of any kind such as […] religion […] (art. 2).
>
> Everyone has the right to life, liberty and security (art. 3).[11]

IV. The Open Letter to his Holiness Pope Benedict XVI[12]: the Co-existence of Different and even Contrasting Interpretations of the "Verse of Tolerance"

The Open Letter, signed by 38 dignitaries and representatives of Islamic countries who confirmed that they want to react to the Pope's lecture "in a spirit of open exchange," starts with the declaration that they "applaud your efforts to oppose the dominance of positivism and materialism in human life," but "must point out" at the same time "some errors in the way you mentioned Islam […]."

The first chapter of the "Open Letter" is dedicated to the "verse of tolerance" and its interpretation by the Pope, which is criticised as being erroneous:

> You mention that 'according to experts' the verse which begins, There is no compulsion in religion (al Baqarah 2: 256) is from the early period when the Prophet 'was still powerless and under threat,' but this is incorrect. In fact this verse is acknowledged to belong to the period of Quranic revelation corresponding to the political and military ascendance of the young Muslim community. There is no compulsion in religion was not a command to Muslims to remain steadfast in the face of the desire of their oppressors to force them to renounce their faith, but was a reminder to Muslims themselves, once they had attained power, that they could not force another's heart to believe. There is no compulsion in religion addresses those in a position of strength, not weakness. The earliest commentaries on the Qur'an (such as that of At-Tabari) make it clear that some Muslims of Medina wanted to force their children to convert from Judaism or Christianity to Islam, and this verse was precisely an answer to them not to try to force their children to convert to Islam. Moreover, Muslims are also guided by such verses as Say: The truth is from your Lord; so whosoever will, let him believe, and whosoever will, let him disbelieve. (al-Khaf 18:

---

10 http://www.msnbc.msn.com/id/14861689/ns/world_news-europe/t/pope-sincerely-regrets-he-offended-muslims/#.TzzTi4Gadu4.

11 http://www.un.org/en/documents/udhr.

12 http://www.ammanmessage.com/media/openLetter/english.pdf.

29); and Say: O disbelievers! I worship not that which ye worship; Nor worship ye which I worship. And I shall not worship that which ye worship. Nor will ye worship that which I worship. Unto you your religion, and unto me my religion (al-Kafirun: 109: 1-6).

The criticism of the Pope's interpretation is certainly correct, insofar as it constitutes not "the" but only one of many traditional interpretations of the "verse of tolerance." But since there is a plurality of interpretations within the Muslim tradition itself, even the authors of the Open Letter cannot pretend to give us the only interpretation accepted generally as correct by the Muslim world. We are naturally ready to accept as correct what Muslims present to us as an accurate interpretation, but in this case, as in many others, the interpretations made by Muslim experts offer an extremely varied picture. Yohanan Friedmann has tried to classify the confusing plurality of interpretations.[13] His list has been augmented by Daniel Pipes.[14]

The verse in question has been interpreted as:

Abrogated: The passage was overridden by subsequent Koranic verses (such as 9: 73: 'O Prophet! Struggle against the unbelievers and hypocrites and be harsh with them').

Purely symbolic: The phrase is a description, not an imperative. Islam's truth is so obvious that to coerce someone to become a Muslim does not amount to 'compulsion,' or else being made to embrace Islam after defeat in war is not viewed as 'compulsion.'

Spiritual, not practical: Governments may indeed compel external obedience, though they, of course, cannot compel how Muslims think.

Limited in time and place: It applied uniquely to Jews in Medina in the seventh century.

Limited to non-Muslims who live under and accept Muslim rule: Some jurists say it applies only to 'Peoples of the Book' (Christians, Jews and Zoroastriens); others say it applies to all infidels.

Excludes some non-Muslims: Apostates, women, children, prisoners of war, and others can indeed be compelled. (This is the standard interpretation that has applied in most times and places.)

Limited to all non-Muslims: Muslims must abide by the tenets of Islam and may not apostatise.

---

13 Friedmann, Y., *Tolerance and Coercion in Islam. Interfaith Relations in the Muslim Tradition*, Cambridge, Cambridge University Press, 2003, pp. 102-120.

14 Pipes, D., *The Issue of Compulsion in Religion: Islam is What is Followers Make of it*, available at http://www.danielpipes.org/2110/the-issue-of-compulsion-in-religion-islam-is-what-its-followers-make-of-it.html.

Limited to Muslims: Muslims may shift from one interpretation of their faith to another (such as from Sunni to Shia), but may not leave Islam.

Applied to all persons: Reaching the true faith must be achieved through trial and testing, and compulsion undercuts this process.

The variety of interpretations developed by Islamic experts throughout history demonstrates that the lecture proposed by the Open Letter is not at all valid for every Muslim.[15] Its authors have made the encouraging choice of deciding in favour of a message of tolerance instead of presenting a less tolerant interpretation. This alone, should be applauded. And it allows institutions and persons engaged in interreligious dialogues to confront representatives of the Muslim world who deny the validity of the tolerance-message, with the fact that the Qur'an exegesis has produced different and even contrasting messages. Such an ambiguity is not reproachable. To acknowledge the ambivalence of the Quranic messages means only that the possibility for deriving unambiguous prescriptions for religious policies from the Quranic text is excluded – at least logically.

Similar conclusions are suggested by a comparison of "A Common Word between Us and You" and the Quranic text.[16]

V. "A Common Word between Us and You"[17]

In "A Common Word between Us and You," 138 Muslim scholars and clerics have declared the common ground between Christianity and Islam (13 October 2007). This letter was given support by 460 Islamic organisations and associations and was applauded nearly unanimously by representatives of the Christian world. The message wants to point out that the most fundamental faith articles of Christianity, the love of God and the love of the neighbour, have their counterparts in the tradition of Islam.

---

15 Thomas Bauer has studied traditional ambiguity in Islam, even with regard to Quranic exegesis: Bauer, T., *Die Kultur der Ambiguität. Eine andere Geschichte des Islam*, Berlin, Verlag der Weltreligionen, 2011, *passim*. The divergent interpretations of the verse of tolerance prove that one can no longer maintain the universal validity of this verse as supposed by Th. Koury, A., *Was sagt der Koran zum Heiligen Krieg*, Gütersloh, Gütersloher Verlagshaus, 2007, p. 61, or by Lewis, B., *Islam in History: Ideas, Peoples and Events in the Middle East*, Chicago, Open Court Publishing, 2002, p. 272.

16 For more details see Thomas, J., "Toleranz versus Intoleranz im Islam," in A. Rauscher (ed.), *Toleranz und Menschenwürde, op. cit.*, pp. 219-255; Noth, A., "Möglichkeiten und Grenzen islamischer Toleranz," in *Saeculum*, vol. 29, 1978, pp. 190-204; Paret, R., "Toleranz und Intoleranz im Islam," in *Saeculum*, vol. 21, 1970, pp. 344-365.

17 http://www.acommonword.com.

The first quotation, the only one taken from the Qur'an, underlines inter alia the social responsibility and obligations of the believers as one of the conditions to be fulfilled, in order to be considered "righteous":

> It is not righteousness that ye turn your faces Towards east or West; but it is righteousness- to believe in Allah and the Last Day, and the Angels, and the Book, and the Messengers; to spend of your substance, out of love for Him, for your kin, for orphans, for the needy, for the wayfarer, for those who ask, and for the ransom of slaves; to be steadfast in prayer, and practice regular charity; to fulfil the contracts which ye have made; and to be firm and patient, in pain (or suffering) and adversity, and throughout all periods of panic. Such are the people of truth, the Allah fearing. (s. 2: 177)

Similar exhortations to love someone's neighbour are quoted from some of the most authoritative collections of the prophet's sayings (Hadith).

> None of you has faith until you love for your brother what you love for yourself. (al-Bukhari, Hadith no. 13)

> None of you has faith until you love for your neighbor what you love for yourself. (Muslim, Hadith no. 45)

Most of the Christian reactions to the message of "A Common Word between Us and You," expressed the hope that those who are carrying out interfaith dialogue all over the world, would find in them a starting point for a better co-operation. They believed that the message is based on "the most solid theological ground possible: the teachings of the Qur'an and the Prophet, and the commandments described by Jesus Christ in the Bible,"[18]

The above quoted list with many different and contrasting interpretations of the verse of tolerance, however, has already shown that "the teachings of the Qur'an and the Prophet" are, to say the least, somehow ambiguous and not "the most solid ground." This is furthermore proven also by the extremely intolerant, aggressive and murderous advice in the Qur'an and in the collections of sayings of the prophet, for example those that regard apostasy.

VI. Apostasy[19]

That intolerance preaching verses (and Hadith) have proven to be more influential than tolerant ones on the practical behaviour of Muslims – at least on the behaviour of the official representatives of Islam in modern times – is demonstrated by the lack of religious freedom in most Islamic countries or countries with a Muslim majority.

---

[18] *Ibidem.*

[19] The following passages are quoted from http://www.islamicity.com/mosque/quran.

Apostates for example can be sentenced to the death penalty in Egypt (but here only by religious courts, not by law), in Afghanistan, Iran, Yemen, Mauretania, Pakistan, Qatar, Saudi Arabia, Somalia and the Sudan.

The governments of these countries can feel legitimated to act this way insofar as there are many verses and Hadith that contradict the affirmation of religious freedom based on 18: 29. According to the following verses and Hadith, those who have been converted to Islam and after having known the truth reject the faith, should be killed:

> [I]f they turn renegades, seize them and slay them wherever ye find them; and (in any case) take no friends or helpers from their ranks (4: 89; see also for example 9: 74).

The Sunni-collections of sayings and reports about practices of the prophet provide us with further examples of intolerance against apostates. To start with a quotation from the same at-Tabari, who has served to explain the "verse of tolerance," we read:[20]

> As Abu Bakr, Muhammad's closest companion, explained in a letter at the time, his prophet 'struck whoever turned his back to Him until he came to Islam, willingly or grudgingly.' Thus did Abu Bakr promise to 'burn them with fire, slaughter them by any means, and take women and children captive' [...] (at-Tabari v.10, pp. 55-57; see even v. 17, p. 191).

The collection of the prophet's sayings by al-Bukhari that was quoted by A Common Word, with one Hadith that prescribes to love one's brother, contains several sayings which prescribe the killing of a renegade. Such a renegade, evidently, is not considered to be a "brother."

> The Prophet said, 'If somebody (a Muslim) discards his religion, kill him.' (al-Bukhari, 52: 260; further examples of Hadith with the same prescription: 83: 37; 84: 57; 84: 64-65).

It is not possible to present the Muslim teachings about apostasy throughout history, but in order to give at least an idea of what is the present-day Sunna-teaching about apostasy, it might be worth quoting from a recently published manual of Islamic Law that was endorsed by the Al-Azhar Islamic Research Academy, i.e. by one of the highest authorities of Sunna-theology:

> Leaving Islam is the ugliest form of unbelief (kufr) and the worst [...]. When a person who has reached puberty and is sane voluntarily apostasises from Islam, he deserves to be killed. In such a case, it is obligatory [...] to ask him

---

20 http://www.thereligionofpeace.com/Quran/012-apostasy.htm.

to repent and return to Islam. If he does it is accepted from him, but if he refuses, he is immediately killed.[21]

Furthermore, leaving Islam is not the only possible reason for being declared an apostate. It is sufficient to speak of Jesus as God's son, to deny the validity of certain Quranic prescriptions, to declare as allowed what is forbidden, for example alcoholic beverages, to offend the prophet, to deny his existence, to omit the prayers because of laziness, to read the Qur'an in a way that historicises or contextualises the text and so on.[22] Thus, we are confronted again with the co-existence in the Qur'an (and in the Sunna) of divergent and even contrasting positions.

VII. Holy War?

The signatories of the Open Letter criticise the Pope for having interpreted jihad as Holy War. Their own explanation of jihad demonstrates, however, that the Pope was not entirely wrong:

> We would like to point out that 'holy war' is a term that does not exist in Islamic languages. Jihad, it must be emphasised, means struggle in the way of God. This struggle may take many forms, including the use of force. Though a jihad may be sacred in the sense of being directed towards a sacred ideal, it is not necessarily a 'war.'

But it "can" be a "war" and even a "sacred" one. One misses here a similar unconditioned refusal of violence in the name of religion as that expressed by the pope in his answer.

A. No Tolerance for Pagans and Unbelievers

Classical sunnah-authors have declared that the following verse alone has abolished or abrogated more than a hundred verses that speak in more positive or even tolerant terms about non-Muslims:[23]

---

21 *Reliance of the traveller (Umdat al-salik): A Classical Manual of Islamic Sacred Law (Fiqh)* by Ahmad ibn al-Naquib al-Misri (d. 769/1386). Transl. by N. Ha Mim Keller, English/Arabic, Cairo, Sunna book, 1991, pp. 595-596.

22 Griffel, F., *Apostasie und Toleranz im Islam. Die Entwicklung zu al-Ġazālīs Urteil gegen die Philosophie und die Reaktionen der Philosophen*, Leiden, Boston, Köln, Brill, 2000, pp. 44 *et seq.*

23 Sami Awad Aldeeb Abu-Sahlieh, *Le Coran. Texte Arabe et Traduction Française par Ordre Chronologique selon l'Azhar avec Renvoi aux Variantes, aux Abrogations et aux Écrits Juifs et Chrétiens*, Vevey, Éditions de l'Aire, 2008, p. 23; Powers, D. S., "The Exegetical Genre nāsikh al-Qur'ān wa mansūkhuhu," in A. Rippin (ed.), *Approaches to the History of the Interpretation of the Qur' ān*, Oxford, Clarendon Press, 1988, pp. 117-138; Rippin, A., "Al-Zuhrī, naskh al-Qur'ān and the Problem of Early tafsīr Texts," in *Bulletin of the School of Oriental and African Studies*, vol. 47, 1984, pp. 22-43.

> But when the forbidden months are past, then fight and slay the Pagans wherever ye find them, and seize them, beleaguer them, and lie in wait for them in every stratagem (of war); but if they repent, and establish regular prayers and practise regular charity, then open the way for them: for Allah is Oft-forgiving, Most Merciful. (9: 5; further example: 3: 56)

In the Hadith-tradition one finds an infinite amount of examples and (sometimes contradictory) prescriptions for wars against unbelievers on behalf of the religion. In the collection of Muslim ibn Hajjāj al-Qushayrīal-Naysabūrī (d. 261/875) we read for example:

> [...] the messenger of Allah [...] would say: Fight in the name of Allah and in the way of Allah (jihad). Fight against those who disbelieve in Allah. Make a holy war; [...] When you meet your enemies who are polytheists, invite them to three courses of action. If they respond to any one of these, you also accept it and withhold yourself from doing them any harm. Invite them to (accept) Islam; if they respond to you, accept it from them and desist from fighting against them [...]. If they refuse to accept Islam, demand from them the Jizya. If they agree to pay, accept it from them and hold off your hands. If they refuse to pay, seek Allah's help and fight them.[24]

The Hadith-reader just quoted, contains hundreds of prescriptions related to jihad.

B. Holy War and/or "Common Grounds" with "Peoples of the Book"

The relations with and attitudes towards Christians and Jews are characterised by divergent prescriptions and declarations. There is only one sura that prescribes in unmistakable terms the war against them until they submit to the Muslims:

> Fight those who believe not in Allah nor the Last Day, nor hold that forbidden which hath been forbidden by Allah and His Messenger, nor acknowledge the religion of Truth, (even if they are) of the People of the Book, until they pay the Jizya with willing submission, and feel themselves subdued. (9: 29)

On the other side, a great number of suras of the Qur'an underline the friendship with Christians and the common ground of Muslims and the "peoples of the book" (2: 62, 19; 3: 48; 4: 116, 163, 171; 5: 44-47, 69; 9: 30-31). I would like to quote here at least one striking example:

> And dispute ye not with the People of the Book, except with means better (than mere disputation), unless it be with those of them who inflict wrong (and injury): but say, 'We believe in the revelation which has come down to

[24] Peters, R., *The Jihad in Classical and Modern Islam: a Reader*, Princeton, Markus Wiener Publishers, 2004, pp. 10-11.

> us and in that which came down to you; Our Allah and your Allah is one; and it is to Him we bow (in Islam).' (29: 46).

On the other hand, Christians who believed in the divinity of Jesus, were classified not as "people of the book" but as unbelievers in the same way as if they were polytheists:

> They do blaspheme who say: '(Allah) is Christ the son of Mary.' But said Christ: 'O Children of Israel! worship Allah, my Lord and your Lord.' Whoever joins other gods with Allah, – Allah will forbid him the garden, and the Fire will be his abode. There will for the wrong-doers be no one to help. (5: 72)

> They do blaspheme who say: Allah is one of three in a Trinity: for there is no god except One Allah. If they desist not from their word (of blasphemy), verily a grievous penalty will befall the blasphemers among them. (5: 73; see further 4: 171)

Verses like these can help to explain why most of the Imams teaching Islam in Europe speak of Christians as unbelievers and not as people of the book. They have made the message of the Qur'an unequivocal in their sense, cancelling out or passing over the suras that express a positive attitude towards Christians. Their intolerant positions, however, are well founded insofar as they are in accordance with the Hadith-literature, which has privileged throughout history a hostile attitude towards Christians.[25]

VIII. Complexity and Openness

The messages of the Muslims declaring a common ground with Christians, religious tolerance and love for one's neighbour, seem to be unambiguous, but they cannot be acknowledged as representing "the" Islamic position. Those who defend intolerant and murderous actions as required by the Qur'an and the sunnah, can present their position with a very similar clearness as based on the prescriptions of the only true religion.[26]

Therefore, dialogues with Muslims cannot be conceived of as purely intellectual exercises. Given the strong conviction of most people to

---

[25] Goldziher, I., *Über mohammedanische Polemik gegen Al al-kitāb*, in *id.*, *Gesammelte Schriften*, edited by J. Desomogyi, vol. 2, Hildesheim, Olms Reprint, 1968, pp. 341-378; *id.*, *Introduction to Islamic Theology and Law*, translated by A. and R. Hamori, with an introduction and additional notes by B. Lewis, Princeton, Princeton University Press, 1981, pp. 33 *et seq*.

[26] For a survey of Islamic fundamentalist and progressive positions with regard to Human Rights see: Denny, F. M., "Muslim Ethical Trajectories in the Contemporary Period," in W. Schweiker, *The Blackwell Companion to Religious Ethics*, Malden, MA and Oxford, Blackwell Publishing, 2005, pp. 268-277.

dispose of the only true religion, it seems necessary, in order to maintain an open exchange, to debate about these questions in a climate of friendship, seeing the other as a person whose autonomy is shaped, exactly like ours, by reciprocity, by shared concerns for the common good, and acknowledging that Islam, as every other religion, is what its followers make of it.

Notes on contributors

LÉONCE BEKEMANS, MA in Economics and BA in Philosophy (University Leuven), MA in International Studies (Bologna & Washington) and PhD in International Relations (EUI Florence/ University Leuven) is the Jean Monnet Chair for "Globalisation, Intercultural Dialogue and Inclusiveness in the EU," at the University of Padua and academic co-ordinator of its Jean Monnet Centre of Excellence "Intercultural dialogue, Human Rights and Multi-level Governance," which collaborates with its Interdepartmental Centre on Human Rights and the Rights of Peoples. He is a visiting Professor at various universities in Europe; a member of various European projects dealing with education and citizenship, a research fellow at the Pázmány University in Budapest, the President of "Ryckevelde," an organisation for active citizenship (Bruges, Belgium) and current secretary general of ECSA-world.

LUK BOUCKAERT is emeritus Professor of ethics at the Catholic University of Leuven (K.U. Leuven, Belgium). He is a philosopher and an economist by training. His research and publications fall within the fields of business ethics and spirituality. In 1987 he founded, with some colleagues, the interdisciplinary Centre for Economics and Ethics at Leuven. In 2000 he started the SPES Forum (Spirituality in Economics and Society) and some years later the international European SPES Forum. He has written several books in Dutch. Recent publications in English include: Spirituality as a public good (co-edited with L. Zsolnai, 2007), Frugality. Rebalancing material and spiritual values in economic life (co-edited with H. Opdebeeck and L. Zsolnai, 2008), Imagine Europe (co-edited with J. Eynikel, 2009), Respect and Economic Democracy (co-edited with Pasquale Arena, 2010), The Palgrave Handbook of Spirituality and Business (co-edited with L. Zsolnai, 2011).

ULRICH BUNJES is Head of the Youth Department, Directorate of Democratic Citizenship and Participation of the Council of Europe. He was one of the members of the team who prepared the "White Paper on Intercultural Dialogue" and is Director of the Council of Europe Campaign against Discrimination. He is the author of several reports and studies such as the *Final Evaluation Report of the European Year of Languages 2001* (2002).

CHRISTOPH EBERHARD is researcher and invited Professor in Anthropology and theory of Law at the Facultés universitaires Saint Louis (Brussels) where he occupies the FPH (Charles Léopold Mayer Foundation for the Progress of Humankind) chair of Law, Governance, and Sustainable Development. He is guest Professor at the European Academy of Law Theory in Brussels and a member of the Legal Anthropology Laboratory of Paris. He has worked for many years on the question of the Law in cross-cultural dialogue and his main research interests include globalisation, law, governance and sustainable development in intercultural perspectives.

JOSÉ MARIA GIL-ROBLES is a Spanish politician. He holds a Jean Monnet Chair at the Complutense University of Madrid where he is also co-ordinator of the Jean Monnet Centre of Excellence. He has been both Member (1989–2004) and President (1997–1999) of the European Parliament, and was the President of the Parliament's Former Members Association. He is also President of the Jean Monnet Foundation in Lausanne and the European University Council for the Jean Monnet Programme. He was President of the International European Movement. He studied Law at the Universities of Deusto (Bilbao) and Salamanca.

THOMAS JANSEN studied Political Sciences, Sociology and Modern History at universities in Bonn and Munich, concluding in 1967 with a PhD degree. He has been an academic assistant and lecturer at the Institute of Political Science, University of Mainz, Assistant to Walter Hallstein MP and Adviser on European policy to the CDU/CSU Parliamentary group in the Bundestag, 1970-71; Personal adviser to Rainer Barzel MP; Secretary general of the European federalist movement in Germany (Europa-Union Deutschland), 1975-80; Editor-in-chief of 'Dokumente. Zeitschrift für den deutsch-französischen Dialog', 1978-80; Director of the Konrad Adenauer Foundation in Rome/ Italy, 1981-83; Secretary general of the International European Movement, 1981-83; Secretary general of the European People's Party (EPP) and of the European Union of Christian Democrats (EUCD), 1983-94; Member of the Forward Studies Unit of the European Commission (1995-2000); Head of the President's Office, European Economic and Social Committee, (2000-2004) and retired in 2004.

WOLFRAM KAISER is Professor of European Studies at the University of Portsmouth in England and Visiting Professor at the College of Europe in Bruges in Belgium. He has recently held positions as visiting Professor or senior fellow at the Free University of Berlin and the Netherlands Institute for Advanced Studies in Wassenaar. His most recent publications include: (with S. Krankenhagen and S. Poehls) "Europa ausstellen. Das Museum als Praxisfeld der Europäisierung"

(Cologne: Böhlau 2012 – forthcoming April); (ed. with A. Varsori) "European Union History. Themes and Debates" (Basingstoke: Palgrave, 2010); (ed. with B. Leucht and M. Gehler) "Transnational Networks in Regional Integration. Governing Europe 1945-83" (Basingstoke: Palgrave, 2010); "Christian Democracy and the Origins of European Union" (Cambridge: Cambridge University Press).

FERENC MISZLIVETZ is a Jean Monnet Professor at the West Hungarian University and Director of the Institute for Global and European Studies of the Corvinus University, Koszeg – Budapest. He is a scientific advisor of the Institute for Political Sciences at the Hungarian Academy of Science and president of the board of ISES Foundation, an independent postgraduate research centre and a Jean Monnet Centre of Excellence. Professor Miszlivetz teaches Bologna University's MIREES masters program and is affiliated to the Péter Pázmány Catholic University as research Professor. His research interests include world system theory, the post 1989 transition in East Central Europe, the European construction in global context, the theory and practice of civil society.

ANTONIO PAPISCA is Professor Emeritus of the University of Padua where he teaches "International Organisation of Human Rights and Peace" in the Master's Degree in "Institutions and Policies of Human Rights and Peace." He holds the UNESCO Chair "Human Rights, Democracy and Peace." He is director of the Review "Pace diritti umani/Peace human rights," published by Marsilio (Venice). He promoted in 1982 the establishment of the Interdepartmental Centre on Human Rights and the Rights of Peoples within the University of Padua. In the period between 1994 and 2002 he was a member of the Italian Inter-ministerial Committee of Human Rights at the Ministry of Foreign Affairs and of the Italian Human Rights Commission at the Presidency of the Council of Ministers.

RICCARDO SCARTEZZINI is the President of the "Martino Martini Study Centre for China-Europe Cultural Relations." Former Director of the Jean Monnet European Centre of Excellence, Prof. Scartezzini holds the Jean Monnet Chair *ad personam* "The Social Construction of Europe" at the University of Trento, Italy. His main research interests are European Integration, European identity and regionalism, International Relations, Migrations and inter-ethnic relations.

JOHANNES THOMAS is Prof. emeritus of Romance Philology and Culture at the Institute of Romance Literature at the University of Paderborn. He studied Romance Philology and Philosophy at the Universities of Köln, Bonn and Geneva (1961-1966). He accomplished his PHD in Philosophy and in Comparative Culture Studies at the

Universities of Aachen and Köln (1967-1974). He chaired the Institute of the Konrad Adenauer Foundation in Rome (1985-1988). Between 1993 and 2008 he chaired the journal "Documente. Zeitschrift für den deutsch-französischen Dialog." From 1999 until 2002 he was a Senate Chairman of the University of Erfurt. In recent years he has researched Islamic Spain and related questions.

LUC VAN DEN BRANDE is Chair of the CIVEX Commission (Citizenship, Governance, Institutional and External Affairs) of the Committee of the Regions of the European Union, President of the Flanders-EU Liaison Agency and special advisor to the European Commissioner of regional policy, former President of the Committee of the Regions 2008-2010, former President of the EPP/CD-group of the Parliamentary Assembly of the Council of Europe, former Minister-president of Flanders 1992-1999, former Federal minister of Labour and Employment of Belgium 1988-1992, former member of the Flemish parliament and former Belgian Community Senator.

DARIO VELO is Chairman of the Jean Monnet Centre of Excellence and Professor of Business Economics and Management at the University of Pavia. He has taught at the Universities of Bordeaux, Strasbourg, Nice-Sophia Antipolis and Bocconi. He was Dean of the Faculty of Economics at the University of Pavia and Chair of the Italian Economic Faculty Deans' Conference. He is a board member of the European Community Studies Association, Brussels and editor of "The European Union Review."

PETER XUEREB is Professor of European and Comparative Law, and Jean Monnet Professor of EU Law and European Integration at the University of Malta. Since 1993 he has been the Chairman of the European Documentation and Research Centre (EDRC), which became a Jean Monnet Centre of Excellence in 2004 and is now renamed the Institute for European Studies, of the University of Malta. Prior to 1993, Professor Xuereb was Senior Lecturer at Queen Mary College University of London, in the Department of Law and the Centre for Commercial Law Studies. Prior to that he lectured in the Department of Law at the University of Exeter (UK). He actively collaborates with the Jean Monnet Centre of Excellence of the University of Padua.

Series titles

Vol. 1. Mark Dubrulle et Gabriel Fragnière (dir.), *Identités culturelles et citoyenneté européenne. Diversité et unité dans la construction démocratique de l'Europe*, 2009.

Vol. 2. Gily Coene et Chia Longman (dir.), *Féminisme et multiculturalisme. Les paradoxes du débat*, 2010.

Vol. 3. Muriel Rouyer, Catherine de Wrangel, Emmanuelle Bousquet et Stefania Cubeddu (dir.), *Regards sur le cosmopolitisme européen. Frontières et identités*, 2011.

Vol. 4. Lénia Marques, Maria Sofia Pimentel Biscaia and Glória Bastos (eds.), *Intercultural Crossings. Conflict, Memory and Identity*, 2012.

Vol. 5. Léonce Bekemans (ed.), *A Value-Driven European Future*, 2012.

Kolibri 360 GmbH
Ferdinand-Jühlke-Straße 7
99095 Erfurt, Deutschland
produktsicherheit@kolibri360.de